The Twilight of Ancient Egypt

The Twilight of Ancient Egypt

FIRST MILLENNIUM B.C.E.

BY KAROL MYŚLIWIEC

translated from the German by David Lorton

12/01

Cornell University Press

ITHACA AND LONDON

English translation first published 2000 by
Cornell Univerity Press
First printing, Cornell Paperbacks, 2000

Printed in the United States of America

Library of Congress Cataloging-in-Publication Data
Myśliwiec, Karol.
The twilight of ancient Egypt : first millennium B.C.E / by
Karol Myśliwiec; translated from the German by David Lorton.
p. cm.
Includes bibliographical references and index.
ISBN 0-8014-3716-4 (cloth)—ISBN 0-8014-8630-0 (paper)
1. Egypt—History—332 B.C.   I. Title.
DT83.M97 2000
932—dc21   00-034039

Cornell University Press strives to use environmentally
responsible suppliers and materials to the fullest extent
possible in the publishing of its books. Such materials
include vegetable-based, low-VOC inks and acid-free papers
that are recycled, totally chlorine-free, or partly composed
of nonwood fibers. Books that bear the logo of the FSC
(Forest Stewardship Council) use paper taken from forests
that have been inspected and certified as meeting the highest
standards for environmental and social responsibility. For
further information, visit our website at
www.cornellpress.cornell.edu.

1 2 3 4 5 6 7 8 9 10 Cloth printing
1 2 3 4 5 6 7 8 9 10 Paperback printing

Contents

Translator's Note   ix

Introduction   xi

THE DUALISTIC VISION OF THE WORLD AND THE PARADOX OF ANCIENT EGYPT'S HISTORY

Dualistic Concepts   1
The Uniting of the Two Lands   6
Egypt's Imperialistic Era: The New Kingdom   14
The Decline of the New Kingdom   17
The Report of Wenamun   22

AMUN'S TWO CAPITALS: THEBES AND TANIS (DYNASTIES 21–24)

Dynasty 21   27
Mummy Caches   35
Tanis and Israel   40
Dynasty 22   41
Shosheng I's Campaign to Israel   44
The Bubastid Portal of Osorkon II   46
Domestic Policy   47
The Chronicle of Prince Osorkon   51
Political Fragmentation and Threat from Abroad   56
Discovery of the Serapeum   58
Preserved Temple Structures   64

Fresh Currents from the African Interior: Kushites in Egypt (Dynasty 25)

Nubia	68
Piye's Campaign to Egypt	73
Piye's Successors	85
Shabaka's Piety	89
The "Kushite Cap"	91
The Reign of Taharqa	93
Assyrians in Egypt	105

The Saite Renaissance (Dynasty 26)

Psammetichus I	110
Artistic Developments	117
Psammetichus II	119
Herodotus on Saite Kings	122
Archaeology and the Saite Period	127
Thebes in the Saite Period	130
The End of the Dynasty	131
Challenges to Art Historians	132

Persians and Greeks on the Throne of the Pharaohs (Dynasty 27–Ptolemaic Period)

Cambyses and Darius	135
The Temple of Hibis	137
The Naos from Tuna el-Gebel	144
The Statue of Darius from Susa	146
Foreigners in Egypt	156
Struggles for Independence	158
Ritual Confirmation of Royal Power	159
The Final Decades of Independence	162
The Art and Architecture of Dynasty 30	169
The Second Persian Occupation	177
Alexander's Conquest	178
The Ptolemaic Dynasty	179

Contents

The Divine "Lords of the Two Lands": The Last Thousand Years of Pharaonic Egypt; Polish Archaeology on the Nile

The Tombs of Alexander   185
Egypt and Rome   188
Polish Archaeology in Egypt   191
Athribis   195
Artisans' Workshops   200
A Public Bath   202
A Private Bath   203
The Cultic Aspect of Baths   204
Political Symbolism   207

Bibliography   212
Comparative Chronology   219
Index   225

[vii]

Translator's Note

In this book, the following conventions have been followed in the citations from ancient texts:

Parentheses ( ) enclose words or brief explanations that have been added for clarity.

Square brackets [ ] enclose words that have been restored in a lacuna.

An ellipsis . . . indicates that a word or words in the original text have been omitted in the citation.

An ellipsis in square brackets [. . .] indicates the presence of a lacuna for which no restoration has been attempted.

There is no single set of conventions for the English rendering of ancient Egyptian and modern Arabic personal and place names. Most of the names mentioned in this book occur in a standard reference work, John Baines and Jaromír Málek, *Atlas of Ancient Egypt* (New York: Facts on File, 1980), and the renderings here follow those in that volume. Of the two exceptions here, one is the omission of the typographical sign for ayin; this consonant does not exist in English, and it was felt that its inclusion would serve only as a distraction to the reader. The other is the divine name Amun-Re, which is more consistent with the form Amun than is the Amon-Re of the *Atlas*.

This volume was originally published in Polish under the title *Pan Obydwu Krajów*. The English translation, which was reviewed by the author, was prepared from the German edition, *Herr beider Länder* (Mainz am Rhein: Philipp von Zabern, 1998).

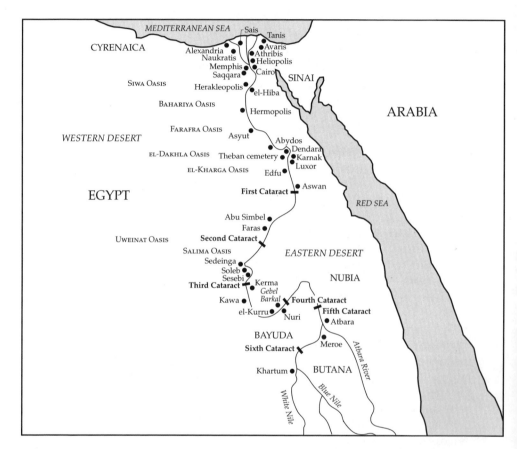

Egypt and Nubia, with the principal sites where finds have been made.

Introduction

Scholars and laypeople alike typically connect the idea of pharaonic Egypt with three great periods in its history: the Old, Middle, and New Kingdoms. The first of these epochs saw the construction of huge stone pyramids, which the Greeks would later view as one of the wonders of the world. The most famous monuments of this era are the Step Pyramid of Djoser at Saqqara, which dates to the beginning of Dynasty 3, and the three pyramids of Dynasty 4 at Giza, which were built for Khufu, Khephren, and Menkaure.

The Middle Kingdom, the pharaonic state's second epoch of imperial grandeur, is viewed by Egyptologists as its "classical" period. The finest works of Egyptian literature, works that would be copied and emulated for centuries to come, were composed at this time, under the rule of kings with the oft-repeated names Amenemhet, Senwosret, and Mentuhotpe. Among them was the well-known Story of Sinuhe, which served the ancients as a model of good style.

The last of these three great periods, the New Kingdom, saw the reigns of pharaohs named Amenophis, Tuthmosis, and Ramesses. These names are most often associated with the famed Valley of the Kings, the burial place of these rulers at Thebes (modern Luxor) on the west bank of the Nile. The world was stunned when the tomb of Tutankhamun was discovered there, the only one that still contained its burial treasure, including hundreds of gold or gilded objects.

The era that included the three major periods just mentioned and the so-called Intermediate Periods that separated them lasted from c. 2700 to 1070 B.C.E., that is, more than sixteen centuries. The pharaonic era, however, continued down to the conquest of Egypt by Alexander the Great in 332 B.C.E. The Ptolemies and the Roman emperors also ruled as pharaohs and were depicted as such in Egyptian art, but the history of dynastic Egypt ended with the assumption of power by the *diadochi*, the successors of Alexander the Great, toward the end of the fourth century B.C.E.

What happened in Egypt between 1070 and 332 B.C.E., that is, during the more than seven centuries from the fall of the New Kingdom to the conquest of Alexander the Great? This is a question seldom raised by readers interested in the history of ancient Egypt. They are not to be faulted, however, for this period, which comprises nearly a third of the dynastic period and often receives the general designation "Late Period," finds scant mention in the popular literature. How is this so? Many traces that would have led to a better understanding of the preserved sources were wiped out during this highly turbulent period. These sources include not only texts but also the remains of cities, temples, and tombs. In many cases, we can admire the beauty of the statues and reliefs, while we are able to say but little regarding the historical events contemporary with their creation. This is in fact the case when inscriptions—or, as rather more often happens, their fragmentary remains—are preserved on monuments, while we find ourselves deprived of the links that could enable us to connect the events they describe with other known facts.

One might wonder why this period holds so many puzzles and why Egyptologists approach the reconstruction of its history so cautiously, as though they were treading in the shadow of ruins that threaten to collapse at any time. There are several reasons.

The first is the ongoing situation in this period. Constantly changing political constellations, caused by both the internal collapse of the state and invasions from neighboring lands, resulted in a series of essential facts either not being set down in writing or being recorded in a way that impedes our understanding and interpretation of them. Often, therefore, we must read between the lines in order to distinguish historical events from mere propaganda or literary fiction. The constant repetition of literary or iconographic patterns in sources that could create an impression of being historical leave us skeptical as to their credibility.

It was the rule for the Egyptians to portray themselves as victors in wars against their enemies, while inscriptions left behind by the latter speak of victory over Egypt. We nevertheless rely on the sources from both sides, their partiality notwithstanding, less in search of objective information than to establish the chronology of the facts they describe. In this regard, the Egyptian and Asiatic sources come together like the words in the solution to a crossword puzzle. But their contents seldom jibe or remove the question marks, with the result that historians often feel as though they are holding a coffer full of valuables, to which they have no key.

The state of preservation of the sources is as much a hindrance as their partiality. Since decisive political events were played out chiefly in the north of the land—that is, in Lower Egypt, the Nile delta—in this era, monuments discovered there are of the utmost importance in clarifying the historical facts. Unfortunately, it is precisely in the north that the fewest remains of the past are preserved. The humid climate of the delta led not only to the swift collapse of mud brick structures, such as dwellings and defensive walls, but especially to the destruction of important documents written on papyri. We can only imagine how much more comprehensive our knowledge would be if temple or palace archives had been preserved in Heliopolis, Memphis, Tanis, Bubastis, Sais, Athribis, Mendes, or Pithom. But neither the monumental structures nor the papyrus rolls once stored in them have been preserved down to our time. It is only from the descriptions of Greek travelers, such as Herodotus and Strabo, that we have some knowledge of what these magnificent, age-old cultural centers actually looked like toward the end of antiquity.

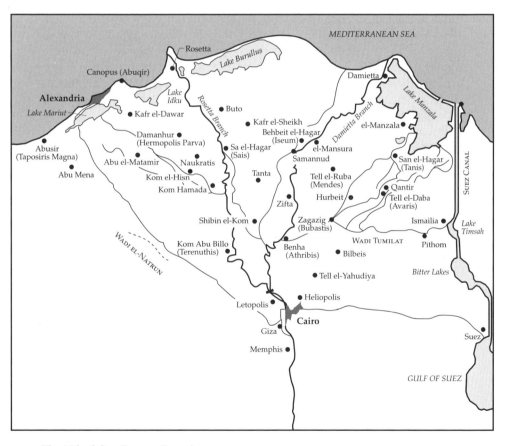

The Nile delta: (Lower Egypt)

The climate of the Nile delta is not the only cause of the poor condition of the preserved monuments in this part of Egypt. Because of its political importance, this region was in special danger of enemy invasions from the east (western Asia), the west (Libya), or by water from the north. From a strategic point of view, Lower Egypt is particularly reminiscent of the location of Poland on the map of Europe, and the fate of both political entities proved similarly stormy. From the middle of the second millennium B.C.E. on, the delta was often the stage for hard-fought battles in which monumental constructions were razed or burned down and objects of the greatest value were plundered and carried off. Warfare was particularly intensive in this region during the first millennium B.C.E. The stratigraphy of the excavated portions of ancient cities displays layers of burning that alternate with remains of ancient construction activity.

For archaeologists, digging in the Nile delta is neither easy nor rewarding. The humid climate and the high water table make it difficult to distinguish ancient mud brick walls from the surrounding earth or ordinary fill. Objects dug up are often in bad condition and in immediate need of conservation. It is frequently necessary to employ different excavation techniques from those used in Upper Egypt, where the dry sand acts as an excellent, albeit accidental, preservative for reliefs and paintings. The remains of the monumental temples that once graced the cities of Lower Egypt are mostly now mere heaps of relief-decorated stone blocks.

Excavation in the delta is often precluded by the destruction of the monuments by adverse climatic conditions, as well as by the ongoing expansion of modern towns and settlements in the vicinity of the ancient cultural centers. Among such excavations is the Polish-Egyptian mission at Tell-Atrib, ancient Athribis, which is now a suburb of the industrial city of Benha.

To excavate in the delta, archaeologists must be thoroughly versed in the area, and they must sometimes employ special, costly equipment. Combined with the prospect of relatively unspectacular discoveries, notwithstanding the great scientific importance they might have, these difficulties discourage many archaeologists from undertaking work in Lower Egypt, where the quest is not for magnificent monuments but for relics that can shed new light on the history of Egypt. Though each International Congress of Egyptologists ends with an appeal to take up research in this area, the intensity of excavation in the delta lags far behind that of archaeology in Upper Egypt.

As a result, our knowledge of Egypt in the first millennium B.C.E. remains less than that of the earlier periods. This epoch is often spoken of as one of "decadence" characterized by a general decline in or ossification of tradition. The brief "renaissance" under Dynasty 26 is viewed as a mechanical, academic imitation of age-old models. Creative individuality is disallowed for most areas of cultural expression during this millennium.

It is the intention here to demonstrate to the reader that this is a superficial evaluation. Original, creative elements made their appearance on Egyptian soil in this period, and they also flowed into Egypt from outside on the crest of political events at the same time as they brought the cultures of other lands ever closer to Egyptians while spreading pharaonic civilization beyond the borders of Egypt. This exchange resulted in phenomena that were unprecedented in the history of Egypt. My goals in undertaking this topic are to represent the complexity of these phenomena, to indicate the interplay between their political, social, and cultural aspects, and to give an account of the most recent archaeological efforts and discoveries related to the period treated here.

Our topic is thus one of the lesser-known epochs in Egyptian history, which comprises the period from the eleventh to the fourth century B.C.E. Egyptologists divide this era into the Third Intermediate Period (from the collapse of the New Kingdom to the end of the Kushite Dynasty 25) and the Late Period (from the Saite "Renaissance" of Dynasty 26 to the conquest of Egypt by Alexander the Great), and this terminology has been adopted in the present treatment.

The last chapter highlights Polish archaeological work in Egypt related to the final phases of this era and its cultural continuation into the following centuries, that is, the Ptolemaic, Roman, and Byzantine Periods.

The Twilight of Ancient Egypt

The Dualistic Vision of the World and the
Paradox of Ancient Egypt's History

DUALISTIC CONCEPTS

The ancient Egyptian outlook was dominated by a conviction that every unity was composed of two contrasting elements. This resulted, first, from observation of natural phenomena: night follows day, death follows life. Dormant in every human being were elements of good and order associated with the god Horus, along with negative qualities personified by the god Seth.

Similar antitheses make their appearance in geographical, religious, and political concepts. Flowing from south to north, the Nile divides the entire land into two parts: east and west. The west was viewed as the realm of the dead, and cemeteries were thus for the most part located to the west of cities. Among the most important of these were Saqqara and Giza, the burial places of kings and officials who resided in Memphis, along with the Valley of the Kings, the Valley of the Queens, and the cemeteries of the nobles on the west bank of Thebes. We assume it was for this reason that in the earliest burials of the dynastic period, the bodies already faced west, either lying on their left side with their head oriented south, or on their right side with their head to the north. The concepts West and East were personified by two goddesses whose heads bore insignia and hieroglyphic signs designating east (*'I3bt*, read: *Iabet*) and west (*'Imntt*, read: *Imentet*).

The division of the land into north and south was political in nature, recalling that the Egyptian state originated in the unification of these two geographical entities at the beginning of the third millennium B.C.E. Recent research seems to confirm the hypothesis that the unification was accomplished by aggressive tribes of nomads and hunters from Upper Egypt,

[1]

who apparently dominated and subjugated the sedentary, agricultural tribes of the prehistoric Nile delta. The Egyptians thus divided their land into Upper Egypt, which stretched from Aswan to the tip of the delta, and Lower Egypt, which comprised the area of the delta from Memphis north. These were the "Two Lands" (Figure 1), whose existence loomed large in Egyptian thought and which were symbolized in various ways in Egyptian iconography.

Temples, which were usually erected on an east-west axis, had a symmetrical or near symmetrical arrangement of rooms, so that their northern and southern portions corresponded to each other. The ritual, mythological, and historical scenes carved in raised or sunken relief on the walls of the sacred edifices were subject to this same principle. The concept of symmetry required that the more important scenes in the northern portion have their counterparts in the southern portion. Special importance in this regard was accorded to the scenes along the temple axis, such as those on the doorjambs, the portals, the pylons, and the rear walls of rooms that directly faced the entrance. The composition of these scenes is often symmetrical and consists of two analogous or similar elements, such as the king entering the temple, offering to its deity, slaughtering an enemy, and the like. Such scenes tend to be didactic or even propagandistic in nature.

The doorjambs and rear walls of rooms often display two scenes that, taken together, form a symmetrically composed whole, with their contrasting elements represented antithetically. We thus see important figures on either side of the axis with their backs turned toward one another, such as Osiris, god of the dead, with his back turned toward the Heliopolitan god Atum. Entire ritual scenes are sometimes composed antithetically. Parallelism, symmetry, and antithesis dominate these compositions, and we often encounter them in the decoration of the tombs of officials and kings as well. An example is furnished by the two analogous representations of Anubis lying on a naos—a small chapel containing the figure of a deity— that we often find in tombs of the New Kingdom. In the period that interests us here, these principles also predominate in the decoration of sarcophagi (Figures 2 and 3) and tomb stelae: the latter often present the appearance of the two facing pages of an open book.

It would be an error, however, to jump to the conclusion that the Egyptians classified the entire world according to a simple black-and-white scheme. They were capable of recognizing much finer gradations than would seem apparent from the examples just cited. The mortuary god Osiris was also a symbol of resurrection, and sanctuaries were thus erected for him on the east bank of Thebes, especially in the first millennium B.C.E. Amun-Re, who stood at the head of the Theban pantheon, was also venerated in the land of the dead: as a form of manifestation of the sun god, in

[2]

Figure 1. Two uraeus-serpents wearing the royal double crown on either side of a cartouche containing the name of Ramesses III. Below them are the heraldic plants of Upper and Lower Egypt. Relief decoration of a column in the mortuary temple of Ramesses III at Medinet Habu on the west bank of Thebes. Photo by the author.

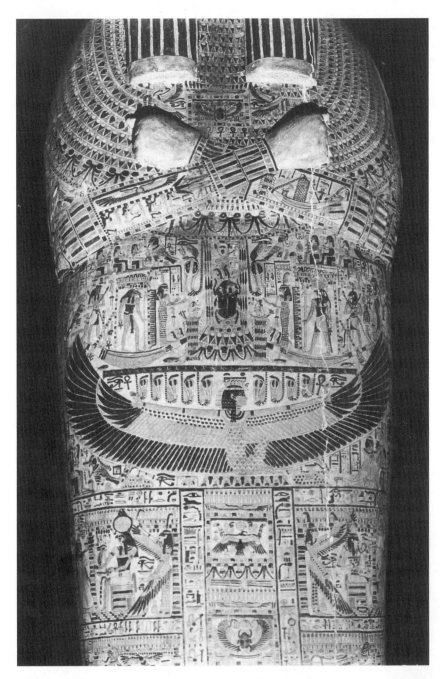

Figure 2. Religious scenes in symmetrical and antithetical composition. Upper register: barges with falcon-and ram-headed sun gods symbolizing day and night. Painted decoration of the wooden coffin of Shed-su-Amun (Dynasty 21) from Thebes. Egyptian Museum, Cairo. Photo by Waldemar Jerke, Polish Center of Mediterranean Archaeology, Warsaw University.

Figure 3. Mummies of the deceased and his wife along with two representations of the deified king Amenophis I (Dynasty 18). Antithetical scene on the wooden coffin of Bekenmut (Dynasty 21 or 22). Photo © The Cleveland Museum of Art, gift of John Huntington Art and Polytechnic Trust, 1914.561.A.

the course of his ongoing journey through the sky, he "died" each evening and was resurrected at dawn.

The relative value of contrasting concepts was expressed with especially subtle nuances in the question of gender. The Egyptians were of the opinion that every creator god was androgynous. Alongside his masculine form, there also existed, albeit in the shadows, a feminine form, whose name was composed by adding the feminine suffix -*t* to his masculine name. Thus, Amun had his Amaunet, while Atum sometimes appeared in the form of Atumet. These goddesses were hypostases, not consorts, of their masculine counterparts. These gods had intimate relations with other goddesses, and in the case of Amun—so it was believed—also with mortal princesses who fulfilled the function of God's Wife of Amun. We shall devote our attention to the institution of God's Wife later in this book.

Gender distinction was also reflected in the color conventions of Egyptian painting. In representations of women, their bodies have a yellow color, while male figures are distinguished by a red skin color. There are, however, exceptions to this rule. On a stela of the First Intermediate Period, we see a deceased man who is represented twice. In one case, his body is red, while in the other, it is yellow. Other details of his appearance also differ. The yellow color characterizes his form in advanced old age, with a large paunch and a bald head, while the "masculine" color accompanies a youthful, slender silhouette with long hair. Here, there is clearly a stress on two alternative aspects of human nature that are present in every man: the calm and passivity of the god Horus—qualities that usually characterize advanced old age—are contrasted with the dynamic, restless, active nature of the god Seth. This contrast is also reflected in Egyptian literature; in the oldest known work of religious literature, the Pyramid Texts, one chapter contains a naturalistic description of Seth's violation of Horus.

Even the hieroglyphic writing system is not free of such associations. The sign with the phonetic value *her*, which might have been associated with Horus because of the similar sound of his name, and which depicts a man's face shown frontally, is yellow in painted inscriptions, while the sign *tp* that often accompanies it and represents a man's head in profile is painted red in the same inscriptions.

THE UNITING OF THE TWO LANDS

The examples just given illustrate the various means used to symbolize the notion that every unity is composed of two contrasting elements. The institution of kingship was an area in which dualistic concepts assumed considerable importance and found expression in especially varied symbols. Just as the greatness of his forebears had been based on their uniting of Upper and Lower Egypt into a single state, so the legitimation of the power of an individual monarch rested on his maintenance of this unity—an especially important task, inasmuch as in the conviction of the ancient Egyptians, history began anew with each pharaoh's assumption of power. From this point on, a new year was reckoned. The first task of a new king was thus the symbolic repetition of the act of uniting Upper and Lower Egypt.

This very act was the "calling card" of the first regnal year of each ruler in the famous royal annals from the time of Dynasty 5, carved on stone and today generally called the Palermo Stone after the city where it is now located. In these annals, each regnal year was designated by the most important event it witnessed, and the year a king ascended the throne was invariably the "year of the Uniting of the Two Lands."

This historical act was represented by a hieroglyphic sign that attained the status of a graphic symbol and appeared frequently in Egyptian heraldry. In variants that are sometimes quite complex, it appears on the walls of temples and tombs, and it adorns the throne of Pharaoh, the bases of statues, and the stands for ritual barques. There are even beautiful alabaster vessels in the form of this sign, known especially from the tomb of Tutankhamun. It is thus time to describe the *sm3–t3wy* (read: *sema-tawy*) sign that symbolized the uniting of Upper and Lower Egypt. It is a symmetrical composition whose axis was the representation of a windpipe flanked by two lungs, which together form the hieroglyph for the word *sema*, "to unite." Around this central element are intertwined heraldic plants that symbolize the north (papyrus) and the south (water lily) of Egypt.

A more elaborate variant on this symbol appears most often on the sides of royal thrones. There, we see two personifications of the Nile, figures with large bellies and pendulous breasts, who hold the ends of the heraldic plants in their hands. A clump of these respective plants on the head of each figure provides an additional topographic accent. So that the beholder will not forget who performed this work of uniting and who is to be thanked for the gifts of the Nile, oval cartouches containing the names of the pharaoh are often placed above or beside the sign (Figure 4).

An unusually beautiful variation on this symbol was conceived by an artist in the reign of Amenophis III (Figure 5). He created a vase crowned by a scene depicting the king seated in a thicket of heraldic plants, holding a papyrus stalk in one hand and a water lily in the other. In this instance, Pharaoh himself is the symmetrical axis, replacing the windpipe and lungs. The vessel was one of the gifts for Amenophis on the occasion of the festival celebrating the thirtieth anniversary of his rule, and it is known to us from a relief on a wall of the tomb of a high official named Kheruef on the west bank of Thebes.

Every anniversary of an accession to the throne was festively celebrated, but special importance was accorded to the thirtieth anniversary of a reign.

[7]

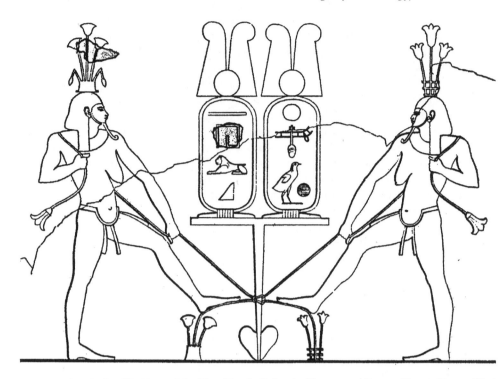

Figure 4. Symbolic "Uniting of the Two Lands," that is, Upper and Lower Egypt. Personified Nile gods with heraldic plants on their heads stand on either side of cartouches containing names of Taharqa. Relief on a barque stand in the temple of Gebel Barkal.

This was the occasion of a jubilee, the so-called *sed*-festival, which was distinguished by a special ritual whose episodes were represented in the reliefs decorating the walls of a sacred building constructed specifically for this occasion. One of the most important sources for our knowledge of this ritual is the reliefs of Osorkon II on an edifice erected in the Lower Egyptian city of Bubastis on the occasion of his jubilee.

We have good reason to think that not every pharaoh had the patience or the leisure to wait for his thirtieth regnal year to celebrate a *sed*-festival. Many of these jubilees were celebrated in Heliopolis, the Lower Egyptian center of the sun cult. There, for example, was enacted the ceremony in which the king's name was written on the leaves of the *ished* tree by one of

Figure 5. Pharaoh Amenophis III uniting the heraldic plants of the Two Lands, that is, Upper and Lower Egypt. Decoration of a sumptuous vessel. Relief in the tomb of Kheruef at Thebes. Photo by Zbigniew Doliński, Polish Center of Mediterranean Archaeology, Warsaw University.

Figure 6. Double scene with the *ished*-tree. The kneeling kings are Osorkon III and Takelot III (Dynasty 23). The god Atum is writing the names of Takelot on the leaves of the tree. Relief on a wall of the chapel of Osiris Heqadjet at Karnak. Photo by Dieter Johannes, German Archaeological Institute, Cairo.

the most important deities (Figure 6). In the representations of this episode on the walls of Egyptian temples, we generally see the king kneeling in front of the *ished* tree in the presence of a creator god, who sits on a throne as he writes the name of the king or hands him the insignia of his power. A second god, standing behind the pharaoh, sometimes functions as scribe. The most beautiful example of this iconographic motif is the double, antithetically composed scene carved on a wall of the temple of Osiris Heqadjet ("Osiris, Ruler of Eternity") at Karnak, which dates to Dynasty 23.

Some Egyptologists are of the opinion that the scenes with the *ished* tree do not illustrate an actual ritual but rather a sort of mythological "wonder," one of the many to be found in the repertoire of ancient Egyptian political theology. But the fact remains that Heliopolis was of great religious and political importance, from the beginning of Egyptian civilization down through the Graeco-Roman Period. The chief god of the local pantheon, Atum—viewed as the primeval god who rose out of a hillock in the primeval ocean and created the first divine pair by pleasuring himself—was as much venerated throughout Egypt as Ptah or Amun-Re. Though Heliopolis in Lower Egypt had its counterpart in Upper Egyptian Hermonthis (also called "southern Heliopolis"), where the god Montu stood at the head of the local pantheon, the city of Atum remained virtually without a competitor as an age-old center of religious thought.

Thus, in dualistic geographical-religious-political conceptions, the primeval god of Heliopolis often appeared as a symbol of Lower Egypt, for the most part in conjunction with an Upper Egyptian counterpart. This role was especially accorded to him when stress was placed on the double character of the kingship. One of the iconographic motifs that often appear in the reliefs of Egyptian temples depicts the ruler in the company of two gods who symbolize the north and the south of the land. Atum usually represents Lower Egypt, while the role of his Upper Egyptian partner is played either by Montu, the god of Hermonthis (e.g., in the relief of Ramesses IV that graces the temple of the god Khons at Karnak, Figure 7), or by Khons, the youngest member of the Theban triad, son of Amun-Re and the goddess Mut.

Because of his unusual authority, Atum was brought into special connection with the kingship, and he was even identified with Pharaoh. As early as the Pyramid Texts, which were recorded in the second half of the third millennium B.C.E. and carved on the walls of the royal burial chambers toward the end of the Old Kingdom, we read the following witness to the identity of the deceased ruler:

> Your (= the king's) arm is (the arm) of Atum,
> Your shoulders are the (shoulders) of Atum,
> Your belly is the (belly) of Atum,
> Your back is the (back) of Atum,
> Your hinder-parts are the (hinder-parts) of Atum,
> Your two legs are the (legs) of Atum,
> Your face is the (face) of Anubis.

This theological interpretation of the royal anatomy points to the Heliopolitan origin of the Pyramid Texts and shows how far the identification of the king with Atum had progressed at a very early date. The theologian associated only the king's face with a god other than Atum, namely Anubis, who was responsible for the mummification of the corpse.

[11]

Figure 7. Pharaoh Ramesses IV led by gods representing Upper and Lower Egypt: the falcon-headed Theban god Montu and Atum, "Lord of the Two Lands and of Heliopolis." Relief in the temple of Khons at Karnak. Photo by the author.

In later periods, Pharaoh was provided with such epithets as "living image of Atum," "incarnation of Atum," "messenger of Atum," and even "egg of Atum." It is thus no wonder that the iconography of the ruler approached the representation of this god to the point of confusion. In ritual scenes, Atum is anthropomorphic and wears on his head a double crown that symbolizes the royal power; it consists of the red crown of Lower Egypt and the white crown of Upper Egypt (Figure 8). In Egyptian art,

[12]

Figure 8. Ramesses II, "Lord of the Two Lands," crowned by the god Atum, "Lord of Heliopolis," who is wearing the double crown. Quartzite naos (shrine) from Pithom in the eastern delta. Now in the court of the Egyptian Museum, Cairo. Photo by Waldemar Jerke, Polish Center of Mediterranean Archaeology, Warsaw University.

only the shape of their beards makes it possible to distinguish the two figures.

But the essential element in this identity was the epithet Lord of the Two Lands, which was ascribed both to the king and to Atum. Rulership over all Egypt, as expressed by the double crown, defined Pharaoh as an emanation of the Heliopolitan sun god. As already noted, maintaining the unity of the land was the holiest task and the passionate endeavor of every monarch.

EGYPT'S IMPERIALISTIC ERA: THE NEW KINGDOM

From the middle of the second millennium on, after the beginning of the New Kingdom, Pharaoh's gaze was ever more often cast beyond the borders of Egypt, especially toward Nubia, which bordered the pharaonic realm on the south, and toward Palestine, which was a bridgehead between the great powers of the ancient Near East. Imperialistic inclinations were awakened in the pharaohs by their consciousness of their own economic power and their drive to plunder costly materials.

Thus began subjugations and prolonged wars that sometimes brought rich booty and cheap labor but which just as often weakened Egypt itself (Figures 9 and 10). In the reign of Tuthmosis III, Egypt's borders extended briefly as far as the kingdom of Mitanni in northern Mesopotamia. To the south was Nubia, called Kush in antiquity, which lay on the route to the interior of Africa and was especially rich in gold. It had already been partially colonized by Egypt during the Middle Kingdom, and at the beginning of the New Kingdom, after further conquests, the office of viceroy was created there; its holders bore the title King's Son, which was later altered to King's Son of Kush. The ultimate victim of these imperialistic tendencies was Egypt itself. The first symptom of a weakening of the internal cohesion of the state was the so-called religious revolution of Akhenaten toward the end of Dynasty 18.

Everything points to the conclusion that the sudden outbreak of this monotheistic heresy, as some historians interpret the phenomenon, had a deep-seated political cause whose roots reached back more than a century into the past. It seems that the throne was already somewhat shaky early in the New Kingdom when it was occupied by a woman, the first "iron lady" in history. Her minor stepson was obliged to wait for a long time to succeed her as Tuthmosis III. The determination with which he later had the queen's name hacked out from the walls of her temple at Deir el-Bahri allows us to suspect the humiliation he must have suffered during the reign of his ambitious stepmother. Perhaps these early difficulties encouraged his fighting spirit and led him to make up for his former humiliation with wars that brought him to the northern limits of the civilized world. His pride in his

[14]

conquests is shown by the fact that he had the chronicle of his military expeditions carved on the walls of the temple of Amun-Re at Karnak.

His successors attempted to emulate his warlike deeds, for the most part with ever less success. The written documents from each reign clearly suggest that the rulers did not feel all too secure on the throne and that they sought additional legitimation for their power. Literature was thus pressed into the service of political-religious propaganda, and there are narratives in which a god—usually Amun-Re—appears to the king in a dream and entrusts the rulership over Egypt to him in recognition of his special virtue and service. Piety also counted; it found its expression inter alia in the construction of temples and in the restoration of the great sphinx statue that lies in front of the pyramids at Giza.

Notwithstanding the lack of unequivocal written evidence, we sense a gradual increase in the importance of the cult of the sun and, closely bound up with it, that of the Heliopolitan clergy. The decoration of tombs at Thebes, especially those from the reign of Amenophis III,

Figure 9. Tuthmosis III (Dynasty 18) smiting bound foreign enemies of Egypt and offering them to Amun-Re. Relief on the Seventh Pylon of the temple of Amun-Re at Karnak. Photo by the author.

Figure 10. Amenophis II (Dynasty 18) smiting bound prisoners before Amun-Re. Relief on the Eighth Pylon of the temple of Karnak. Photo by the author.

suggests a flight into religious themes—a typical phenomenon in conditions of mounting crisis. The expansion of the solar cult must have led inevitably to conflict with the clergy of the Theban Amun-Re. The "Amarna revolution," which for a short time accorded the sun disk the status of the most important and practically the only deity, was only a brief episode in Egyptian history, but it had unforeseeable consequences for the futher development of the land. Like every political disruption, it altered social relationships and enabled the rise of groups of people who had previously remained in the shadows. Today, we call this a process of democratization.

Profiting most from the weakening of the land after the period of religious heresy was the military elite of Lower Egypt, who succeeded in founding a new dynasty. With his scant two years of rule (c. 1306–4 B.C.E.), Ramesses I, who stemmed from a family in the eastern delta, inaugurated the lengthy Ramesside Period, which lasted more than two hundred years and encompassed Dynasties 19 and 20. Most—eleven in all—of the rulers of this period bore the name Ramesses, which means "the one created by Re." This very name bears witness to the return to the religious orthodoxy of the pre-Amarna era.

The Ramesside kings displayed an exaggerated military ambition. Innumerable campaigns, mainly against Asiatics, were represented on the outer walls of the temples of the period, so that everyone could marvel at Pharaoh's deeds. The Residence of the Ramessides was Pi-Riamsese ("House of Ramesses") in the eastern delta. Thebes, however, retained its role as a major center of culture and especially of religion. There, in the cliffs on the west bank of the Nile, tombs were prepared for the deceased pharaohs.

But history, which is rich in paradoxes, soon showed that the tombs in the Valley of the Kings, whose excavation and decoration required years of labor, would assure a comfortable but by no means eternal rest. Toward the end of the New Kingdom, violations of the burial chambers, theft of the rich burial goods, and desecration of the corpses had already become so frequent that the high priests of Dynasty 21 were obliged to collect the mortal remains of their great forebears in a special hiding place and to store them there in a manner far removed from Egyptian conceptions regarding the fate of the "sons of the sun god."

The greatest rulers of the Ramesside Period were Ramesses II, who defeated the Hittites in the year 1286 B.C.E. in the famous Battle of Qadesh and erected an unusually large number of temples in Egypt, and Ramesses III, who left behind the largest preserved mortuary temple of the New Kingdom at Medinet Habu, not far from the Valley of the Kings. This edifice originally bore the name "United with Eternity."

As early as the reign of Ramesses III, Egypt was threatened by intruders from the north, today called the Sea Peoples, that is, the Philistines and the Sherden (from whom the modern name Sardinia evidently is derived). This king also battled with the Libyans, the Hittites, and the Syrians. In his reign, the waging of war became the ruler's most important concern; small wonder, then, that the internal order of the state was destroyed.

From documents preserved on papyri and ostraca, we learn of problems with provisioning that led to unrest. Toward the end of Ramesses III's thirty-year reign, there were insufficient means at Thebes to pay the semi-monthly wages of the necropolis workers who lived in Deir el-Medina. The hungry men gathered at the Ramesseum, the mortuary temple of Ramesses II. A vizier named Ta, who was traveling via Thebes with divine statues that had to be brought from the south for the celebration of the royal jubilee, the *sed*-festival, attempted to save the situation by making a small distribution of rations, but soon thereafter, the strikes were renewed. We also learn of the dismissal of a vizier at Athribis in the north of the land, where the king ordered a review of the allocations to the temples. There must have been trouble there, perhaps fraud or just ordinary theft.

Corruption became an ever more common phenomenon. Even in his own court, the king was no longer capable of controlling the situation. Toward the end of Ramesses III's life there was the famous harem conspiracy, which is described in well-known papyri. We are not informed whether the king lost his life as a result of this conspiracy, but we know that his corpse found no rest. Ramesses III was buried in a splendid tomb in the Valley of the Kings, whose construction had been begun by his father, Sethnakhte. Along with other royal mummies, Ramesses was found a century ago in the cache at Deir el-Bahri, where his body had been hidden from tomb robbers by the priests of Amun during Dynasty 21.

THE DECLINE OF THE NEW KINGDOM

Further diminution of Pharaoh's authority and a general decay of the state ensued under Ramesses III's successors. Hunger and unrest were the order of the day. Violations of the tombs of kings and officials on the west bank of Thebes bore dramatic witness to this situation. In the accounts of legal proceedings against the violators, we read how cynically and with what determination sarcophagi covered with gold foil were smashed to pieces and how valuable objects were stolen from the tombs. For many, the deities, along with Pharaoh, their "living image," had become hollow words or meaningless images painted on the walls of tombs, while for the influential priests, they served as an instrument to mask their corruption and caprice.

A priest in the temple of Khnum at Elephantine was accused of theft, corruption, the commission of sacrilege, and even of having sexual relations with married women. One of the most serious accusations against him was the sale of the sacred Mnevis bulls, who had been raised at Heliopolis and were believed to be incarnations of the sun god Re. No less serious an infraction was his taking part in processions of divine statues without first completing the requisite ten days of purification, which included the drinking of natron, and his bribing a servant of the vizier to arrest his accuser while he was fulfilling his priestly duties. The corruption of yet other persons led to substantial losses from the grain delivered to the temple of the god Khnum.

An even clearer indication of the weakness of the king toward the end of the New Kingdom was immortalized on one of the walls of the temple of Amun-Re at Karnak. There, we behold a scene that would have been un-

[17]

thinkable in earlier periods, when the temple was decorated chiefly with representations of the king making offerings to the gods. A large relief carved directly opposite the sacred lake depicts Ramesses IX honoring the high priest Amenhotpe with lavish gifts. Leaving aside the merits of the priest, both the content and the form of the representation are shocking. At an earlier date, in the reign of Sethos II, the high priest of Amun-Re had been represented on a wall of the temple of Karnak, but he was depicted there in a moment of prayer to the god for long life and the handing down of his office to his descendants. In Egyptian art, where there was a particular concern to maintain correct proportions in representing persons from different levels of the social hierarchy, it was unprecedented to depict the priest as a figure precisely as large as the pharaoh—and on such a large scale and in so visible a place! Unequivocally propagandistic in its character, this scene is of the utmost importance for our understanding of social relationships toward the end of the Ramesside Period.

The high priests exploited the weakness of royal authority to assume a leading position in the political arena. While the kings conducted wars, leaving their capital in Lower Egypt for long periods of time, the priests of Amun-Re at Thebes increased their power. In this period, the office of high priest was an inherited one, which led to the rise of a theocratic dynasty that functioned parallel to the royal one. The Amenhotpe rewarded by Ramesses IX was the brother of his predecessor Nesamun and the son of the high priest Ramessesnakht. Their theophoric (containing a divine name) names alone testify to the almighty authority of the Theban Amun-Re: every one of them contains either the element "Ra" (for "Re") or the element "Amun." The priests of this god acquired ever more political power, gradually usurping Pharaoh's authority in Upper Egypt.

The written sources lead us to presume that the King's Son of Kush challenged the royal power. Toward the end of the reign of Ramesses XI, the last ruler of Dynasty 20, Egypt was embroiled in civil war by the Nubian viceroy, who bore the name Panehsy. This ambitious rebel had already trod the political stage ten years earlier, when he lent assistance to the high priest Amenhotpe, who had been temporarily ousted from power by one of his rivals. His rebellion against royal authority met with resistance from Theban loyalists, but it smoothed the way to power for the high priest, who was the de facto ruler not only of Thebes but also of a considerable portion of Upper Egypt.

Herihor was the first high priest (Figure 11) to find the courage to enclose his name in a royal cartouche; we can still see it today on the walls of the temple of Khons at Karnak. Herihor's titles Commandant of the Army and Great Commandant of the Armies of Upper and Lower Egypt point to the combining of religious functions with military power, which in practice was what rulership over the southern portion of the land came down to. We do not know Herihor's origin or what qualifications predestined him to assume

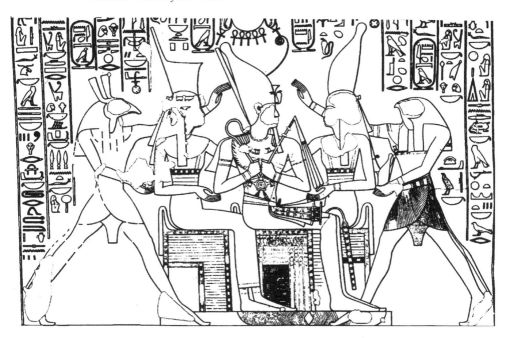

Figure 11. Herihor between the goddesses Wadjit (left) and Nekhbet and the gods Seth (left) and Horus. Relief in the temple of Khons at Karnak.

the highest office in the theocratic state, but we may suppose that an essential role was played by his marriage to Nodjmet, who was evidently a daughter of the high priest Amenhotpe. This was one of the many times in history when the social rank of a wife smoothed the way for her husband's political career. Her high rank in no way hindered the highborn Nodjmet from fulfilling her marital duties in an exemplary fashion: it has been reckoned that she bore nineteen sons and five daughters. Since many of Herihor's sons had Libyan names, it is supposed that their father, the high priest, might have been descended from a family of Libyan military officers.

Of special interest, from a historical standpoint, is the relationship between Herihor and Ramesses XI, who was still at least nominally viewed as the ruler of Egypt and who resided in the eastern delta. Instructive in this regard are the reliefs decorating the walls of the southern portion of the temple of Khons, which was under construction at just this time. Some of the preserved scenes still depict Ramesses in the customary pose of offering to the deities. In others, however, Herihor (Figure 12) already appears performing ritual activities previously reserved for the king as the highest priest, such as the burning of incense before the barque containing the image of the highest god. It is almost astonishing to see Ramesses' name men-

[19]

Figure 12. Herihor kneeling before the god Amun-Re with a tray of offerings. Relief in the temple of Khons at Karnak.

tioned in speeches expressing the god's satisfaction with the construction of a beautiful temple by the king, and not by Herihor. Still more significant are the scenes carved on the columns in this portion of the temple. Half of the eight central columns depict Herihor making divine offerings in the same manner as the king. In most of the dedicatory inscriptions that run along the lower portion of the walls of this area, only Herihor, and not Ramesses, is named as the dedicator of the edifice.

The apogee of this development is revealed by the content of the scenes on the walls of the court that was built to the south a bit later. Herihor, still dressed in priestly garb, is depicted with uniquivocal insignia of royal authority: a uraeus-serpent adorns his brow, and we sometimes see the ruler's double crown on his head. In the inscriptions accompanying these scenes, Herihor's figure is accompanied by a full royal titulary, with a Horus name of his own, along with names enclosed in cartouches. The high priest of Amun-Re was now "Horus, Mighty Bull, Son of Amun, King of Upper and Lower Egypt, King of the Two Lands, First Prophet of Amun, Bodily Son of Re, Son of Amun."

Ramesses XI is not mentioned even once in these inscriptions. To what

[20]

extent was he still king of Egypt? What was he doing, and by whom was he recognized? Perhaps we could speak of these matters if we had written sources from the delta referring to the rule of the last Ramesses. Texts from Thebes, however, indicate that the Libyan tribes of the Meshwesh and Libu in particular profited from the internal troubles during the reigns of the last Ramessides. As a result of their gradual infiltration—perhaps by means of conquests, or perhaps through the social climbing of military colonists— the Libyans already controlled a considerable portion of the delta, Middle Egypt, and the oases west of the Nile valley toward the end of the New Kingdom.

To save the hopeless situation, Herihor attempted to carry out a radical reform, a sort of "renaissance," whose traces can be found only in written documents. In Ramesses XI's nineteenth regnal year, unknown events caused a new year count to be begun. Instead of indicating the regnal year of the king, a new era called Repeating of Births was suddenly introduced. Its inspiration might have lain in two rulers who used this expression at much earlier dates. The usurper Amenemhet I (c. 1991–1962 B.C.E.), who founded Dynasty 12, had a similar-sounding Horus name, while Sethos I (c. 1309–1291 B.C.E.), the second ruler of Dynasty 19, supplemented the dates referring to the first and second years of his reign with this concept. Imitating them, Herihor evidently attempted a program of renewal that he did not succeed in carrying out. Inscriptions from Thebes lead us to suspect that the high priest died at least a year before the king passed away. That did not mean, however, that Ramesses XI's power was restored in Thebes. His tomb in the Valley of the Kings was not completed, nor did it serve as his burial place.

We still do not know where Herihor was buried, but we have evidence of his care for the mummies of his great predecessors. The coffins of Sethos I and Ramesses II found in the cache at Deir el-Bahri bear inscriptions stating that Herihor had both kings buried in a new place, though not the one where they were discovered toward the end of the nineteenth century C.E. The posthumous wanderings of the second of these rulers are especially interesting; they did not end the moment he was transferred from Deir el-Bahri to the Cairo Museum. Twenty years ago, the mummy of the greatest (though rather small in stature) of the Ramessides traveled to Paris, where it was subjected to painstaking research and conservation efforts.

The atmosphere of the era in which Herihor rivaled Ramesses XI and gradually assumed royal authority over Upper Egypt was excellently captured by Boleslaw Prus in his novel *Pharaoh*. Notwithstanding anachronisms relating to political history, which are undeniably conditioned by the state of knowledge a century ago, this literary work paints a faithful picture of the growth in the power of the Theban clergy and the transformation of the temple of Amun-Re into the capital of a theocratic state that neither the king nor any other power was able to resist.

THE REPORT OF WENAMUN

In ancient Egyptian literature, this period finds its best reflection in the account of the adventures of Wenamun, an Egyptian who was dispatched by Herihor on a trade mission to Phoenicia. It is written on a papyrus that was acquired in Cairo in 1891 and is now in the Pushkin Museum in Moscow. This document is all the more precious in that it is the only preserved copy of this historical novel, which is today called the Report of Wenamun. We do not know how much in this account of the adventures of an Egyptian envoy is true, but we can establish that its author anchored it securely in the historical realities of the final years of the New Kingdom. From this standpoint, the story of Wenamun has value for us as a historical document. It is also distinguished by its simple composition, the lively pace of its narrative, and its outstanding characterization of the psyches of its protagonists via dialogue. Unfortunately, the last part of the work, which would have described Wenamun's return to Egypt, is not preserved.

We first learn that Wenamun, a high official of the temple of Amun, was to sail to Phoenicia, by order of Herihor, to purchase cedar wood for the construction of a ritual barque in which the statue of the god would journey on the Nile. Such barques, richly decorated with reliefs and three-dimensional figures made of the costliest materials, are often depicted on the walls of Egyptian temples. In "year 5," doubtless reckoned from the beginning of the Renaissance, Wenamun journeyed to the north of the land and first paid a visit to Nesubanebdjed, the governor of Lower Egypt, who resided in Tanis. It is striking that before setting out on so important a mission, Wenamun had no communication with Pharaoh. The king is referred to only once in the story, and that without mention of his name; in contrast, Amun-Re, King of the Gods, is constantly spoken of as wielding the highest authority.

We have thus to do with a theocratic state ruled by Herihor at Thebes on the one hand, and on the other, with an independent power center at Tanis, where the royal governor Nesubanebdjed was sovereign. Everything suggests that the latter had himself proclaimed king after the death of Ramesses XI: in the work written by Manetho, who systematized the history of Egypt in the Ptolemaic Period, Nesubanebdjed is viewed as the first ruler of Dynasty 21. The story of Wenamun thus conveys an authentic witness to the collapse of the state into two independent entities already in the reign of the last Ramesses. The two power centers remained on friendly terms, but as a state, Egypt did not inspire as much respect abroad as it had enjoyed in the past, as we also learn from Wenamun's report.

[22]

Provided with valuable goods and with a statue of the god Amun to serve as a patron saint of travelers, Wenamun journeyed by ship and reached the city of Dor in the land of the Tjeker, which lay on the eastern coast of the Mediterranean. And there began his troubles. Robbed by a member of his own crew, who made off with a considerable amount of silver and gold, Wenamun appropriated the silver belonging to the sailors, with whom he continued his journey. He cynically explained to the members of the crew: "I have taken the silver from you. I shall keep it if you do not find my silver and the one who stole it. You did not steal it, but I am taking it nevertheless. Now, go and do what I have told you."

When Wenamun finally arrived at the Phoenician city of Gubla (Byblos), with which Egypt had had ongoing relations from time immemorial, its prince, Tjekerbaal, evinced no desire to speak with him and ordered him to leave his territory immediately. The cunning Wenamun, who well knew the tricks of the priests, organized a sort of oracle. A speech on his behalf sounded forth from the mouth of a native priest while divine offerings were being made. The Egyptian was finally received in his capacity of envoy of Amun by Tjekerbaal, whom he informed of the purpose of his mission. The dialogue between the Egyptian priest and the Phoenician merchant is an example of in-depth psychological analysis, characterizing the two figures with the help of their own words and an escalation of the dramatic tension. It also conveys the mistrust and even the disdainful attitude of the Phoenician toward his guest, conditioned by the diminished authority of the Egyptian state. Wenamun describes the dialogue:

> I found him seated in his upper chamber with his back against a window, and the waves of the great sea of Syria broke behind his head. I said to him: "Blessings of Amun!" He said to me: "How long is it to this day since you came from the place where Amun is?" I said to him: "Five whole months till now." He said to me: "If you are right where is the dispatch of Amun that was in your hand?" I said to him: "I gave them to Smendes and Tentamun." Then he became very angry and said to me: "Now then, dispatches, letters you have none. Where is the ship of pinewood that Smendes gave you? Where is its Syrian crew? Did he not entrust you to this foreign ship's captain in order to have him kill you and have them throw you into the sea? From whom would one then seek the god? And you, from whom would one seek you?" So he said to me.
>
> I said to him: "Is it not an Egyptian ship? Those who sail under Smendes are Egyptian crews. He has no Syrian crews." He said to me: "Are there not twenty ships here in my harbor that do business with Smendes? As for Sidon, that other (place) you passed, are there not another fifty ships there that do business with Werekter and haul to his house?"
>
> I was silent in this great moment. Then he spoke to me, saying: "On what

[23]

business have you come?" I said to him: "I have come in quest of timber for the great noble bark of Amen-Re, King of Gods. What your father did, what the father of your father did, you too will do it." So I said to him. He said to me: "True, they did it. If you pay me for doing it, I will do it. My relations carried out this business after Pharaoh had sent six ships laden with the goods of Egypt, and they had been unloaded into their storehouses. You, what have you brought for me?"

He had the daybook of his forefathers brought and had it read before me. They found entered in his book a thousand *deben* of silver and all sorts of things. He said to me: "If the ruler of Egypt were the lord of what is mine and I were his servant, he would not have sent silver and gold to say: 'Carry out the business of Amun.' It was not a royal gift that they gave to my father! I too, I am not your servant, nor am I the servant of him who sent you! If I shout aloud to the Lebanon, the sky opens and the logs lie here on the shore of the sea! Give me the sails you brought to move your ships, loaded with logs for (Egypt)! Give me the ropes you brought [to lash the pines] that I am to fell in order to make them for you [. . .] that I am to make for you for the sails of your ships; or the yards may be too heavy and may break, and you may die (in) the midst of the sea. For Amun makes thunder in the sky ever since he placed Seth beside him! Indeed, Amun has founded all the lands. He founded them after having first founded the land of Egypt from which you have come. Thus craftsmanship came from it in order to reach the place where I am! Thus learning came from it in order to reach the place where I am! What are these foolish travels they made you do?"

I said to him: "Wrong! These are not foolish travels that I am doing. There is no ship on the river that does not belong to Amun. His is the sea and his the Lebanon of which you say, 'It is mine.' It is a growing ground for Amen-user-he, the lord of every ship. Truly, it was Amen-Re, King of Gods, who said to Herihor, my master: 'Send me!' And he made me come with this great god. But look, you have let this great god spend these twenty-nine days moored in your harbor. Did you not know that he was here? Is he not he who he was? You are prepared to haggle over the Lebanon with Amun, its lord? As to your saying, the former kings sent silver and gold: If they had owned life and health, they would not have sent these things. It was in place of life and health that they sent these things to your fathers! But Amen-Re, King of Gods, he is the lord of life and health, and he was the lord of your fathers! They passed their lifetimes offering to Amun. You too, you are the servant of Amun!

"If you will say 'I will do' to Amun, and will carry out his business, you will live, you will prosper, you will be healthy; you will be beneficent to your whole land and your people. Do not desire what belongs to Amen-Re, King of Gods! Indeed, a lion loves his possessions! Have your scribe brought to me that I may send him to Smendes and Tentamun, the pillars Amun has set up for the north of his land; and they will send all that is needed. I will send him to them, saying: 'Have it brought until I return to the south; then I shall refund you all your expenses.' " So I said to him.[1]

After a while, goods constituting the payment for the Phoenician wood came from Egypt. They consisted of vessels of gold and silver, royal and Upper Egyptian linen, rolls of papyrus, ox hides, ropes, sacks of lentils, and baskets of fish. The trees destined for Egypt were thus felled, and it seemed as though Wenamun could return serenely home. But eleven Tjeker ships appeared on the horizon, intent on settling with the Egyptian traveler over his theft of their silver. Wenamun experienced a moment of utter terror:

> Then I sat down and wept. And the secretary of the prince came out to me and said to me: "What is it?" I said to him: "Do you not see the migrant birds going down to Egypt a second time? Look at them traveling to the cool water! Until when shall I be left here? For do you not see those who have come to arrest me?"
>
> He went and told it to the prince. And the prince began to weep on account of the words said to him, for they were painful. He sent his secretary out to me, bringing me two jugs of wine and a sheep. And he sent me Tentne, an Egyptian songstress who was with him, saying: "Sing for him! Do not let his heart be anxious." And he sent to me, saying: "Eat, drink; do not let your heart be anxious. You shall hear what I say tomorrow."
>
> When morning came, he had his assembly summoned. He stood in their midst and said to the Tjeker: "What have you come for?" They said to him: "We have come after the blasted ships that you are sending to Egypt with our enemy." He said to them: "I cannot arrest the envoy of Amun in my country. Let me send him off, and you go after him to arrest him."
>
> He had me board and sent me off from the harbor of the sea. And the wind drove me to the land of Alasiya.[2]

The clever Tjekerbaal thus avoided scandal in his own territory, but in doing so, he consigned Wenamun to yet more wandering. Fleeing the Tjeker, the Egyptian landed on Cyprus (the land of Alasiya), where death again threatened him, this time from the natives. But he was saved from these dire straits by the local princess, Hatiba, who was evidently influenced by his words:

---

[1] M. Lichtheim, *Ancient Egyptian Literature: A Book of Readings*, Vol. 2: *The New Kingdom* (Berkeley, 1976), pp. 226–27. Werekter, who resided in Djanet/Tanis, was a Phoenician merchant and shipowner, probably in Egyptian service. The same name occurs in that of a shipping company of the second century B.C.E.; see Eisler, "Barakhel Sohn et Cie," *ZDMG* 78 (1924): 61–63. Seth is here a storm god; when he rages, he summons up a storm.
[2] Lichtheim, *Ancient Egyptian Literature*, 2:228–29.

"If the sea rages and the wind drives me to the land where you are, will you let me be received so as to kill me, though I am the envoy of Amun? Look, as for me, they would search for me till the end of time. As for this crew of the prince of Byblos, whom they seek to kill, will not their lord find ten crews of yours and kill them also?"[3]

The remainder of the papyrus is not preserved, so we do not know how the further adventures of Amun's envoy unfolded or whether he returned safely to Egypt. It is certain, though, that in Egypt, the state had completed the process of splitting into two parts. Its last act was the passing of Ramesses XI.

Nothing unusual or surprising occurred after his death. In the political power game, all the cards had already been dealt during his lifetime. At Thebes, the high priests of Amun continued to reign, often placing their names in royal cartouches, while Lower Egypt was ruled by Dynasty 21, whose founder was the Nesubanebdjed known from the Report of Wenamun. His name clearly shows that his origin lay in Mendes, not far from Tanis, the city that became the Residence of the new dynasty. His name is given as Smendes in the Greek sources, and this is the form most often used by historians today.

Neither the kings of Dynasty 21 nor the high priests of Amun-Re ruled over all of Egypt: the age-old epithet Lord of the Two Lands, though still used of them, was devoid of any meaning. Paradoxically, the reunification of the land under a single scepter occurred more than a century later, thanks to rulers of foreign origin. They would be Libyans, descended from the military elite of tribes that had settled in the delta toward the end of the New Kingdom.

And that was not all. In the first millennium B.C.E., Egypt, weakened but still in possession of its age-old culture and its fertile delta area, became an object of interest on the part of great powers on the lookout for rich booty and an impressive "calling card" to advertise their power. In consequence of warfare, a series of Kushites, Persians, and Greeks mounted the throne of Egypt. In certain cases, this signified a genuine rebirth of the land, in particular, economically and culturally. The title Lord of the Two Lands would regain its ancient meaning and even—here is another paradox—take on added meaning, for these pharaohs of foreign origin would combine rulership over all Egypt with kingship in their own lands.

---

[3] Ibid., p. 229.

Amun's Two Capitals: Thebes and Tanis
(Dynasties 21–24)

Toward the end of the second millennium B.C.E., the god Amun-Re reigned supreme over all Egypt. He was the real Lord of the Two Lands, a figure who united the two parts of the divided pharaonic state. The rulers in the south and the north collaborated and maintained friendly relations with each other.

The kings of Dynasty 21 had their capital at Tanis, a city of great strategic importance because of its proximity to Egypt's northeastern border. This former Lower Egyptian nome capital was soon expanded by Smendes and his successors to such an extent that it was regarded as a second Thebes. The architecture of Djanet, as Tanis was called in pharaonic times, imitated the monumental constructions of Thebes. Huge temples were erected there for various deities, though the sanctuary of Amun-Re had pride of place. The fact that the tombs of the kings of Dynasties 21 and 22 were located within its enclosure wall testifies to the unusual importance accorded to this temple.

From an archaeological standpoint, Tanis is not only one of the most fascinating but also one of the most mysterious places in Egypt. Not long ago, it was thought that it was Avaris, the capital of the Hyksos, the Asiatic infiltrators who had occupied the eastern delta in the Second Intermediate Period, as well as Piriamsese, the capital of the Ramessides. The excavations carried out by Auguste Mariette and William Matthew Flinders Petrie in the nineteenth century investigated only a small portion of the huge area, which lay on a hill cut through the middle by sandy mounds. They uncovered tons of worked stone: blocks decorated with reliefs, columns, fragments of obelisks, and huge statues of deities and kings. The monarch most often represented was Ramesses II, who had left traces of his activity nearly everywhere in Egypt.

But the inscriptions carved on the stone blocks—that is, the written sources from which we normally expect the answers to our questions—this time led the investigators into a cul-de-sac. They clearly show that most of the material stemmed from various periods and had been usurped at a later date and thus been obtained by demolishing earlier constructions (Figures 13 and 14). Statues dating to Dynasty 12 bear inscriptions that were altered in the Ramesside Period, while the names of New Kingdom rulers were hacked out to make room for the cartouches of kings of Dynasties 21 and 22. Certain objects bear traces of recurrent use. It has also been established that the overwhelming majority of the sculptures and reliefs were not manufactured at Tanis but were transported there from elsewhere. Why, whence, and when? These questions remained unanswered for years.

Convinced that San el-Hagar, as the Arabs now call the site, was the original seat of the Ramessides, which is also mentioned in the Hebrew Bible, the French Egyptologist Pierre Montet commenced excavations at Tanis in 1929. He was chiefly concerned with investigating the role of this city in the period described in the Bible, hoping to find documents relating to the so-

Figure 13. Statues and fragments of reliefs of the Ramesside Period at Tanis. Photo by the author.

[28]

journ of the Hebrews in Egypt and to their Exodus. His persistence and stamina were crowned by a success he himself had not foreseen. In a particularly unimpressive area of the Amun enclosure not far from the southeastern corner of the temple, under a heap of ruined bricks beneath which the remains of some miserable chapels and what was left of a sculptor's workshop could be discerned, Montet discovered, completely unexpectedly, the tombs of the kings of Dynasties 21 and 22. This event, however, did not arouse the response received by the discovery of the tomb of Tutankhamun in the Valley of the Kings at Thebes, for it was overshadowed by another historical event—the outbreak of World War II some months later. The treasures he found at Tanis are now on the top floor of the Egyptian Museum in Cairo, immediately next to the gold objects from the tomb of Tutankhamun.

Figure 14. Head of a colossal sandstone statue of Ramesses II (Dynasty 19) at Tanis. Photo by the author.

The royal tombs at Tanis constitute a valuable historical resource. They afford an idea of the importance of the rulers of Tanis in comparison to the pharaohs of the New Kingdom, whose tombs are preserved at Thebes. How modest these small rooms are, with their unappealing relief decoration, compared to the subterranean labyrinths excavated in the Valley of the Kings for the Tuthmosids and the Ramessides, whose rich paintings cast their spell to this very day!

As at Thebes, most of the Tanite royal tombs fell victim to robbers. Only one of them survived undisturbed to our time: the tomb of Psusennes, the third ruler of Dynasty 21. The splendid tableware found by Montet provides some corrective to the poverty suggested by the architecture of the tombs at Tanis. So elegant in the simplicity of their form, these golden vessels engraved with the royal titulary testify to the continuation of the finest traditions of the New Kingdom; in the perfection of their technique, they rival the masterpieces found in the tomb of Tutankhamun.

[29]

The pharaoh's mummy, adorned with a gold mask and covered with foil of the same material, rested in three nested sarcophagi. Only one of them, the innermost, was actually prepared for him. It has the form of a mummy with hands crossed over the breast, holding the insignia of Osiris: the bent *heqa*-scepter and the *nekhekh*-flagellum. A uraeus-serpent of pure gold is attached to the headdress, the broad *nemes*-headcloth that falls over the chest and arms. The head of the uraeus rises over the ruler's brow, and its coils form a wavy line on the headcloth. The upper surface of the silver sarcophagus is engraved with motifs recalling those painted or embossed on sarcophagi from Thebes: three birds with the heads of a vulture, a ram, and a falcon cover the mummy's torso with their outstretched wings, and the goddesses Isis and Nephthys are depicted as mourning women at the foot of the mummy. The inscription accompanying these figures is an invocation of the king to the goddess Nut, who is here called his mother. The ruler asks her to spread her wings over him, so that he will be "indestructible" and "unwearying," like the circumpolar stars that never disappear. On the floor of this sarcophagus is a huge representation of a goddess with half-opened wings, and along the edges are the words of comfort she addresses to the king (Figure 15). The silver coffin was placed in an anthropoid (human-shaped) sarcophagus of black granite and the latter in a rectangular chest of pink granite (Figure 16).

Neither of these stone coffins was an original work of Dynasty 21. The outer coffin, decorated with a beautiful figure of the goddess Nut in raised relief, was originally prepared for Merneptah, the successor of Ramesses II, while the usurped anthropoid sarcophagus had belonged to a noble of the Ramesside Period. The very fact of this reuse of older—and not just royal—sarcophagi in the burial of a pharaoh testifies to the impoverishment of the Lower Egyptian crown.

The same conclusion is demanded by the fact that the tomb of Psusennes, notwithstanding its modest size, was a collective one: buried with the pharaoh were one of his generals, named Undjebaundjed, and king Amenemope, his successor, who found their final resting place there. The mummy of Amenemope was found in a wooden coffin placed in a stone sarcophagus that had originally been prepared for queen Mutnodjmet, the wife of Smendes and the mother of Psusennes. This is all the more astonishing as the thoroughly plundered tomb of Amenemope was found in this same necropolis.

Who placed the body of the successor in the undisturbed tomb of his predecessor, in a sarcophagus made for the latter's mother? This is only one of the hundreds of mysteries concealed by Tanis. The monuments recently excavated there raise fresh questions more often than they help to solve old ones. After World War II, the French archaeological mission resumed excavations there and has continued them to this day. The city area to be inves-

tigated is so vast that various problems will probably have to wait
many years for their resolution.

Other questions related to the
history of Tanis have been solved
with the help of material found at
other sites in the delta. This was the
case not many years ago, for instance, when the question of why
the rulers of Dynasty 21 chose Tanis as the capital of Lower Egypt
was answered by the Austrian and
German excavations at Tell el-Daba
and Qantir, respectively, two sites
located southwest of Tanis.

As early as the 1960s, the eminent
Egyptian scholar Labib Habachi
had ventured the daring hypothesis
that neither the Hyksos capital of
Avaris nor the Ramesside Residence
of Piriamsese had been located in
the region of modern San el-Hagar.
In his opinion, the great majority of
decorated blocks and statues,
chiefly of the Ramesside Period,
had been transported to Tanis in the
Third Intermediate Period, and especially in Dynasty 22, from a place
that lay further to the west and that
was the actual Piriamsese. His "suspect" was modern Qantir, where a
large number of colored faience
tiles that could only have belonged
to the decoration of a royal palace
had already been found. They depict bound prisoners representing
various foreign peoples, and they

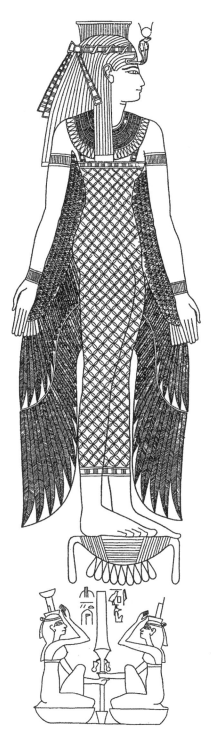

Figure 15. The winged goddess Nut. Below her are the mourning goddesses
Isis and Nephthys with the fetish of
Anubis. Relief decoration of the silver
sarcophagus of Psusennes from Tanis.

[31]

Figure 16. The goddess Nut in a star-covered dress, between the barques of the third and fourth hours and the stars of the south and the north. Relief on the outer granite sarcophagus of Psusennes from Tanis.

are also inscribed with royal cartouches containing the names of the great Ramesside rulers. Entire wall and floor surfaces were covered with such tiles in especially prestigious buildings. Labib Habachi's suspicions were confirmed by the work then being carried out by a German mission at Qantir, which discovered further remains of palaces and temples that had been erected in Dynasties 19 and 20 and subsequently destroyed. Blocks and statues from these edifices are today scattered over the whole of the eastern delta.

But why were the buildings of Piriamsese degraded to the status of a quarry as early as the period of the Tanite rulers, and why were such quantities of their blocks transported to Tanis? An unexpected answer was supplied by the painstaking investigations of Austrian archaeologists in the eastern delta, conducted for over twenty years now under the direction of Manfred Bietak, which are concentrated at the site of Tell el-Daba, near Qantir. The first sensation there was the discovery of the Hyksos capital of Avaris. Splendid palaces like those in neighboring Piriamsese did not come to light, but rather more modest constructions of mud brick. The objects found in them, however—scarabs with the names of Hyksos kings, ceramics characteristic of the Second Intermediate Period, and animal burials—constitute an invaluable find for historians. We now know where the Hyksos capital was located and that the Ramessides resided in another, neighboring city.

Not many years ago, an archaeological sensation was created by the discovery of splendid, though unfortunately only fragmentarily preserved, paintings in Minoan style that graced a palace at Avaris. They testify to close relationships between Egypt and the Aegean world, in particular Knossos and Thera, early in Dynasty 18.

The Austrians also concentrated their investigations on the paleogeography of the eastern delta, including geology, hydrology, climatology, stratigraphy, and so forth. Never before had the eastern delta of the pharaonic period been so meticulously investigated from the point of view of the natural sciences.

It came to light that a historical development could be traced in these matters as well, for interrelated changes in hydrology, the structure of the terrain, and the mineralogical composition of the soil are layered like the cultural strata of an ancient city. There were many indications that toward the end of the New Kingdom, the Pelusiac branch of the Nile sanded up and that, as a result, its waters combined with those of the Tanite branch, which flowed somewhat further to the west. The Ramesside capital, which lay north of the place where the branches now flowed together, thus lost its access to the sea, impeding its normal functioning, for it was now cut off from an important trade route. Evidently, there were also problems with water supply. We may assume that the city gradually died out. The rulers of the new dynasty had no choice but to move their capital to Tanis, the nearest center suited to be a royal Residence.

Located on a plateau near a bay of the Mediterranean—the very spot where Wenamun set out by ship for Phoenicia—Tanis was also well linked to the interior of the land, thanks to its branch of the Nile, whose waters were now increased by its being joined with a second branch. This might have led to a rise in the height of the water table, and perhaps this is the reason why the royal tombs at Tanis were located just below the surface of the ground, with very low ceilings. Everything points to a greater concern on the part of the rulers at Tanis with constructions that were connected with life in this world. Among these were especially the temples, for which enormous numbers of stone blocks were transported from the abandoned Piramsese.

The same god Amun reigned supreme in Upper Egypt, and his cult was probably the most important factor in the peaceful relations between the two parts of the land during Dynasty 21. On a secular level, these relationships were effected by marriages between members of the Theban priestly dynasty and the royal family at Tanis. The political role of royal daughters became unusually important in this period. Diplomatic marriages—an important instrument in dynastic politics—were concluded not only with kings but also with gods. This has to do with the institution of Divine Adoratrice or God's Wife of Amun, which had already been inaugurated in Egypt at the beginning of Dynasty 18 but which only now assumed special importance. While the princesses who bore this title in the New Kingdom had been able to have normal marriages, from the time of the high priest Pinudjem on, they were required to be faithful to the god and thus, in practice, to remain chaste. In many respects, their authority and social status approached the rank of a pharaoh.

Maatkare-Mutemhet, daughter of Pinudjem and his Tanite wife Henuttawy, was the first of the series of virgin brides of the Theban god. Not long ago, the maidenhood of this priestess was cast into doubt, for in her coffin, along with her embalmed corpse, there was found a small mummy that was assumed to be her child, who died after she gave birth. Upon examination by x-ray, however, the mummy proved to be that of a monkey, perhaps the only true companion of the God's Wife. In light of this evidence, the hypothesis that there was "sacred prostitution" in ancient Egypt proved to be unfounded. There is every reason to think that the participation of the God's Wife of Amun in the regularly repeated "engendering" of Khons, who played the role of child-god in the Theban triad, was purely symbolic.

After the death of Herihor in the seventh year of the Renaissance era, Piankh was named as the new high priest at Thebes; as in the case of his predecessor, his origin is passed over in silence in the Egyptian sources. The practice of dating years to the Renaissance was discontinued after the death of Ramesses XI, when Smendes assumed power at Tanis and was also recognized as king by the Thebans. But the next high priest of Amun, a son of Piankh named Pinudjem, had himself proclaimed king. His ambition is in no way surprising, for he was, after all, the husband of Henuttawy, a daughter of Ramesses XI, and the "father-in-law" of the god Amun, to whom he had given the hand of his daughter Maatkare in marriage. In his own court, he ended up enjoying as much authority as queen Nodjmet, the widow of the priest and royal usurper Herihor.

Pinudjem's power assumed such proportions that he was able to place his son Psusennes on the throne of Lower Egypt. Though this filiation is not a hundred percent certain, it remains a fact that behind the Greek form Psusennes lies an Egyptian name meaning "star that has risen in Thebes" and that along with the classical royal titulary, inscriptions at Tanis accord him the title of high priest of Amun-Re, King of the Gods. At this point, Egypt was ruled by a priest-king at Thebes and a king-priest at Tanis. Did this mean, then, that a reunification of the land was only a step away?

This might have happened if the high priests had concerned themselves only with religious matters. But their second, military function was every bit as important—and political—as their priestly office. Each one of them was a general and bore the title Great Commandant of the Army and even Great Commandant of the Army of the Entire Land.

The geographical boundaries of the Theban realm were precisely marked, and its northern limit was Teudjoi (modern el-Hiba) in Middle Egypt (Plate Ia). The high priest Menkheperre had a fortress built there, at a distance of about nineteen miles from Herakleopolis, on the east side of the river, in a place where the rocky desert embankment reaches nearly to the riverbank. It was intended to protect Egypt's theocratic southland not only from thoughts of conquest on the part of the Tanite rulers but also—and with time, ever more so—from attacks by the Libyan tribes that had by this time imposed their sovereignty on the areas west of the Nile valley. The most influential of these tribes was the Meshwesh, called Ma for short. Similar fortresses towered along the Nile throughout the area controlled by Thebes. They conjure up the sense of threat that must have prevailed in the southern portion of the land, and they show that this state was every bit as much military as it was theocratic.

MUMMY CACHES

Another major problem for the Theban priests was the constant violations of the tombs on the west bank of the Nile. They were plundered, and the corpses were desecrated, which in the case of the royal mummies was especially gruesome: these were gods, after all, incarnations of Osiris, and special care on the part of the priesthood was due them. The desperate search for a secure place for the royal mummies is a hallmark of the period. From the reign of Herihor to the pontificate of Pinudjem II, that is, through the century that comprised Dynasty 21, the royal tombs were inspected and the mummies of the great predecessors were restored and transferred, until finally, fourteen of these divine bodies were hidden in the subterranean rock tomb of Amenophis II in the Valley of the Kings, while twenty others were collected in a cache excavated deep in the rock south of Deir el-Bahri (Figure 17). In Egyptological literature, this secret repository is referred to by the French term *cachette*.

The discovery of the cachette—one of the most sensational finds in the archaeology of Egypt—was an event that smacked of a detective novel. It seems so because the mummies, already ignominiously treated in antiquity, were again robbed and desecrated in modern times, toward the end of the nineteenth century. When valuable objects started to appear on the antiquities market at the beginning of the 1870s, objects that gave every appearance of deriving from an unidentified royal tomb, the Egyptian Antiquities Service, at that time under the direction of the French Egyptologist Gaston Maspero, was alerted. All the classical methods of catching tomb robbers with the help of antiquities dealers had failed. It was necessary to proceed with utmost caution, for the organization of the sale of these ob-

Figure 17. The Dynasty 11 and Dynasty 18 temples at Deir el-Bahri, where many coffins of the Third Intermediate Period were hidden. Photo by the author.

jects pointed to a master thief. Where was the tomb? Who had been its fortunate discoverer? What had been destroyed, and what could still be saved? The French scholar responsible for saving the pharaonic monuments spent sleepless nights over these questions.

In January 1881, Maspero began by sending a telegram to the Luxor police, ordering them to keep an eye on the local antiquities dealers. Then he dispatched one of his colleagues to do detective work there. He was supposed to play the role of a rich tourist ready to buy. Without drawing attention to himself, he purchased a valuable object and won the trust of the dealer. Later, when he was brought a small statue that belonged to the equipment of a tomb from Dynasty 21, no doubt remained: this was a royal tomb. After much haggling, he purchased the statuette. It was thus that he happened upon Ahmed Abd el-Rassul, who together with his brother Mohammed had long been supplying dealers with objects from the Theban necropolis, which they smuggled into Luxor under their clothing or in baskets of vegetables. The Abd el-Rassul family had distinguished itself by its activity in this trade, which rendered them especially suspect in the eyes of the Luxor police and Maspero's delegate. The other suspect was Mustafa Aga Ayat, a Turk in the service of the Belgian, British, and Russian con-

[36]

sulates. Since he was provided with diplomatic immunity, Aga Ayat encountered no obstacles in purchasing mummies and other objects.

In April 1881, the Rassul brothers were arrested and taken in chains to the police station at Qena. They swore by all the saints that they were innocent, which appeared to be verified by the failure to find any antiquities in their home. When neither torture nor persuasion yielded any result, the brothers were soon released. Today, it is suspected that Daud Pasha, the police chief, had ties with the Rassul family. There would have been a happy ending had a violent family quarrel not broken out over the division of the loot from the royal cache. It is time to lift the veil of secrecy: it was Ahmed Abd el-Rassul who had accidentally discovered the cachette while searching for a lost goat. A plain, empty shaft led to the subterranean chamber containing the mummies of the great pharaohs and the remains of their sumptuous burial equipment. For nearly ten years, the brothers mined this vein of gold, avoiding the dangers of storing the objects at home and a fall in their price. Dealers at Luxor quickly resold the objects to rich foreign tourists.

When Ahmed demanded a larger share of the loot in compensation for the torture he had suffered at the hands of the police, a family quarrel broke out. News of this dispute quickly spread throughout the locale, once again drawing the attention of the Antiquities Service to the Rassul family. In a fit of rage when he was unable to come to terms with his brother, Mohammed—only three months after their interrogation—returned to the police, admitted to his deeds, and recounted the story of their tomb robbing in all its details. Some days later, he led a group of people to the royal cache; among them was the Egyptologist Emil Brugsch, who was the official representative of the government. The members of this expedition were armed to the teeth, for fear of vengeance on the part of the locals. We can easily imagine Brugsch's feelings as he was being lowered by rope into the deep shaft. He had with him a supply of candles. What terror he must have felt when suddenly, in their dim, flickering light, he found himself face to face with the greatest rulers of ancient Egypt. Among them was Ahmose, who had defeated the Hyksos, the renowned Tuthmosis III, and the first two rulers of Dynasty 19, Sethos I and Ramesses II. The coffins of the great queens were stacked in a heap, and canopic jars (jars in which the viscera of mummified bodies were stored) and drinking vessels were strewn everywhere. It was difficult to convince himself he was not dreaming.

Three hundred workers were immediately set to the task of salvaging the treasure. The undertaking was carried out under strict supervision, and all possible precautionary measures were observed. In the course of forty-eight hours, the first group of venerable dead and a number of valuable objects were loaded onto a ship. Maspero wrote that at Thebes, the ship *el-Menshieh*, serving as the largest hearse in history, was bid farewell by a crowd of mourning women and men firing salvos from rifles. Cynics wondered whether these demonstrations of grief at their departure referred to the source of income that was floating away. The mummies were taken to the Egyptian Museum in Cairo, where they have remained to this day. They were thoroughly investigated and precisely documented, and—as we have already mentioned—one of them made a posthumous journey, this time overseas. It was taken to Paris by plane, where it underwent further conservation treatment. Proof of illnesses furnished by x-rays and anthropological investigation, to which the other mummies were also subjected, suggests that more than just toothaches could sometimes make the pharaohs forget that they were gods.

A scant ten years after the discovery of the royal chachette south of Deir el-Bahri, the Theban necropolis yielded yet another archaeological sensation. Another cache of mummified bodies was discovered, this time of Theban priests. It was located at Deir el-Bahri itself, not far from the temples of Hatshepsut and Tuthmosis III, which are today being investigated by Polish archaeologists. This was a simple rock tomb, excavated in the time of Dynasty 19 and then deepened and expanded in Dynasty 21 by the high priest Menkheperre, who intended it as the resting place for his family. Somewhat later, it was reused as a cachette for the bodies of the priests of Amun from the end of Dynasty 21. There, in the year 1891, the French archaeologist Georges Daressy found no more and no less than 153 wooden coffins, including 101 double coffins, as well as a huge number of objects belonging to the equipment of the burials, among them 200 statuettes and more than seventy papyri.

The tomb is entered via a shaft 49 feet deep, at the bottom of which begins a gallery that is 394 feet long and has a side corridor. The coffins of the priests and priestesses, which were stacked on top of one another along the walls, filled the space to its ceiling. They are now in Cairo and in other museums around the world. The Polish Egyptologist Andrzej Niwiński has been investigating this unusually rich material, and he has succeeded in improving our knowledge of the history of this period with a series of new conclusions. In his opinion, all these coffins, which contain, among others, the bodies of many children and grandchildren of the high priest Menkheperre himself, were collected in the Bab al-Gasus (the modern name of the cache) at the same time that the royal mummies were placed in the *cachette royale* south of Deir el-Bahri, and thus when Pinudjem II was high priest and Siamun reigned at Tanis.

But these were only two components of a gigantic scheme to rescue the threatened mummies. Several other caches prepared at that time have also been discovered on the west bank of Thebes, for instance at the Asasif, where sixty mummies had been stored in nine shafts, and again at Deir el-Bahri, where Auguste Mariette—who paved the way for French archaeology in Egypt—found no fewer than seventy-one coffins of priests of the

[38]

god Montu in 1858. All indications are that the subterranean tombs in the hidden recesses of the temple of Hatshepsut afforded the best protection for the endangered mummies. The preparation of these caches best shows the sense of danger that prevailed in the theocratic Theban state of the high priests of Amun, especially toward the end of Dynasty 21.

The sheer quantity of these secondary burials indicates a collapse in the social order. A century earlier, every one of these deceased persons had rested in a tomb of large proportions excavated in the cliffs of western Thebes and decorated with beautiful paintings. But at the beginning of the second millennium B.C.E., this was no longer the case. Instead, there was a hasty, feverish attempt to save the most valuable objects, as though things might fall apart at any time.

The decoration of the wooden coffins of the Theban priests shows, however, that the finest traditions of the past had not fallen into oblivion. There was a concern to cover them with a miniature version of everything that was missing from the walls of the tombs. Every inch of these anthropoid coffins is covered with colorful paintings and inscriptions whose form and content are reminiscent of the decoration of Theban tombs of the Ramesside Period. The themes of the mythological scenes are especially rich, including excerpts from the great iconographic programs of the past, such as that of the Book of the Afterlife called the Amduat, which is known from royal tombs, and that of the Book of the Dead, which was for the most part copied down on papyri that accompanied the mummies of these high officials. Freed from the rigid schemes that had been considered important in times of greater religious orthodoxy, the imaginations of the artists created surprising new compositions, which they sometimes arbitrarily interspersed with elements of classical archetypes.

An indication of a longing for the good old days is provided by the many representations that were made of the greatest kings of Dynasty 18, in particular Amenophis I—the founder of that dynasty, who had already been deified in the Ramesside Period—and Tuthmosis III, during whose reign Egypt experienced a golden age. Identified with the mummiform Osiris, these rulers were often represented in large proportions on the floor of the wooden coffins, as though there was a desire to place the deceased under the magical protection of a divine predecessor or even to guarantee them a similar incarnation after death. Figures of falcons with their wings stretched around the depiction of the ruler, as well as the latter's feathered garment, which is reminiscent of the body of a falcon and is associated with Horus, son of Osiris, serve as symbols of rebirth in these scenes. In the inscriptions on the walls of the coffins, Amun-Re is often combined with the Heliopolitan sun god into a single entity and even spoken of in terms of the latter's various aspects: Khepri, the morning sun; Atum, the evening sun; and Horakhty, "Horus of the Two Horizons."

[39]

This process of syncretism, which opened the possibility of identifying nearly any deity with any other, came close to being a monotheism, though its character was completely different from that of the cult of the sun disk Aten in the reign of Akhenaten. At this time, the solar form of Amun had an omnipotent, magical power. Carried on the shoulders of his priests, his statue could decide any question by leaning in a certain direction—this was the usual form taken by oracles, which were extremely popular in this period. Trivial questions were addressed to them, such as who had stolen an article of clothing or a piece of pottery, as well as important problems, such as political and military decisions. Invoking the divine "will," the priests could thus decide everything. Since they essentially had greater knowledge than anyone else, they were practically lords over life and death for each and every Egyptian. With a bow, the divine statue could decide who assumed priestly functions in the temple and who might exercise the office of God's Wife of Amun.

Oracles had assumed such importance that some of the questions asked were even inscribed on temple walls. Among these is a rather long text preserved at Karnak, from the time of Pinudjem II. From it, we learn that the high priest himself turned to the oracle with a question regarding the dishonesty of an official, for the god evidently "had no desire" to participate in the annual procession at the temple of Luxor until the matter was decided. Two documents were placed before the divine statue, one containing a positive response, the other a negative one.

Even the dead were in the care of the magical words of Amun-Re, as evidenced by one of the papyri found at Deir el-Bahri. The papyri placed in the tombs of the deceased priests and priestesses are today, along with their wooden coffins, our most important sources of knowledge regarding the religion of this stormy period. Especially interesting are the Mythological Papyri. In many cases, we do not see their motifs used again until the temple reliefs of the Ptolemaic Period. We do not know what happened in the meanwhile, for few comparable sources are preserved from the intervening centuries.

TANIS AND ISRAEL

Like Thebes, Tanis also experienced a significant crisis in the second half of Dynasty 21, that is, at the beginning of the first millennium B.C.E. Of the five successors of Psusennes, only Siamun (c. 978–959 B.C.E.) left traces of significant architectural undertakings. His works included a large chapel of granite, while the many foundation stones of his that were found in the temple of Amun and Mut testify to an élan that presupposes the availability of considerable means and a corresponding self-confidence. The tombs

[40]

of Psusennes' successors, however, are small and unassuming. In no case are we certain whether these kings belonged to the same genealogical line. It is supposed that one of them, Osorkon, might have been the first ruler of Libyan descent.

During Dynasty 21, Israel, which began to play an ever greater role in Egypt's foreign policy, stepped into the political arena. Toughened by its wars with the Philistines and consolidated by Saul, its first king, the state increased in power during the reign of David (c. 1010–970 B.C.E.), who moved his capital from Hebron to Jerusalem. In the biblical book of Samuel, which contains a report of David's deeds, Egypt is mentioned only in connection with the king's expedition to northern Sinai, where he rescued an Egyptian, the slave of Amalekite bedouins, from starvation (1 Sam. 30:11–13).

Somewhat later, the royal court at Tanis granted asylum to the young Hadad, the successor to the throne of Edom in Transjordan. Hadad, who had been disinherited by David, then came to Egypt, where he married the sister of the queen (1 Kings 11:14–22). David's successor Solomon (c. 970–930/929 B.C.E.) also received a daughter of Pharaoh as bride: the Hebrew monarch's wife was the daughter of Siamun, and her dowry included the Philistine city of Gezer in the foothills of Judea, which had previously been conquered by the same pharaoh (1 Kings 9:16–24).

The laconic information contained in the Hebrew Bible tells us a great deal about the status of Egypt on the international stage. How very different it was from the imperial might of the pharaohs of the New Kingdom, who took Asiatic princesses as brides! How weak the ruler at Tanis must have felt when he gave a city conquered from the Philistines to the Hebrew king along with his daughter!

There is every indication that the last Tanite rulers, like the high priests of Amun at Thebes, slowly lost their power over their realm. A series of provinces gradually fell under the sway of Libyan tribes. The most important of them, that of the Meshwesh (Ma), exerted an increasingly greater influence over the development of events at Tanis and Memphis. In Middle Egypt, where the fortress at Teudjoi defended the border of the Theban theocracy of Amun, this tribe built a fortress of its own and brought the city of Herakleopolis under its control. The threatening atmosphere that accompanied the decline of authority and the collapse of social structures facilitated the rise of this new political power.

DYNASTY 22

Around 950 B.C.E., Shoshenq, one of the leaders of the Libyans who already resided on the Nile, marched his army into Thebes; shortly thereafter, he had himself proclaimed pharaoh. So as not to contravene the for-

malities, he consulted the oracle of Amun as to whether he should intro-
duce the cult of his father, Nimlot, at Abydos. This chief center of the Osiris
cult, which was situated north of Thebes, was a city where cult chapels for
deceased ancestors had traditionally been erected. The text of this unusual
decree was carved on a granite stela whose lower portion has been preserved to us. In conformity with the principles of the Theban theocracy, the
reigning monarch Psusennes II posed the question to the oracle. The costs
of the endowment, which included the baldachin and the statue of the deceased, were shared by Shoshenq as ruler of the Ma and the Egyptian king.
We are witness to an act of political violence, concealed under the mantle of
piety and the affected rhetoric of the Egyptian literary language. Amun
was of course "delighted" with the proposal, and he directed words of
highest praise to Shoshenq. Thus were laid the theological grounds for the
latter's assumption of power. In the reliefs representing Shoshenq, only the
feathers on his head and his title of tribal chief betray the origin of the new
ruler of Egypt. This pharaoh, who stemmed from a line of five Great Chiefs
of the Ma, was already completely Egyptianized.

Shoshenq I (Figure 18) founded a new line, Dynasty 22. In the history
written by Manetho, it was called the Bubastid dynasty, for the seat of the
new ruler was the city of Bubastis, located southwest of Tanis in the Nile
delta. In the period of these Libyan rulers, many monumental constructions
were erected in this principal center of the goddess Bastet, whose sacred
animal was the cat.

Nothing leads us to suppose that the assumption of the pharaonic throne
by someone of foreign origin upset the land or in any way harmed it. Quite
the contrary, the energy of the Libyan neophyte proved to be healthy
for the land, which had been weakened and overcome by corruption. Under the scepter of the Bubastids, Egypt was once again united and the title
Lord of the Two Lands regained its old meaning. In conformity with tradition, the tombs of the kings were erected in the precinct of the temple of
Amun at Tanis; like those of their predecessors, they assumed the form of
hypogea.

Thebes did not, however, lose its status as the central cult city of Amun-
Re. A large priestly class continued to prosper there, with a high priest and
the God's Wife of Amun at its head. To maintain his power, the king ruling
over the south had to be concerned with the goodwill of these priests, while
also taking care lest the Theban center become a source of unrest and attempts at separatism. It was watched over by a royal governor, usually one
of Pharaoh's sons, whose seat was at Teudjoi in Middle Egypt. The fortress
there was expanded during Dynasty 22, as shown, for instance, by the
beautiful temple reliefs discovered some decades ago by a German mission. Now in the collection at Heidelberg University, the reliefs depict
Shoshenq I, the founder of the dynasty, in the company of various deities.

Figure 18. The goddess Mut nursing king Shoshenq I. Relief on the "Bubastite Portal" at Karnak. Photo by Dieter Johannes, German Archaeological Institute, Cairo.

The erection of a temple at Teudjoi, which geographically and strategically linked Upper and Lower Egypt, was probably an expression of gratitude on the part of the king for the goodwill of these deities. For us, it has the value of a symbol that, like the *sema-tawy* sign, represents the uniting of the two parts of the land under the scepter of a single pharaoh.

The very style of the reliefs found at el-Hiba/Teudjoi constitutes important information for us. The modeling of the king's face, along with various iconographic details, show clearly that the source of inspiration for the artists of that period lay in the extremely subtle and refined forms of the bas-reliefs of the Tuthmosid Dynasty 18. As in the case of the representations of Dynasty 18 kings on wooden coffins of Dynasties 21 and 22, we again see a consciousness of history that found its expression in a longing for "better times" associated with the first half of the New Kingdom. The art of the pharaohs named Tuthmosis and Amenophis became a model that was emulated five centuries later in the reigns of the Shoshenqs, Osorkons, and Takelots—as most of the rulers of the Libyan dynasty were called.

According to the most recent research, six pharaohs named Shoshenq, three Osorkons, and three Takelots ruled during the period from the middle of the tenth century to the end of the eighth century B.C.E. Because of their repeated names and titles and the fragmentary condition of the preserved record, it can be difficult to determine whether we are dealing with one and the same pharaoh or with two distinct individuals. Even more complicated is research into the genealogy, the chronology, and the connections between the officials who are named in the documents of this period. Even establishing their identities poses a major challenge to the historian of the Third Intermediate Period. It is only in the last four decades that we have seen detailed historical investigation and comprehensive treatments of this period.

SHOSHENQ I's CAMPAIGN TO ISRAEL

The Egyptian state consolidated by Shoshenq I and his successors and administered by persons descended from military families developed into a political and military power capable of striking fear in the hearts of its Asiatic neighbors. An expression of this was Egypt's active policy vis-à-vis Palestine: information derived from Egyptian sources supplements the evidence of the Hebrew Bible in this regard. Thus the Hebrew Jeroboam, whom Solomon sought to kill because he viewed him as a rival heralded by the prophets (1 Kings 11:29–43), found asylum at the court of Shoshenq I. After Solomon's death (c. 930 B.C.E.), Jeroboam returned home and created a rupture between the tribes, between Judea and Israel, between Jerusalem and Samaria. Around 925 B.C.E., the pharaoh took advantage of this circumstance to march into Palestine with a powerful Egyptian army reinforced by Nubian and Libyan troops. The Egyptian force thoroughly plundered the land of the Philistines, the two Hebrew kingdoms, and the Negev. Shoshenq forced his way into Jerusalem, where he seized the treasures of the Temple and the royal palace (1 Kings 14:25–27). He even took the golden shields that Solomon had had made; the Judean king Rehoboam subsequently replaced them with shields of bronze.

The surrender of these treasures to the Egyptians probably saved Jerusalem and its people from total destruction. The belief that the army of Shoshenq took the famed Ark of the Covenant is a product of modern fantasy. The biblical text is silent on the matter, while the opinions of present-day scholars differ. Archaeologists have never sought the Ark in the region of Tanis. From the Hebrew Bible, we learn that in the end, Shoshenq's expedition had a positive result, for it induced Rehoboam and his court to a piety that enabled them once again to enjoy the grace of God and to prosper.

A huge scene carved on the south wall of the temple of Amun at Karnak illustrates Shoshenq's victory. But we would search in vain there for concrete episodes of the Palestinian campaign or even for the names of the conquered cities of Jerusalem and Gezer. This is because the ruler is depicted wielding his mace in a thoroughly conventional manner, following the iconographic tradition of the New Kingdom, smiting predominantly Asiatic captives who are bound by their hair to a tall pole. Facing him is Amun-Re, who holds a short sickle-sword in his right hand and, in his left, ropes that fetter the figures representing the defeated peoples. The body of each of these figures has the form of an oval fortification wall that encloses a geographical name. But this lengthy list, which contains the names of more than 150 cities, is of little value as a historical document.

The sequence of the geographical names does not enable us to establish the topography of the conquests. Quite striking is the lack of any traces of Shoshenq's presence in the center of Israel, in contrast to the peripheral Samaria and the mentions of Edom. Were we to depend only on this information, we would be obliged to doubt that Shoshenq penetrated as far as Jerusalem. The opinion is that the relief does not depict historical reality but rather is modeled after an original from the time of Tuthmosis III, Amenophis II, or one of the great Ramessides. Once again, propaganda prevailed over fact.

Though there is little agreement in the information from the biblical and the Egyptian sources regarding Shoshenq's campaign to Palestine, archaeological discoveries have confirmed that such a campaign occurred and that Egypt's relations with its Asiatic neighbors were quite lively at this time. A fragment of an inscription mentioning Shoshenq has been discovered at Megiddo, a city in the north of Palestine, and at Byblos, fragments of statues of this king and his successor, Osorkon I. The latter were undoubtedly sent as gifts to the rulers of Byblos by these pharaohs of Dynasty 22, who had resumed friendly relations with that city. Carved on the red quartzite statue of Osorkon I, which today is in the Louvre, is a cartouche containing the name of the king, written in hieroglyphs, along with a Phoenician inscription ascribing the object to Elibaal, king of Byblos. The iconography and style of this beautiful statue do not permit the slightest doubt as to its identification. The pharaoh is depicted wearing a long wig, with a uraeus-serpent on his brow, and his youthful features seem to radiate serenity and self-confidence.

The sources we have to date do not allow us to determine whether Shoshenq's campaign to Palestine was intended to assist Jeroboam's efforts in his struggle for power, or whether it was an ordinary raid whose goal was to heighten the prestige of Egypt and its new pharaoh. The rich booty Shoshenq took from Jerusalem and other cities guaranteed affluence for him and his successor, as is evident, for instance, in the monumental constructions whose remains are preserved to this day at Tanis and Bubastis.

THE BUBASTID PORTAL OF OSORKON II

Bubastis, in particular, flourished remarkably at this time. Among its ruins, which are located at Tell Basta in a suburb of Zagazig, special attention is merited by the many blocks stemming from a portal erected on the occasion of the *sed*-festival of Osorkon II (c. 874–850 B.C.E.), the successor of Takelot I. This monumental gateway of red granite stood in the area of the great temple dedicated to the goddess Bastet. The portal is decorated with reliefs of the highest interest, for they document various rituals connected with the royal jubilee (Figures 19 and 20).

The condensed content and abbreviated form of these representations prevent us from fully understanding all the scenes. Nevertheless, Osorkon II's gateway at Bubastis constitutes one of our most complete representations of the *sed*-festival in a single cycle of reliefs from ancient Egypt. On this occasion, the king wore a long, simple garment, while the insignia of Osiris in his hands identified him with this god, who was a personification of rebirth. Renewed, the king mounted the throne of Upper and Lower Egypt, as emphasized by the symbolism of his headdresses, which are alternately the white and the red crowns.

Processions, dance, song, and recitations of religious texts were integral parts of this ritual. The masters of ceremonies were priests, as can be immediately recognized from their clothing. The most important of these, who were often sons of the king, are distinguished by the panther skins that grace their bodies. The king himself, who was viewed as the highest priest, sometimes appears in Egyptian art wearing a panther skin and more often

[46]

still with an amulet in the form of a panther head attached to his belt. During festivals, the roles of anthropomorphic deities with animal heads were played by priests who wore the scalp of an animal or a mask of similar form on their head.

DOMESTIC POLICY

Military successes in Palestine were not the only basis for Egypt's prosperity under the Bubastids. Even more important was a shrewd domestic policy that followed the best traditions of the past. An indication that the assumption of power by the new dynasty was essentially free of conflict is furnished by the marriage of Osorkon I to Maatkare, daughter of Psusennes II, the last king of Dynasty 21. Maatkare was the mother of Shoshenq II, one of the next kings of the Libyan dynasty. A single stela found in el-Dakhla oasis, which stems from the fifth regnal year of Shoshenq I, informs us of internal unrest at the beginning of this dynasty.

These parvenus of Libyan blood displayed great generosity toward the priests of the most important

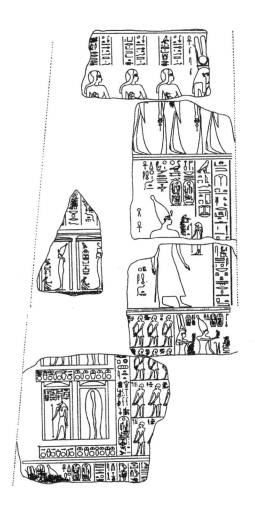

Figure 19. (top) Ritual scenes from the *sed*-festival of Osorkon II. Relief from the king's jubilee portal at Bubastis.

Figure 20. (bottom) Osorkon II in a procession at his *sed*-festival. Relief from the king's jubilee portal at Bubastis.

[47]

Egyptian deities, who represented a potential source of political resistance. We learn of this, for instance, from a stela found in Middle Egypt at Herakleopolis, the cult center of the ram-headed god Herishef (Greek Harsaphes). The text carved on the stela reports the charity of Nimlot, one of the sons of Shoshenq I. This worthy bore the title Commandant of the Entire Army. Nimlot informed the king that the temple of the Herakleopolitan god did not have its usual tribute in the form of the bulls that were indispensable for the many sacrifices made in the course of an entire year.

To make up for this blatant carelessness, Nimlot committed himself to deliver sixty cattle, while the surrounding cities and towns, along with their high officials, were required to supply the remainder. Shoshenq was presented with a precise list of these obligations. The king accepted the proposal and showered the official with praise. Military order, loyalty, and efficiency, indeed—or perhaps just a diplomatic measure to earn the goodwill of the clergy of Herishef?

The military successes and architectural achievements of the first Bubastids might create the impression that the two parts of the land were

Figure 21. Osorkon II (depicted twice), Isis, and Nephthys adoring the *djed*-pillar and the *ankh*-sign. Double scene in the tomb of Osorkon II at Tanis.

now integrated and that unity prevailed in Egypt. The situation, however, was much more complicated.

After the reigns of Shoshenq I, Osorkon I, and Osorkon II (Figure 21), which together comprised nearly a century (c. 945–850 B.C.E.), ever deeper rifts were noticeable on the political map of Egypt. New generations of great commandants of the Meshwesh (Ma) sprang up in certain important administrative and religious centers. Related to the king by blood or marriage, they continuously strove to loosen the ties that bound them to the center of authority. The inheritance of rule in the provincial centers was one factor that stimulated their independence. To win the loyalty of the local rulers, the kings often bestowed large gifts of land on them, a shortsighted policy that increased the assets of these power holders. In the end, there emerged several strong, competitive centers of power. Royal gifts in the form of large estates led to the appearance of, among others, independent centers at Athribis and Pharbaethos in the delta.

Toward the end of Dynasty 22 and during Dynasty 23, only two of the largest cities in the eastern delta belonged securely to the crown: Tanis and Bubastis. In their vicinity lay an ever more independent center of power: Leontopolis, ancient Egyptian Taremu, located in the vicinity of modern Tell el-Muqdam. Here were worshiped a lion goddess and her fierce son Mahes, and the tomb of one of the queens of this period was discovered in the precinct of their temple (Plate Ib).

A political center that slowly turned into an independent kingdom made its appearance in the western delta. This was Sais, the city of the warrior goddess Neith, who was depicted with a bow and arrows in her hand. As time passed, the rulers of Sais gained control over an area extending west as far as Libya and north to the Mediterranean, that is, more than a third of the entire delta.

These princedoms competed with Pharaoh for influence in the area of Memphis, the ancient capital of the land at the apex of the delta, south of modern Cairo. Here ruled the clergy of the temple of Ptah, where a son of the king usually served as high priest. In this period, it was the custom to locate the tombs of the priests within the temple enclosure. One of the most beautiful is that of the high priest Shoshenq, a son of Osorkon II, in the form of a chapel made of sandstone blocks. Discovered at Memphis several decades ago, this chapel now graces the garden in front of the Cairo Museum (Figures 22 and 23). Reliefs carved on its walls depict the young Shoshenq wearing a panther skin and praying to the god Ptah, who has the form of a mummy with a royal beard.

One of the most important functions of the priests at Memphis was the care of the Apis bull, an incarnation of Ptah. The dead Apis bulls, who were identified with Osiris, god of the netherworld, were mummified and ceremonially buried in subterranean galleries in the vicinity of the royal

[49]

Figure 22. Shoshenq, son of Osorkon II and high priest of the god Ptah at Memphis, offering ointment to the god Harendotes. Relief from the tomb chapel of Shoshenq at Memphis. Now in the court of the Egyptian Museum, Cairo. Photo by the author.

cemeteries. Small wonder, then, that power over this important religious and strategic center was in the care of dignitaries of Libyan origin who ruled in their delta principalities. Memphis fell briefly into the hands of the ruler of Sais, in whose army soldiers from Libya also served.

The administration of Middle Egypt and the Theban region was reserved for royal children. Their seat was the fortress of Teudjoi, which lay in the vicinity of Herakleopolis. From there, they were supposed to maintain control over Upper Egypt, keeping a special eye on the development of events at Thebes, a potential center of rebellion. These royal governors even bore the title of high priest of the Theban Amun, but how could they have exercised this function from a practical point of view, when they resided some 250 miles to the north? They appeared in Thebes on the occasion of the most important religious festivities, which gave them an opportunity to take stock of the mood there and to demonstrate that an authentic king still resided in Lower Egypt.

In reality, the duties of the high priest in the temple of Amun were fulfilled by one of the most influential local dignitaries. In the course of time, the Theban priesthood felt an increasing desire for independence from royal authority. We have indications of the loyalty of the high priest Iuput, the third son of Shoshenq I, but the high priest Osorkon, a son of Takelot II, was obliged to struggle to maintain order at Thebes. The first of these two broke with the tradition of the inheritance of this most important priestly office. This afforded a strong king the possibility of manipulating the office, but it also created an opportunity for the pharaoh's enemies at a moment when he was weak. Already in the reign of Osorkon II, a certain Harsiese had himself proclaimed king at Thebes, and a tomb was prepared for him in the enclosure of the mortuary temple of Ramesses III at Medinet Habu.

THE CHRONICLE OF PRINCE OSORKON

To this day, this confused period in Egyptian history has left more questions open than have been answered. Relatively few hieroglyphic texts are preserved to impart information regarding the development of political events during the reigns of the later Bubastids. The chronicle that the high priest Osorkon, a son of Takelot II, had carved on the walls of the temple of Karnak is thus all the more valuable. This text adorns the walls of the so-called Bubastite Portal, a sort of high gateway that was erected of sandstone by command of Iuput, a son of Shoshenq I. To obtain the raw material for its construction, a special quarry was opened at Gebel el-Silsila.

Figure 23. Shoshenq, son of Osorkon II, adoring the god Anubis. Relief from his tomb chapel. Now in the court of the Egyptian Museum, Cairo. Photo by the author.

Squeezed in between the older temple of Ramesses III and the great pylon of the temple of Amun-Re, the Bubastite Portal today goes almost unnoticed in the thicket of edifices at Karnak. In the time of Dynasty 22, however, it was intended to play an unusually important propagandistic and political role. Erected at what was at that time the front of the temple of Amun, the portal led from its courtyard into the sacred edifices that stood in the southern portion of the temple precinct. It was thus a sort of show-

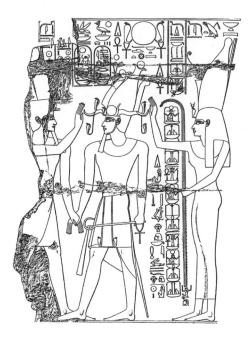

Figure 24. The Theban divine couple Amun and Mut crowning King Osorkon I. Relief on the "Bubastite Portal" at Karnak.

case of the Libyan dynasty in the Theban region, intended to remind the priests and the people who still ruled the land.

The reliefs carved on the front wall of the portal depict Shoshenq I, the founder of the dynasty, being nursed by the goddess Mut, Amun's consort. Could a more suggestive means have been found to express the notion that the leader of a Libyan tribe derived his Egyptian essence from the breast of this mother and that none other than the very gods of Egypt had thus designated him pharaoh? Further along, we see his successor, Osorkon I, crowned by the divine couple of Thebes, Amun-Re and Mut (Figure 24).

The decoration of the portal was not finished during the pontificate of Iuput. The next rulers of Dynasty 22, Takelot I, Osorkon II, and Takelot II, contributed little to the completion of the work. Prince Osorkon, a son of Takelot II, decorated the interior walls with a chronicle of the dramatic events that were played out at Thebes during his pontificate. Osorkon bore the title of high priest of Amun, and as royal governor, he resided in the fortress of Teudjoi in Middle Egypt. Around 835 B.C.E., there was a rebellion against royal authority at Thebes, and Osorkon traveled south at the head of his army. It is noteworthy how strongly he emphasizes his virtues and his merits at the beginning of the text, creating an impression that he wishes to make the reader wonder how anyone could have dared to raise a hand against so outstanding a man as he. Despite the badly preserved condition of this lengthy text and its doubtless partial representation of the facts, it is worthwhile to gain some acquaintance with this document, which reflects the internal situation of Egypt in the time of the Libyan rulers.

> Lo, the governor of Upper Egypt and chieftain over the Two Lands, whom Amun appointed according to his own desire, [the first prophet of] Amun in Thebes, generalissimo of the entire land, the leader Osorkon, whom the hereditary noble, great of favour, the king's great wife, mistress of the Two

Lands Karomama [beloved-of-Mut], may she live, bore, was in his residence, in might and victory over his boundaries, (at) The Crag of Amun Great of Roaring—so it shall be called. [. . . greatest of] the great, the eldest son of the Two-Great-of-Magics, one to whom Upper [Egypt] reported, one to whom Lower Egypt petitioned, as the fear of him encircled them, their produce being at his gate through the greatness of his strength which the lord of the Thrones of the Two Lands imparted [to] him. . . .

Now when Thebes rose (in rebellion) against the protector of the land and the gods who were in it, the great god heard the appeal (made) to him. The beneficent ram of He-ninsu came to him in his name conformably to [his wish], so that he might suppress the wrong. Then he came forth at [the head of] his army even as [Horus] coming forth from Chemmis.

Lo, he was at the town of Khmun doing what is praised of its lord, the lord of Khmun, the lord of the god's words, and making content the lords of Upper Egypt. Their braziers were set, their cult-places renewed, their fanes cleansed from all evil things, their walls erected anew, and what had been destroyed in every city of Upper Egypt was re-established. Suppressed were his enemies belonging to the interior of this land, which had fallen into turmoil in his time.

He proceeded southward (?) [. . .] sailing along the stream peacefully, and putting to land at Thebes-is-Victorious. He entered it [as] the child of the Lady, and the gods who were in it rejoiced. He accepted her breasts of fine gold and sucked her milk; [it] entered [into him] with life and dominion, while she gave to him [her might and] her victory.

So it came to pass that he was there doing what is praised of the lord of the gods, Amen-Re, lord of the Thrones of the Two Lands, and bringing [offerings] and things of his victory to Amun, the great god, and then saying, 'Take to yourself'; his hands bearing a million of things and offerings consisting of all good things in order to make an exceedingly great present of divine offerings consisting of everything good and pure, pleasant and sweet, supplied with ten thousands and thousands without end as a daily offering in excess of what existed before. . . .

He (Amun-Re) readily assented in agreement with what he (Osorkon) had said like a father whose son is dear to him. Then there came the prophets, god's fathers, priests, lector-priests of Amun, and the entire temple-priest-hood bearing bouquets to the governor of Upper Egypt; (as well as) this whole city, namely all its districts and every quarter of it, and men [and women] gathered together at the same time.

Lo, they said with one accord crying aloud to the governor of Upper Egypt, thus:

You are the valiant protector of all the gods. Amun appointed you [as] the eldest son of your progenitor; he has chosen you amongst hundreds of thousands in order to carry out what his heart desires throughout. Now (?) we are begging you as we are aware of your affection for him. Behold, he has brought

[53]

you [to us] in order to suppress our misery and put an end to the tempest confronting us; because this land was drowned, its laws having perished in the hands of those who rebelled against their lord and who were his (own) officials. Each scribe in his temples would obliterate his ordinances, which the lord of the *heden*-plant (the god Thoth) had put down on the book (himself), and would wreck the sacred rites of the temples, which had fallen into plunder; yes (all this) was not in the cognizance of the king [. . .] . . . O true image of Osiris, [. . .] who sent you to the land which is called the Eye of Re in order to banish the injurer of its pupil. What, then, would this land be like without [you]? . . .

Thereupon [the governor of] Upper Egypt said, 'Go and bring to me every (case of) transgression against him and the records of the ancestors [. . .] . . . Then the prisoners were brought to him at [once] like a bundle of pinioned ones (?). Then he struck them down for him, causing [them] to be carried like goats the night of the feast of the Evening Sacrifice in which braziers are kindled [. . .] like braziers (at the feast of) the Going forth of Sothis. Everyone was burned with fire in the place of [his] crime [. . .] Thebes.

Then [he] caused the children of the magnates [of] the interior of this land [who] were learned [to be brought to him, in order to] make [them sit on] the seats of their fathers with willing heart for the purpose of causing [the land] to be better off than in its former condition.[1]

At this point, Osorkon begins to issue orders regarding benefactions for various landed estates, such as:

A decree is (herewith) issued in my name as first prophet of Amen-[Re], king of the gods, Osorkon, in order to provide for the estate of Amen-Re, king of the gods, [the estate of Mut the great, mistress of] Ashru, the estate of Khons-

---

[1] The translation is by R. A. Caminos, *The Chronicle of Prince Osorkon*, Analecta Orientalia 37 (Rome, 1958), pp. 17, 26, 29, 31, 33, 35, 42, 48, 51. The "Crag of Amun Great of Roaring" is a fortress on the east bank of the Nile opposite the island of el-Hiba in Middle Egypt, twenty miles south of Herakleopolis Magna. The "Two-Great-of-Magics" are the two uraeus-serpents on the royal crown; Osorkon was thus the son of one who was crowned, that is, a king. The "fear of him encircled them" refers to the fear of people in both parts of the land, that is, Upper and Lower Egypt. He-ninsu was the ancient Egyptian name of Herakleopolis. Chemmis was called Akh-bit in Egyptian; the name means "papyrus-thicket of the king of Lower Egypt," and the place, which was the mythological birthplace of Horus, was associated with an island near Buto. Khmun was the Egyptian name of Hermopolis. The reference to suckling has to do with the statue of a goddess, probably Mut. The "Feast of the Evening Sacrifice" is a festival we encounter at Letopolis (modern Ausim) in the second nome of Lower Egypt; typical of this festival was a ritual in which some sort of ordeal by fire was staged during the night to frighten off enemies and evil spirits. The festival of the "Going Forth of Sothis (the star Sirius)" was the ancient Egyptian New Year's Day.

in-Thebes Neferhotep, the estate of Mont, lord of Thebes, and the harim (?) of
Maet, and the temples and subsidiary temples of its foundation; in order to
cause them to be in accordance with their (proper) standing; in order to add
to what has been done (in the matter of) sustenance and offerings to them
throughout eternity for ever; in order to organize their people, their herds,
and their fields permanently according to their ordinances. All their staffs are
safeguarded and protected, without permitting them to be interfered with by
any [person?], by any count, any official, any controller of the palace, l. p. h.,
concerning any task which may have to be performed in this entire land except [their (own)] work in these temples.[2]

Osorkon's second order concerns the estates of the high priest of Amun,
from which many offerings to Amun were supposed to be donated, such as
incense and honey—scarce commodities, for incense producers and bee-
keepers had been chased away. There are careful specifications of who was
to deliver what and where. There follows an order concerning the donation
of a temple lamp and its fuel.

> . . . issuing a decree [in order to] provide for this castor-oil lamp which I
> have newly instituted for Amen-Re, king of the gods.
>   List thereof:
>   The priests who are in their month (i.e., their monthly service) in the estate
> of Amun for every [year]: 4[85] hin of castor oil. The House of Gold (i.e., the
> treasury) of Amun: 365 hin of castor oil for every year. The Gateway of Al-
> abaster: 365 (hin) of castor oil. Sum-total: 1215 hin of castor oil.[3]

In the conclusion of the text, Osorkon makes the following political declaration regarding the future:

> I have acted for Amun with willing heart on [behalf of] the life, prosperity,
> and health of my father, the son of Re Takelothis beloved-of-Amun son-of-
> Isis, may he live for ever, [in order] to cause his spirit to rejoice until I am
> upon his throne . . . [. . .]
>   As for the one who will upset this command which I have issued, he shall
> be subject to the ferocity of Amen-Re, the flame of Mut shall overcome him
> when she rages, and his son shall not succeed him, whereas my name will
> stand firm and endure throughout the length of eternity.[4]

---

[2] Ibid., p. 54.

[3] Ibid., pp. 62–63. A hin was a measure of capacity, equaling nearly .45 quart. The function of the "Gateway of Alabaster" remains unknown.

[4] Ibid., pp. 70–71. The word translated "spirit" is *ka*, a sort of Doppelgänger believed to
be an aspect of every human being.

Other documents of the period show that Osorkon's triumph over Thebes was temporary, and neither gifts nor acts of mercy secured the loyalty of Upper Egypt to the rulers residing in Bubastis or Tanis. The division of the land into ever smaller chiefdoms had become an irreversible process, and new local rulers constantly had themselves proclaimed king. We do not always know how large their domains were or how long they remained under their control. Though it functioned officially as a single state, by the end of Dynasty 22, Egypt had at least two or three kings reigning simultaneously, counting the years from their accession to the throne, and writing their names in cartouches.

POLITICAL FRAGMENTATION AND THREAT FROM ABROAD

Shoshenq III's most powerful rival proved to be Pedubaste, whom the historian Manetho viewed as the founder of the new Dynasty 23, which reigned concurrently with the last rulers of Dynasty 22, from about 817 to 730 B.C.E. Though Manetho calls Pedubaste a "Tanite" king, no traces of his activity have been found in Tanis to date; on the contrary, modest tombs of the last rulers of Dynasty 22 have been discovered there. Shoshenq III put the entire royal necropolis in order, reorganizing the complex of hypogea and reserving for himself a tomb whose main chamber is decorated with reliefs depicting the resurrection of Osiris and the nocturnal transformations of the sun (Figure 25).

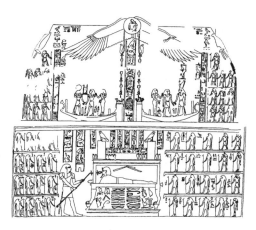

Figure 25. Relief in the tomb of Shoshenq III at Tanis. Upper register: Osiris traveling in two barques. Lower register: Horus waking his father Osiris to life.

Monumental constructions decorated in the reign of this ruler have also been found at Tanis, along with remains dating to the reign of Shoshenq V, who was probably the last pharaoh to bear this name. Are we witness here to attempts to cover up, at all costs, any impression that this dynasty, threatened from all sides, was experiencing its "swan song"?

By around 725 B.C.E., Egypt had five kings simultaneously exercising authority over various parts of the land from Aswan to the Mediterranean. Rulers who added the epithet Son of Isis to their names reigned in Thebes. The best known of these, Osorkon

III, bore the title of king as well as high priest. He controlled an area that stretched north to Hermopolis and Tihna. The office of God's Wife of Amun was held by his daughter Shepenwepet, who would later adopt the princess Amenirdis, daughter of the Kushite king Kashta, as her successor. Eventually, after a victorious campaign against Egypt, the Kushite ruler Piye would assume authority over Thebes.

The situation in the north was more complicated. At the forefront of the small competing princedoms was that of Tefnakhte, the ruler of Sais. He managed to ally three petty kings to himself and to undertake a military expedition against the south whose goal was to reunite the land—under his own scepter, of course. Though it began successfully, his march toward Thebes met with an obstacle in the form of the Kushite army, itself moving north in an effort to restore the unity of Egypt, though under the rule of its own king.

Somewhat later, a new military threat appeared in the north. This was the Assyrian army, which arrived at the border of Arabia around 720 B.C.E. Tefnakhte's son Bocchoris (the Greek form of the Egyptian name Bakenrenef) held sway over the area around Sais and founded, according to Greek tradition, the new Dynasty 24, of which he was the only representative. He was recognized as king by cities as important as Memphis, Herakleopolis, and Tanis.

It is quite clear that in the eighth century B.C.E., there was no longer an Egypt consisting of "Two Lands." Rather, there were many princedoms, united primarily by fear of one another. There were also two military superpowers threatening Egypt from the south and the north: Kush and Assyria. These two powers would decide the fate of Egypt during the century to follow. They regarded the delta and the valley of the Nile as a huge gaming board with pieces in the form of vassals at odds with one another.

There are still many puzzles to be solved by Egyptologists investigating this period. Every new discovery creates still more question marks, and making progress is like solving a complicated crossword puzzle that stretches unendingly in all directions. A source of many problems is the constant reappearance of the same names and titles in the case of both rulers and officials. In imitation of the great and by that time already legendary forebear Ramesses II, many kings of the period bore his prenomen Usermaatre. No fewer than eight rulers bore the name of Ramesses IV, Usermaatre setepenamun. As we shall see later, these pious rulers of centuries past were imitated in many other ways as well, as is reflected in the art of the Third Intermediate Period.

There is also no lack of difficulty in identifying the many women of the ruling family who bore the name Karomama. Until recently, the lovely statue of bronze encrusted with gold and silver that represents one of these noble ladies and is now in the Louvre was regarded as a portrait of the wife of Takelot II, though it actually belonged to the like-named God's Wife of Amun, a granddaughter of Osorkon I. This bronze statue of Karomama is a masterpiece of Egyptian metalwork, created at a time when the technique of casting bronze had reached its acme and objects of the greatest refinement were being produced; there are even statue groups made entirely of gold. The problem of identifying this statue becomes comprehensible when we recall that Karomama was the name of three queens, the wives of Shoshenq I, Osorkon II, and Takelot II. The last of these, a daughter of the high priest Nimlot and the mother of king Osorkon III, is the one best known to us.

Given that there are already so many problems in identifying the kings and queens of this stormy period, we can imagine the labyrinth posed by the names of their officials. It is an endless quid pro quo: who was who— whose child, whose father, whose mother? Are the figures attested in various sources with one and the same name and titles also one and the same person? Who lived earlier and who later?

DISCOVERY OF THE SERAPEUM

An especially valuable aid in solving this complex puzzle was discovered at Saqqara in 1851 by the French Egyptologist Auguste Mariette. Employed by the Louvre, this young man came to Egypt with the task of purchasing, on behalf of the French government, ancient Coptic manuscripts stored at various monasteries. He met with stiff opposition from the monks, however, and there was no assurance he could even get a look at the manuscripts. His mission ended in a fiasco.

Discouraged by this failure, Mariette began to visit the pyramids in the vicinity of Cairo. First, he spent a week at Giza, and then he made his way to Saqqara, where the oldest of the known pyramids, the Step Pyramid, burial place of king Djoser of Dynasty 3, towered over the royal necropolis. One day, while strolling near this pyramid, Mariette noticed a sandstone sphinx statue whose lower part was still buried in the sand. At that moment, he had an inspiration that would decide far more than just his own future.

This scholar remembered what he had once read in the *Geography* of Strabo about a certain place in the vicinity of Memphis. This Greek author of the first century C.E. had mentioned an avenue of sphinxes that was already buried in sand in his own day and that was supposed to lead to the temple of the god Sarapis. Mariette immediately connected this information with similar sphinxes he had seen in Alexandria; he had been told that an antiquities dealer in Cairo had acquired them as objects whose provenance was Saqqara. Guided by brilliant intuition, the Frenchman entertained not the slightest doubt that they must have come from the avenue

[58]

described by Strabo and that they had stood on the very spot where he was gazing at a similar example. He immediately hired thirty laborers and commenced his first excavation.

He did not have to wait long for results. In November 1851, Mariette discovered a chapel erected by the last native pharaoh, Nectanebo II of Dynasty 30, to which the above-mentioned avenue led. But that was just the beginning. As he proceeded west in the desert along the avenue, he came upon the entrance to the subterranean galleries that for fifteen hundred years had served as the burial place of the sacred Apis bulls. The Greeks had called this place the Serapeum, for they connected it with the cult of their god Sarapis, who was none other than the Hellenized form of the Egyptian Osiris-Apis. The syncretistic name of this deity designated the deceased Apis, who was identified with Osiris, the god of the netherworld. Like the king and every other human being, the sacred bull became an incarnation of this god after his death.

Though Apis had originally been connected with the Memphite god Ptah, his cult quickly spread throughout Egypt and became one of the most important in the religion of the land. Decisive in this development was the royal aspect of the bull as symbol. The Pyramid Texts identify the phallus of Apis with that of the king so as to assure the latter continued potency in the afterlife. Pharaoh was traditionally called Mighty Bull, and this epithet was often included in the royal titulary. This association doubtless sprang from the fertility cult practiced by tribes of hunters in the Nile valley before the emergence of the Egyptian state.

Apis was not the only sacred bull worshiped in Egypt. Not far from Memphis, at Heliopolis on the opposite bank of the Nile, the Archaic Period saw the development of the cult of the Mnevis bull, who was regarded as the herald of the sun god Atum. Toward the end of the dynastic period, in the fourth century B.C.E., another rival of Apis appeared in the form of the Buchis bull, whose home was at Hermonthis (modern Armant) in Upper Egypt, and who was identified with the local god Montu.

But of all the bulls worshiped in Egypt, Apis enjoyed the greatest popularity. Numerous Egyptian sources, as well as Greek writers, inform us of his cult. A cemetery of Apis is mentioned already in the Pyramid Texts, the oldest document of religious literature, dating to the second half of the third millennium B.C.E. The ritual for embalming the sacred bull, however, is known only from sources of the Late Period. Unfortunately, the Demotic papyrus describing this ritual, which is now in Vienna, is poorly preserved; the knowledge we gain from it is thus supplemented by the archaeological material found by Mariette at the Serapeum of Memphis.

Apis was a special bull. First and foremost, he was distinguished by his external attributes. He had to be black with white spots, and he had to have a triangular marking on his forehead. He was also required to display certain outlines on his back. As can easily be imagined, finding such a bull was no easy matter. After the death of an Apis bull, a great search was conducted throughout the land for his successor. From the written sources, we know of only a single occasion on which the new Apis was the off-spring of his predecessor. The search was conducted under the supervi-sion of a special commission of priests, and whoever was in possession of a suitable candidate would view this development as an act of divine grace. According to official doctrine, a moonbeam was responsible for en-gendering Apis. The discovery of a young bull who met all the require-ments was a momentous event that was celebrated with great festivities throughout the land, for a new god had made his appearance. Apis quickly freed himself from the burden of royal symbolism and became the object of a cult of his own.

In all haste, a place was set up for the newly chosen bull, where he could remain under the care of "nurses"—that is, milch cows—until he was ready for a further journey. The priestly commission then conveyed him to Nilopolis, a place on the Nile, where, according to Diodorus, he remained for forty days. This was an extremely important time for Egyptian women, who made pilgrimages to the young bull. They were supposed to stand in front of him and expose their genitals so as to direct the god's potency to themselves. This seems all the more probable, in that similar customs per-sisted in Egypt until relatively recent times. Mariette wrote that when he found a statuette of a bull during his excavations, Egyptian women from the nearby village came and sat on the statue to assure themselves of fertil-ity. Diodorus informs us that after completing this symbolic act, the women were not allowed to approach the bull again. Apis sometimes participated in processions during which such exhibitions were not forbidden.

When the moon was full, which was considered a magical time, the bull was taken in a special barque to Memphis, his ultimate home. There, he dwelled in rooms that had been built on the south side of the temple of Ptah. His residence had its own priests, whose task was to serve Apis and to carry out the appropriate rituals. Adjoining the rooms of the sacred bull were those of the cows selected to comprise his harem. According to one of the Greek writers, Diodorus, he enjoyed complete sexual freedom, while others affirm that he was led only once a year to a specially selected cow, who was slaughtered immediately after the sexual act to prevent him from having any offspring. This last-mentioned information does not appear trustwor-thy, for archaeological investigation has revealed that Apis's harem was huge, and moreover, we have the above-mentioned information concerning an immediate succession to the divine office. Special care was also accorded to the mother of the sacred bull. Naturally enough, she was identified with the sky goddess Hathor, who often assumed the form of a cow.

Doubts are raised by the Greek tradition according to which Apis was slaughtered at the end of his twenty-fifth year of life. We have a text from Dynasty 22 stating that an Apis bull lived for twenty-six years. The belief regarding a life cycle of twenty-five years might have had its source in the Egyptian calendar, which was closely bound to astronomical events, for the phases of the moon repeated themselves on the same day every quarter-century. As Herodotus reports, the Persian king Cambyses, who conquered Egypt in the spring of 525 B.C.E., was supposed to have mortally wounded the Memphite Apis by his own hand. This information could also be false, if we recall the antipathy toward the Persians harbored by this Greek traveler and historian of the mid-fifth century B.C.E.

The death of an Apis was as important an occasion as his initial appearance. Passing on to the realm of the dead, the bull became Osiris. The Greeks also transferred this aspect of his divine nature to their Sarapis, whose cult they spread far beyond the borders of Egypt. The bodies of the Apis bulls were embalmed in special rooms on huge beds that were discovered in the course of excavations in 1941. One of them was prepared from an alabaster monolith that comprised a whole together with its base. The side walls were decorated with reliefs representing two extended lions. The upper surface of the stone embalming table slopes toward the rear, which is provided with an opening to channel the blood that flowed from the corpse when it was cut open. As was the case when human corpses were mummified, the viscera were removed from the body of the bull and placed in four stone vessels. To remove the moisture from Apis's corpse, he was covered for several weeks with dry natron. Finally, the desiccated and preserved body was wrapped in mummy bandages. The entire process lasted seventy days, just like the embalming of a deceased human.

Observing strict rules, the solemn funeral procession then made its way to the place of eternal rest. This lasted an entire day, for it was accompanied by various rituals. Above all, the Opening of the Mouth ritual had to be performed over the mummy to quicken the dead beast and enable him to breathe again. A similar ceremony accompanied the burials of humans, the dedications of new edifices, and even the consecration of statues and small sacral objects. A great crowd of people participated in the burial, among them mourning women whose loud wails were supposed to keep evil spirits away from the deceased. The mummified bull was transported in a special wheeled hearse that had the form of a richly decorated naos. Such carriages are also represented in relief on two alabaster plaques found at Memphis, not far from the alabaster bed.

The Apis bulls were buried in the huge galleries at Saqqara discovered by Mariette in the years 1850–1852, and which he, employing Strabo's term for them, called the Serapeum. It was here that from Amenophis III (c. 1402–1364 B.C.E.) to the beginning of our own era, kings buried the corpses of the sacred Apis bulls. At first they were buried in individual tombs, but

[61]

beginning *c.* 1260 B.C.E., in the reign of Ramesses II, it became the custom to place the divine mummies in collective tombs. Down to c. 643 B.C.E., that is, in Dynasty 26, twenty-eight deceased Apis bulls, each in a wooden sarcophagus, were buried in a single gallery. Only the first two burials, both from the reign of Ramesses II, survived intact, without being plundered, until the nineteenth century C.E. Today, we can marvel at their rich grave goods at the Louvre in Paris. These earlier tombs are presently inaccessible to visitors.

The part of the Serapeum that today is visited daily by tourists from the world over is the second large collective burial place, which was established c. 612 B.C.E. It functioned until the end of the Ptolemaic Period and was constantly enlarged. Beginning with the reign of Amasis (c. 570–526 B.C.E.), the mummified bodies were stored there in granite sarcophagi, each fashioned from a single block of stone and weighing up to seventy tons. Such burials were of course quite costly. Thus, immediately after the death of an Apis bull, envoys were dispatched from Memphis to the various regions of the land to collect donations for the financing of his burial. We know that one of the later burials cost the enormous sum of one hundred talents.

Rich Egyptians made these donations gladly, for they guaranteed the privilege of placing votive stelae of their own on the wall of Apis's burial chamber, near his sarcophagus. Those who participated in the burial enjoyed a similar distinction. Thanks to this practice, the walls of the Serapeum were fitted with thousands of plaques of various sizes, made of all sorts of materials and inscribed in various scripts. Since they were connected with the burials of the successive Apis bulls, these stelae are arranged in chronological order.

Of the approximately seven thousand objects found by Mariette in the Memphite Serapeum, these votive stelae are the most valuable to historians. Their donors turned to the deceased bull with various requests, giving their names and titles and sometimes even a lengthy genealogy. The best-known document of this sort is the stela contributed by Pasenhor, a dignitary from the reign of Shoshenq IV. He traces his lineage back in time over sixteen generations, to a Libyan forebear named Buyuwawa. Though he was himself only a priest of the goddess Neith, Pasenhor had four successive kings in his family tree, of whom the first was Shoshenq I, the founder of Dynasty 22.

Certain stelae were jointly contributed by several contemporary individuals. Such documents make it possible to identify the persons precisely, to synchronize the lifetimes of the more important officials, and even to fine-tune the chronology of the reigns of individual rulers. For the whole first millennium B.C.E., the Egyptian sources include no list of kings to tell us the lengths of their reigns. The stelae from the Serapeum are thus all the more valuable in that they mention the dates on which the individual Apis bulls were born and died, along with the lengths of their lifetimes. The dates supplied by these stelae refer, of course, to the reigns of the individual kings. When a bull was born in the reign of one pharaoh and died during the reign of another, the texts containing this information constitute a historical source of the highest importance, for they make it possible to determine the length of the reign of the former. Such stelae began to appear toward the end of Dynasty 22, and they were especially numerous later, particularly in the years of Dynasty 26. On the basis of texts from the Serapeum, Egyptologists have been able to establish that Shoshenq III reigned no fewer than fifty-two years and that his successor was Pimai, whose name means "cat."

What did the donors of these stelae request from Apis? Let us read one of them, evidently inscribed in regnal year 11 of Shoshenq V, which contains a typical modest prayer of this period. The stela was donated by several members of a single family who represented the middle level of the social hierarchy.

> Words spoken by the god's father (a priestly title), prophet of Bastet mistress of Ankh-tawy (i.e., Memphis), prophet of Ptah the august pillar, prophet of the house of Shesmetet mistress of Ankhtawy, Merneptah, son of the *sem*-priest Neswennefer, justified (?—*neb-imakh*), son of the steward and representative of the domain of Ptah, Pasheryenptah: "An offering that the king gives for your *ka*, o Osiris-Apis, (as) a daily offering. May you be strong through the bread, may you be strong through the beer (of this offering). May you go out as a living *ba*. May I be remembered for what I have done for my lord. Sleep and weariness were my abomination, I was constantly in motion like the sun disk, I wore myself out in your service (when) your intention was fulfilled exactly. I went in peace to the Beautiful West, when you were buried in fine condition. Give me therefore the reward of a lord (i.e., that a lord gives): venerable rank, many years of continuity of generations, and enduring in this house forever and ever."
>
> His son, the *sem*-priest and *wen-ra* (another priestly title) Neswennefer; his son, the king's acquaintance, Pasherienptah, born of the lady Dihapisati; and her daughter Tapennut, her daughter Imyenesites, and her daughter Iru: may they endure in this house as your name endures in it![5]

---

[5] J. Vercoutter, *Textes biographiques du Sérapéum de Memphis: Contribution à l'étude des stèles votives du Sérapéum*, Bibliothèque de l'École des Hautes Études 316 (Paris, 1926), pp. 2–3. "Justified" is an epithet indicating a deceased person. "Living *ba*" was an aspect of an individual's being; to see the daylight was a traditional wish of the deceased. "Beautiful West" is a designation of the realm of the dead. "I went forth in peace to the Beautiful West," etc., refers to participation in the funeral procession, which together with its accompanying rituals took an entire day.

The burials of the bulls at Saqqara, the royal tombs of Tanis, and the innumerable priestly tombs of Dynasties 21 and 22 in the enclosures of the New Kingdom temples on the west bank of Thebes supply a wealth of material for our knowledge of the burial customs of this period. Nearly all the sacred edifices of this period now lie in ruins, however. The many decorated blocks of the temples of Bubastis and Tanis either lie in situ or grace the museums of Europe and America.

Only at Karnak are two edifices from Dynasties 22 and 23 preserved in their original location. The first of these is the Bubastite Portal, which we have already discussed. Even more interesting, for certain reasons, is a small temple dedicated to Osiris Heqadjet ("Ruler of Eternity"), which was erected in the eighth century B.C.E. by Osorkon III and his coregent Takelot III of Dynasty 23. Its decoration is like a motion picture whose individual scenes represent a series of stages in the political history of the period before the assault of the Kushite Dynasty 25 and immediately thereafter. In its isolation in the northeastern corner of the Karnak temple enclosure, this modest construction is rarely visited by tourists. Almost no one pauses to think that it is the only preserved architectural monument of this highly exciting period. And what interesting things are to be found in its reliefs (Figure 26)!

On the rear wall of the principal chamber is a huge scene, carved in relief, representing Osorkon III and his son and coregent, Takelot III. The creator of this relief hit upon the brilliant idea that for two kings reigning together, the most suitable representation would be a double scene with a composition that was both symmetrical and antithetical. Moreover, he turned to a motif he knew from the decoration of the pylon at Medinet Habu, where two scenes depicting Ramesses IV during the ceremony involving the *ished*-tree appear on the front on either side of the entrance. Since this model was suited to the somewhat different situation in his own time, the artist, who lived nearly four centuries later, combined two nearly identical scenes into a larger whole, representing the different kings on either side of the scene.

This very fact shows that the traditions of the New Kingdom were still alive. The refined style of the reliefs in this room demonstrates that its creator's source of inspiration was the art of the period of Amenophis III and his successor Akhenaten of Dynasty 18.

These iconographic innovations have been viewed as a blatantly feverish search for original solutions. In another scene, Takelot's wig is decorated with the form of a falcon with outstretched wings (Figure 27), and we see two double crowns on the head of Shepenwepet, daughter of Osorkon III. Was it creative license that led the artist to break with established patterns,

Figure 26. Swamp-god Kheded. Relief of Osorkon III in the chapel of Osiris Heqadjet at Karnak. Photo by Waldemar Jerke, Polish Center of Mediterranean Archaeology, Warsaw University.

Figure 27. King Takelot III wearing a falcon figure of the god Horus on his head. Relief in the chapel of Osiris Heqadjet at Karnak. Photo by Waldemar Jerke, Polish Center of Mediterranean Archaeology, Warsaw University.

or a need for additional legitimation of the ruler? The falcon was, after all, a symbol of Horus, the forebear of the kings, and the double crown identified the lord of Upper and Lower Egypt. A search for such an identification seems especially comprehensible at a time when a divided Egypt was clearly approaching the loss of its independence, the first sign of which is already visible in the next room of the temple. Here, the God's Wife of Amun Shepenwepet appears in the reliefs instead of the king, and her name is enclosed in royal cartouches. To all appearances, she assumed control of the political life of Thebes. But that is not all: along with her, we see Amenirdis, the daughter of the Kushite king Kashta, who was her adopted successor.

Did Egypt lack a candidate for this highest priesthood, so that a foreign woman was named to it? Even greater astonishment is aroused by the decoration of the adjoining wall. Here, royal cartouches with their names hacked out accompany the representation of a ruler who displays all the typical attributes of a king of Kush. An identical portrait executed in relief on an even larger scale on the front wall of the temple of the Ruler of Eternity dispels any doubt: the Kushite king Shebitku is already seated on the throne of Egypt.

Though both of the kings who resided in Sais, Tefnakhte and his son Bocchoris, whom the historian Manetho would later count as Dynasty 24, tried desperately to reunite the pharaonic realm from the north, they proved inferior to the Kushite monarchs whose origin lay in the south.

Fresh Currents from the African Interior:
Kushites in Egypt (Dynasty 25)

Nubia, a land south of Egypt that today comprises northern Sudan, was already the object of special interest to the pharaohs early in the dynastic period. This huge area was first and foremost a veritable mine of valuable raw materials, the most precious being gold. It has even been surmised that the name Nubia, first used by Greek writers (Eratosthenes, Strabo, Pliny, Ptolemy), is derived from the Egyptian word *nub*, which means "gold." Together with the desert east of the Nile in Egypt itself, Nubia was the chief source of this coveted raw material.

The gold mines, which lay in rough, rocky terrain far from water and vegetation, functioned thanks to the backbreaking labor of Nubian subjects, prisoners of war, and criminals banned from Egypt. Carefully prepared expeditions, reminiscent of those sent on punitive raids, were organized and dispatched in search of the precious ore, and they are immortalized in inscriptions chiseled in the rock near the mines or along the routes leading to them. Among the most famous of the Nubian mines of the pharaonic period were the deposits in the Wadi Allaqi, where a Soviet archaeological mission conducted research in the years 1961–63. This work was carried out in the framework of the great international campaign to save the monuments of Nubia, which was organized by UNESCO because of the construction of the High Dam at Aswan and the artificial lake that would be created south of it. The Polish expedition under the direction of Professor Kazimierz Michalowski that took part in this campaign discovered the now famous early Christian art at Faras in the north of Nubia.

But Nubia's riches consisted of more than just gold. The Egyptians also obtained other ores, various stones (such as diorite, to be found some six

[68]

miles from the site of Tushka), ebony and other kinds of wood, incense, oils, ostrich feathers, lances, and even rare animals such as apes and giraffes, not to mention the panther skins worn by Egyptian priests and kings for ritual purposes. Valuable manpower was supplied by Nubian prisoners of war, who were employed in Egypt as police and soldiers. Nubia was a corridor connecting the Mediterranean world with the interior of black Africa. The trade routes leading there, and above all the Nile valley, were of extraordinary economic and strategic importance.

Objects made of Nubian materials found in burials of the predynastic period point to a lively trade exchange between Egypt and the peoples who lived further to the south at this early date. The population of Nubia differed, ethnically and linguistically, from the Egyptians and from the other population groups that surrounded them. With the rise of the Egyptian state at the beginning of the third millennium B.C.E., there commenced a gradual pharaonic expansion toward the south. Rulers of Dynasty 1, such as Hor-Aha and Djer, organized military expeditions to the Second Cataract and left inscriptions in the vicinity of Wadi Halfa. From the royal annals carved on the famed Palermo Stone, we learn of the considerable booty seized in Nubia by Snofru, the founder of Dynasty 4, in the middle of the third millennium. Nearly all his successors, down to the end of the Old Kingdom, left traces of their expeditions into Lower Nubia.

In the Middle Kingdom, especially at the beginning of Dynasty 12, there was a change in Egypt's policy vis-à-vis Nubia. The pharaohs were no longer interested in trade with their southern neighbors, but rather in subjugation and annexation. Thus began a lengthy period of military expansion to the south. Amenemhet I and Senwosret I ruled Nubia as far as the Second Cataract and erected border fortresses there to control trade and migration in both directions. The Nubians offered resistance, and Senwosret III was obliged to suppress several uprisings; the stelae he left at the fortress of Semna serve as his seal, so to speak, at the southern border of Egypt.

During the Second Intermediate Period, Nubia developed independently for a time; a high culture with a character of its own, today called the Kerma culture, made its appearance, and it was not without influence on Egypt. From the stela of the victorious king Kamose, we even learn that toward the end of Dynasty 17, the Nubian state allied itself with the Hyksos in the delta against the Egyptian rump state. Nubia's independence soon ended, however, when Egypt again became a great power during the reign of the first ruler of Dynasty 18. Pharaoh Ahmose placed it under his sway as far as the Second Cataract, and the great Amenophis I introduced a new system of administration. He inaugurated the office of viceroy, called King's Son of Kush, to administer the new province and assure that tribute

[69]

of the appropriate quantity and quality arrived punctually at the royal court.

The name Kush, which at first designated the northern portion of Upper Nubia, then all of the southern portion, and finally Nubia generally, first appears in the inscriptions of Senwosret I of Dynasty 12 (twentieth century B.C.E.), and it was commonly used in the New Kingdom. Tuthmosis I's campaign to southern Nubia definitively ended the local Kerma culture and opened the way to the "Pure Mountain," the name of Gebel Barkal some nine miles distant from the Fourth Cataract. At the foot of this imposing rock massif, which towers more than 325 feet above a sandy plain (Figure 28 and Plate II), was founded a city whose subsequent development would one day decide the future of Egypt itself.

This city is called Napata. An inscription from the reign of Tuthmosis III attests that it was this king who began to erect monumental buildings there. His construction was a fortress that must have been of great strategic and political importance, considering that his successor Amenophis II ordered a captured Syrian ruler brought there to be hanged from the walls of Napata. This event is attested on a stela found at Amada, another Nubian center.

Figure 28. The massif of Gebel Barkal. Photo by the author.

In the course of time, the city developed by the New Kingdom rulers became an important center of the Theban cult of Amun-Re (Figure 29). Imposing temples were built to him or excavated into the rock there. We can thus speak of Napata as a genuine outpost of Theban religion. The local incarnation of Amun, called Amun, Resident on the Pure Mountain, was worshiped independently here. The theoriomorphic form of this deity had a ram's head. To all indications, the representation of the Theban Amun as a ram, which occurs often at a later date, had its origin in an association with the ram-headed Amun of Napata.

The last sacred building erected at Napata by the rulers of the New Kingdom was a temple of Ramesses II, and the last evidence of their presence at the foot of the Pure Mountain is a statue of Ramesses IX that was found there. Many of the temples and chapels in Nubia date back to Ramesses II, the greatest of the Ramessides, who established cults for various Egyptian deities there, but especially for the Theban Amun-Re. Especially famous in modern times are his two temples hewn into the rock at Abu Simbel. One of them was dedicated to the wife of the great ruler, Nefertari, whose tomb in the Valley of the Queens on the west bank of Thebes has survived to the present day. In 1963, because the construction of the High Dam at Aswan would cause the area to be flooded by an artificial lake, the two temples were cut out of the rock and moved to a level about 650 feet higher, where they at least retain their original orientation.

Worshiping Egyptian deities and participating in trade and cultural exchange with Egypt, the Nubian population became partially Egyptianized. This was especially true of the upper levels of society and above all of the elite who lived in the important religious and administrative center of Napata in the New Kingdom. The written language there, and doubtless to a large extent also the spoken language, was Egyptian.

We do not know what happened at Napata after the collapse of the New Kingdom. To date, no inscription has been found bearing on the history of this city during the two centuries that passed between about 1080 B.C.E. and the middle of the ninth century. We can be certain only that the strong, independent state of Kush arose there by about 850 B.C.E. at the latest. It would be difficult to say whether some immigrant population contributed to this development or whether it was the result of an undisturbed evolution of old traditions. The capital of the state was Napata, where the Theban Amun continued to be worshiped.

The first Kushite rulers were buried at el-Kurru, a site near Napata, and their tombs had the form of subterranean chambers surmounted by tumuli and later by mud brick mastabas. The first kings remain anonymous, and the dynastic line begins with Alara, whose son was Kashta. As noted

Figure 29. Ruins of the temple of Amun at the "Pure Mountain," Gebel Barkal. From Dows Dunham, *Recollections of an Egyptologist* (Boston, 1972), fig. 36.

in the previous chapter, the latter's daughter was adopted as God's Wife of Amun at Thebes by her predecessor in the office, Shepenwepet, the daughter of Osorkon III. Kashta's son Piye (c. 747–716 B.C.E.) finally felt strong enough to declare war on Egypt and aspire to the pharaonic throne.

[72]

PIYE'S CAMPAIGN TO EGYPT

The internal situation in Egypt, which was divided into small princedoms, not only made his invasion easier but actually invited it. He could be represented as the defender of the deities of Egypt, who were worshiped in Kush but found ever less respect in Egypt. He could restore the old practice of protecting the tombs at Thebes from robbers. Finally, he could preach the theological-political slogan of the need for a "uniting of the Two Lands." He had an abundance of pretexts, but when he was finally ready to enlist them, an authentic political rival unexpectedly appeared in the north of Egypt. This was Tefnakhte, ruler of Sais, the founder of Dynasty 24. He, too, was concerned with the unification of Egypt—but needless to say, under his own scepter. His first steps in this direction were successful, and he moved ever further south, annexing one district after another to his kingdom.

This was soon too much for the ambitious Kushite. Piye responded to the challenge like a man, though at first, he underestimated his opponent. He sent an army north, but it met with little success. Finally, he saw no other solution than to go to Egypt personally at the head of his troops. The expedition occurred in regnal year 21 of the Kushite ruler, and it is described in full detail on a huge granite stela that was found in 1862 in the temple precinct at Gebel Barkal. One can marvel at it today at the Egyptian Museum in Cairo. It is one of the most important historical documents bequeathed to us by pharaonic Egypt.

Like every account of this sort, the text begins with a date and the titles of the ruler:

Year 21, first month of the first season, under the majesty of the King of Upper and Lower Egypt, Piye beloved-of-Amun, ever living. . . .

One came to say to his majesty: "The Chief of the West, the count and grandee in Netjer, Tefnakht, is in the nome of . . . , in the nome of Xois, in Hapy, in . . . in Ayn, in Pernub, and in the nome of Memphis. He has conquered the entire West from the coastal marshes to Itj-tawy, sailing south with a numerous army, with the Two Lands united behind him, and the counts and rulers of domains are as dogs at his feet.

No stronghold has closed [its gates in] the nomes of Upper Egypt. Mer-Atum, Per-Sekhemkheperre, Hut-Sobk, Permedjed, Tjeknesh, all towns of the West have opened the gates for fear of him. When he turned around to the nomes of the East they opened to him also: Hut-benu, Teudjoi, Hut-nesut, Per-nebtepih.

Now [he is] besieging Hnes. He has encircled it completely, not letting goers go, not letting entrants enter, and fighting every day. He has measured it in its whole circuit. Every count knows his wall. He has made every man besiege his portion, to wit the counts and rulers of domains." His majesty heard [it] with delight, laughing joyously.

Then those chiefs, the counts and generals who were in their towns, sent to his majesty daily, saying: "Have you been silent in order to forget the Southland, the nomes of Upper Egypt, while Tefnakht conquers (all) before him and finds no resistance?" . . .

His majesty wrote to the counts and generals who were in Egypt, the commander Purem, and the commander Lemersekny, and every commander of his majesty who was in Egypt: "Enter combat, engage in battle; surround [. . .], capture its people, its cattle, its ships on the river! Let not the farmers go to the field, let not the plowmen plow. Beset the Hare nome; fight against it daily!" Then they did so.

Then his majesty sent an army to Egypt and charged them strictly: "Do not attack by night in the manner of draughts-playing; fight when one can see. Challenge him to battle from afar. If he proposes to await the infantry and chariotry of another town, then sit still until his troops come. Fight when he proposes. Also if he has allies in another town, let them be awaited. The counts whom he brings to help him, and any trusted Libyan troops, let them be challenged to battle in advance, saying: 'You whose name we do not know, who musters the troops! Harness the best steeds of your stable, form your battle line, and know that Amun is the god who sent us!'

"When you have reached Thebes at Ipet-sut, go into the water. Cleanse yourselves in the river; wear the best linen. Rest the bow; loosen the arrow. Boast not [to] the lord of might, for the brave has no might without him. He makes the weak-armed strong-armed, so that the many flee before the few, and a single one conquers a thousand men! Sprinkle yourselves with water of his altars; kiss the earth before his face. Say to him:

'Give us the way,
May we fight in the shade of your arm!
The troop you sent, when it charges,
May the many tremble before it!' "

Then they placed themselves on their bellies before his majesty:

"It is your name that makes our strength,
Your counsel brings your army into port;
Your bread is in our bellies on every way,
Your beer quenches our thirst.
It is your valor that gives us strength,
There is dread when your name is recalled;
No army wins with a cowardly leader,
Who is your equal there?

[74]

You are the mighty King who acts with his arms,
The chief of the word of war!"

They sailed north and arrived at Thebes; they did as his majesty had said.

Sailing north on the river they met many ships going south with soldiers and sailors, all kinds of fighting troops from Lower Egypt, equipped with weapons of warfare, to fight against his majesty's army. Then a great slaughter was made of them, whose number is unknown. Their troops and ships were captured, and taken as prisoners to where his majesty was. . . .

Then the army that was here in Egypt heard of the anger his majesty held against them. They fought against Permedjed of the Oxyrhynchite nome; they captured it like a cloudburst. They wrote to his majesty—his heart was not appeased by it.

Then they fought against "the Crag Great-of-Victories." They found it filled with troops, all kinds of fighters of Lower Egypt. A siege tower was made against it; its wall was overthrown. A great slaughter was made of them, countless numbers, including a son of the Chief of the Ma, Tefnakht. They wrote of it to his majesty—his heart was not appeased by it. . . .

First month of the first season, day 9, his majesty went north to Thebes. He performed the feast of Amun at the feast of Ipet. His majesty sailed north to the harbor of the Hare nome. His majesty came out of the cabin of the ship. The horses were yoked, the chariot was mounted, while the grandeur of his majesty attained the Asiatics and every heart trembled before him. . . .

He set up camp on the southwest of Khmun. He pressed against it every day. An embankment was made to enclose the wall. A siege tower was set up to elevate the archers as they shot, and the slingers as they hurled stones and killed people there each day.

Days passed, and Un was a stench to the nose, for lack of air to breathe. Then Un threw itself on its belly, to plead before the king. Messengers came and went with all kinds of things beautiful to behold: gold, precious stones, clothes in a chest, the diadem from his (Namart's) head, the uraeus that cast his power, without ceasing for many days to implore his crown.

Then they sent his wife, the royal wife and royal daughter, Nestent, to implore the royal wives, the royal concubines, the royal daughters, and the royal sisters. She threw herself on her belly in the women's house before the royal women: "Come to me, royal wives, royal daughters, royal sisters, that you may appease Horus, lord of the palace, great of power, great of triumph!" . . . [1]

---

[1] M. Lichtheim, *Ancient Egyptian Literature: A Book of Readings*, Vol. 3: *The Late Period* (Berkeley, 1980), pp. 68–72. The name spelled Tefnakht by Lichtheim is otherwise rendered as Tefnakhte in this volume; Namart is our Nimlot. Netjer is modern Behbeit el-Hagar. Anu was a marshy region that belonged to Imau, the capital of the nome of the West. Itj-tawy is Lisht in the twenty-first nome of Upper Egypt. Mer-Atum is Maidum.

The section of the text citing the pleas of the defeated, the compliments and gifts they heaped upon their conqueror, and the submissive speech of Nimlot (Namart) is unfortunately only fragmentarily preserved:

He (Namart) threw himself on his belly before his majesty, [saying, "Be appeased], Horus, lord of the palace! It is your power that has done it to me. I am one of the King's servants who pays taxes into the treasury [. . .] . . . I have done more for you than they." Then he presented silver, gold, lapis lazuli, turquoise, copper, and all kinds of precious stones. The treasury was filled with this tribute. He brought a horse with his right hand, and in his left hand a sistrum of gold and lapis lazuli.

His majesty arose in splendor from his palace and proceeded to the temple of Thoth, lord of Khmun. He sacrificed oxen, shorthorns, and fowl to his father Thoth, lord of Khmun, and the Ogodad in the temple of the Ogdoad. And the troops of the Hare nome shouted and sang, saying:

"How good is Horus at peace in his town,
The Son of Re, Piye!
You make for us a jubilee,
As you protect the Hare nome!"

His majesty proceeded to the house of King Namart. He went through all the rooms of the palace, his treasury and his storehouse. He (Namart) presented the royal wives and royal daughters to him. They saluted his majesty in the manner of woman, while his majesty did not direct his gaze at them.

His majesty proceeded to the stable of the horses and the quarters of the foals. When he saw that they had been [left] to hunger he said: "I swear, as Re loves me, as my nose is refreshed by life: that my horses were made to hunger pains me more than any other crime you committed in your recklessness! I would teach you (?) to respect (?) your neighbors. Do you not know god's shade is above me and does not let my action fail? Would that another, whoever he might be, had done it for me! I would not have to reprimand him for it. I was fashioned in the womb, created in the egg of the god!

Hut-Sobk is Krokodilopolis in the Faiyum. Per-Medjed is Oxyrhynchus in the nineteenth nome of Upper Egypt. Tjeknesh is Greek Takona north of Oxyrhynchus. Hut-benu, "Palace of the Phoenix," was located in the vicinity of the royal palace in the eighteenth nome of Upper Egypt. Teudjoi is el-Hiba. Hut-nesut is el-Kom el-Ahmar Sawaris in the eighteenth nome of Upper Egypt. Per-nebtepih is Atfih in the twenty-second nome of Upper Egypt. Hnes is Herakleopolis, capital of the twentieth nome of Upper Egypt. The Hare nome is the fifteenth nome of Upper Egypt. Ipet-Sut is the temple of Amun-Re at Karnak. Per-Medjed is modern el-Bahnasa. Khmun and Un are names of Hermopolis.

The seed of the god is in me! By his ka, I act not without him; it is he who commands me to act!"

Then his (Namart's) goods were assigned to the treasury, and his granary to the endowment of Amun in Ipet-sut.

There came the ruler of Hnes Peftuaubast, bearing tribute to Pharaoh: gold, silver, all kinds of precious stones, and the best horses of the stable. He threw himself on his belly before his majesty and said:

"Hail to you, Horus, mighty King,
Bull attacking bulls!
The netherworld seized me,
I foundered in darkness,
O you who give me the rays of his face!
I could find no friend on the day of distress,
Who would stand up on battle day,
Except you, O mighty King,
You drove the darkness from me!
I shall serve with my property,
Hnes owes to your dwelling;
You are Harakhti above the immortal stars!
As he is king so are you,
As he is immortal you are immortal,
King of Upper and Lower Egypt, Piye ever living!"

His majesty sailed north to the entrance of the canal beside Rehone, and found Per-Sekhemkheperre with its wall raised, its gate closed, and filled with all kinds of fighters of Lower Egypt. Then his majesty sent to them, saying: "O you who live in death, you who live in death; you poor wretches, you who live in death! If the moment passes without your opening to me, you will be counted slain according to the King's judgment. Do not bar the gates of your life, so as to be brought to the block this day! Do not desire death and reject life! [. . .] . . .

Then they sent to his majesty, saying:

"Lo, god's shade is above you,
Nut's Son gave you his arms!
Your heart's plan happens instantly,
Like the word of mouth of god.
Truly, you are born of god,
For we see (it) by the work of your arms!
Lo, your town and its gates
[. . .];

[77]

May entrants enter, goers go,
May his majesty do as he wishes!"

They came out with a son of the Chief of the Ma, Tefnakht. The troops of
his majesty entered it (the city), and he did not slay one of all the people he
found. [. . .] and treasurers, in order to seal its possessions. Its treasuries
were allocated to the treasury; its granaries as endowment to his father
Amen-Re, lord of the Thrones-of-the-Two-Lands. . . .

[His majesty proceeded to] Memphis. He sent to them, saying: "Do not
close, do not fight, O home of Shu since the beginning! Let the entrant enter,
the goer go; those who would leave shall not be hindered! I shall offer an
oblation to Ptah and the gods of Memphis. I shall sacrifice to Sokar in Shetit. I
shall see South-of-his-Wall. And I shall sail north in peace! [. . .] . . .

They closed their fort. They sent out troops against some of his majesty's
troops, consisting of artisans, builders, and sailors [who had entered] the harbor of Memphis. And the Chief of Sais arrived in Memphis by night to charge
his soldiers, his sailors, all the best of his army, consisting of 8,000 men,
charging them firmly:

"Look, Memphis is filled with troops of all the best of Lower Egypt, with bar-
ley, emmer, and all kinds of grain, the granaries overflowing; with weapons [of
war] of all kinds. A rampart [surrounds it]. A great battlement has been built, a
work of skilled craftsmanship. The river surrounds its east side; one cannot
fight there. The stables here are filled with oxen; the storehouse is furnished
with everything: silver, gold, copper, clothing, incense, honey, resin. I shall go
to give gifts to the chiefs of Lower Egypt. I shall open their nomes to them. I
shall be [. . . in a few] days I shall return." And he mounted a horse (for) he did
not trust his chariot, and he went north in fear of his majesty.

At dawn of the next day his majesty arrived at Memphis. When he had
moored on its north, he found the water risen to the walls and ships moored
at [the houses of] Memphis. His majesty saw that it was strong, the walls
were high with new construction, and the battlements manned in strength.
No way of attacking it was found. Every man of his majesty's army had his
say about some plan of attack. Some said: "Let us blockade [. . .], for its
troops are numerous." Others said: "Make a causeway to it, so that we raise
the ground to its wall. Let us construct a siege tower, setting up masts and using sails as walls for it. You should divide it thus on each of its sides with
ramparts and [a causeway] on its north, so as to raise the ground to its wall,
so that we find a way for our feet."

Then his majesty raged against them like a panther, saying, "I swear, as my
father Amun favors me, . . . according to the command of Amun! This is
what people say: '[. . .] and the nomes of the South opened to him from afar,
though Amun had not put (it) in their hearts, and they did not know what he
had commanded. He (Amun) made him (Piye) in order to show his might, to

[78]

Plate Ia. Landscape in Middle Egypt near
Teudjoi (modern el-Hiba). Photo by the
author.

Plate Ib. Remains of a temple erected by
Osorkon II at Leontopolis (modern Tell el-
Muqdam). Photo by the author.

Plate II. The rock needle of Gebel Barkal. Photo by the author.

Plate III. Horus-Protector-of-His-Father bringing a *djed*-pillar to Osiris. Fragment from the painted wooden coffin of Pensenhor, a high Theban official of the seventh to sixth century B.C.E. British Museum, London. Photo by the author.

Plate IVa. Remains of Sais, capital of Egypt during Dynasty 26. Photo by the author.

Plate IVb. Processions of deities and inscriptions painted on the wooden coffin of the priestess Isunes, from Edfu in Upper Egypt. First century C.E. Photo by the author.

Facing page
Plate V. Naos of Darius I from Tuna el-Gebel. The king is depicted twice, offering the *udjat*-eye. Archaeological Museum, Mallawi. Photo by the author.

Plate VIa. The representation on the rear
wall of the naos from Tuna el-Gebel. Photo
by the author.

Plate VIb. Scene on a side wall of the shrine.
Photo by the author.

Following page
Plate VII. Temple of Hathor and mammisi at
Dendara. Roman Period. Photo by the author.

Plate VIIIa. Ptolemy II offering sacred oil to the goddess Nephthys. Behbeit el-Hagar. Photo by the author.

Plate VIIIb. Ruins of the city of Hermopolis. Photo by the author.

Plate IX. Necropolis of the Ptolemaic and Roman Periods to the west of the pyramid of Djoser (Dynasty 3) at Saqqara. Burials lying on the rock-hewn mastaba of the vizier Meref-nebef. Photo by Zbigniew Kość, Polish Center of Mediterranean Archaeology, Warsaw University.

Plate Xa. Anubis, god of mummification, at work. Painting on a cartonnage of the Roman Period found at Saqqara West. Photo by Zbigniew Kość, Polish Center of Mediterranean Archaeology, Warsaw University.

Previous page
Photo Xb. Painted cartonnage wrapping of a human mummy. Interior of an anthropoid coffin made of terra-cotta (Plate XI). Saqqara West, Roman Period. Photo by Zbigniew Kość, Polish Center of Mediterranean Archaeology, Warsaw University.

Plate XI. Gilded mask of the cartonnage wrapping of the mummy of a girl. Ptolemaic Period. Found in the court of the mastaba of Meref-nebef. Photo by the author.

Plate XII. Tell Atrib. Arab cemetery atop the ruins of the ancient city. Photo by the author.

Plate XIII. Tell Atrib. Buildings of the ancient city excavated within the modern city of Benha. Workshops of the Ptolemaic Period. Field of Polish-Egyptian rescue excavations. Photo by the author.

Plate XIVa. Golden earring in the shape of a cupid from the third century B.C.E. Photo by the author.

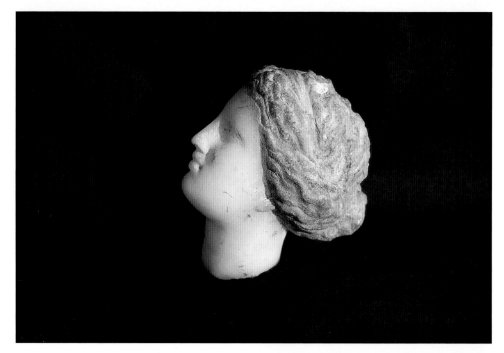

Plate XIVb. Head of a marble statuette of Aphrodite from the third century B.C.E. workshops of Athribis. Photo by the author.

Plate XIVc. Body of another marble statuette of Aphrodite from the third century B.C.E. workshops of Athribis. Photo by the author.

Plate XIVd. Terra-cotta figurine of Bes, an Egyptian god who was considered to be the consort of Aphrodite in Ptolemaic Egypt. From the third century B.C.E. workshops of Athribis. Photo by the author.

Plate XV. Marble head of a statue honoring a notable, probably a gymnasiarch. Found near the Roman Period baths at Athribis. Mid-third century A.D. Photo by the author.

Following page
Plate XVI. Snakes, symbols and protectors of ancient Egyptian gods and kings, enjoy the company of archaeologists as well. This one rested for weeks under a stone used as a step by excavators at Tell Atrib (ancient Athribis) until the end of the campaign. Photo by the author.

let his grandeur be seen.' I shall seize it (Memphis) like a cloudburst, for [Amen-Re] has commanded me!"

Then he sent his fleet and his troops to attack the harbor of Memphis. They brought him every ship, every ferry, every *shry-boat*, all the many ships that were moored in the harbor of Memphis, with the bow rope fastened to its houses. [There was not] a common soldier who wept among all the troops of his majesty. His majesty himself came to line up the many ships.

His majesty commanded his troops: "Forward against it! Mount the walls! Enter the houses over the river! When one of you enters the walls, no one shall stand in his vicinity, no troops shall repulse you! To pause is vile. We have sealed Upper Egypt; we shall bring Lower Egypt to port. We shall sit down in Balance-of-the-Two-Lands!"

Then Memphis was seized as by a cloudburst. Many people were slain in it, or brought as captives to where his majesty was.

Now [when] it was dawn on the next day his majesty sent people into it to protect the temples of god for him. The arm was raised over the holy of holies of the gods. Offerings were made to the Council (of the gods) of Memphis. Memphis was cleansed with natron and incense. The priests were set in their places.

His majesty proceeded to the house of [Ptah]. His purification was performed in the robing room. There was performed for him every rite that is performed for a king when he enters the temple. A great offering was made to his father Ptah South-of-his-Wall of oxen, shorthorns, fowl, and all good things. Then his majesty went to his house.

Then all the districts in the region of Memphis heard (it). Hery-pedemy, Pininewe, Tower-of-Byu, Village-of-Byt, they opened the gates and fled in flight, and it was not known where they had gone.

Then came King *Iuput*, and the Chief of the Ma, Akanosh, and Prince Pediese, and all counts of Lower Egypt, bearing their tribute, to see the beauty of his majesty.

Then the treasuries and granaries of Memphis were allocated as endowment to Amun, to Ptah, and to the Ennead in Memphis.

At dawn of the next day his majesty proceeded to the East. An offering was made to Atum in Kheraha, the Ennead in Per-Pesdjet, and the cavern of the gods in it, consisting of oxen, shorthorns, and fowl, that they might give life-prosperity-health to the King of upper and Lower Egypt, *Piye* ever living.

His majesty proceeded to On over that mountain of Kheraha on the road of Sep to Kheraha. His majesty went to the camp on the west of Iti. His purification was done: he was cleansed in the pool of Kebeh; his face was bathed in the river of Nun, in which Re bathes his face. He proceeded to the High Sand in On. A great oblation was made on the High Sand in On before the face of Re at his rising, consisting of white oxen, milk, myrrh, incense, and all kinds of sweet-smelling plants.

[79]

Going in procession to the temple of Re. Entering the temple with adorations. The chief lector-priest's praising god and repulsing the rebels from the king. Performing the ritual of the robing room; putting on the *sdb*-garment; cleansing him with incense and cold water; presenting him the garlands of the Pyramidion House; bringing him the amulets.

Mounting the stairs to the great window to view Re in the Pyramidion House. The king stood by himself alone. Breaking the seals of the bolts, opening the doors; viewing his father Re in the holy Pyramidion House; [adoring] the morning-bark of Re and the evening-bark of Atum. Closing the doors, applying the clay, sealing with the king's own seal, and instructing the priests: "I have inspected the seal. No other king who may arise shall enter here." They placed themselves on their bellies before his majesty, saying: "Abide forever without end, Horus beloved of On!"

Entering the temple of Atum. Worshiping the image of his father Atum-Khepri, Great one of On.

Then came King *Osorkon* to see the beauty of his majesty.

At dawn of the next day his majesty proceeded to the harbor at the head of his ships. He crossed over to the harbor of Kemwer. The camp of his majesty was set up on the south of Keheny, in the east of Kemwer.

There came those kings and counts of Lower Egypt, all the plume-wearing chiefs, all viziers, chiefs, king's friends from the west, the east, and the isles in their midst, to see the beauty of his majesty. Pediese threw himself on his belly before his majesty, saying: "Come to Athribis, that you may see Khentikhety, that Khuyet may protect you, that you may offer an oblation to Horus in his house, of oxen, shorthorns, and fowl. When you enter my house, my treasury will be open to you. I shall present you with my father's possessions. I shall give you gold as much as you wish, turquoise heaped before you, and many horses of the best of the stable, the choicest of the stall."

His majesty proceeded to the house of Horus Khentykhety. An offering of oxen, shorthorns, and fowl was made to his father Horus Khentykhety, lord of Athribis. His majesty went to the house of Prince Pediese. He (Pediese) presented him with silver, gold, lapis lazuli, and turquoise, a great quantity of everything, and clothing of royal linen of every number, couches laid with fine linen, myrrh and ointment in jars, and stallions and mares, all the best of his stable.

He (Pediese) purified himself by a divine oath before these kings and great chiefs of Lower Egypt: "Anyone who hides his horses and conceals his wealth (?) shall die the death of his father! I have said this in order that you bear out your servant with all that you know of me. Tell if I have concealed from his majesty anything of my father's house: gold bars (?), precious stones, vessels of all kinds, armlets, bracelets of gold, necklaces, collars wrought with precious stones, amulets for every limb, headbands, earrings, all royal adornments, all vessels for the king's purification of gold and precious stones. All

[80]

these I have presented to the King, and garments of royal linen by the thousands of the very best of my house. I know you will be satisfied with it. Proceed to the stable, choose what you wish, all the horses you desire!" Then his majesty did so.

Then said these kings and counts to his majesty: "Let us go to our towns to open our treasuries, that we may choose according to what your heart may desire, and bring to you the best of our stables, the finest of our horses." Then his majesty did so.

List of their names:

King *Osorkon* in Perbast and the district of Ranofer,

King *Iuput* in Tentremu and Taan, . . . [2]

The remainder of the list enumerates many other provincial rulers, whom the text calls generals, counts, chiefs, and prophets. For us, the most important thing is that each name is accompanied by the designation of the

---

[2] Ibid., pp. 72–78. The Hermopolitan Ogdoad consisted of four pairs of primeval deities; Khmun, one of the Egyptian names of the city, means "eight." The name Peftuaubast means "his breath is in the hand of (the goddess) Bastet." Rahone is el-Lahun at the entrance to the Faiyum. Shetit is the name of the sanctuary of Ptah-Sokar in Memphis. South-of-his-Wall is an epithet of the god Ptah. At Memphis, when the Chief of Sais says, "I shall go to give gifts to the chiefs of Lower Egypt. I shall open their nomes to them," he is evidently renouncing his dominion over nomes he had previously conquered in order to have a free hand in the struggle against Piye. "Balance-of-the-Two-Lands" is a poetic name of Memphis that recollects its location at the border of Upper and Lower Egypt; it might also have a figurative meaning, designating the age-old city as guarantor of the equal status of the Two Lands. Kheraha was a locale between Memphis and Heliopolis where Atum was venerated in the form of an ape shooting with bow and arrows. On is Heliopolis. The "camp on the west of Iti" was located at Ain Shams in Matariyah, a section of modern Cairo. The "river of Nun" bears the name of the primeval ocean out of which the creator god emerged. The *sdb*-garment is evidently the band that adorned the head of the Kushite rulers, though it is difficult to imagine it being introduced into the Egyptian ritual before the subjection of the land by the Kushites; its mention here is perhaps a bit of propaganda on the part of the author of the text. The Pyramidion House of Heliopolis contained a stone or mound upon which the primeval god Atum was supposed to have manifested himself at the beginning of creation; the object was also a manifestation of the god. Kemwer ("great black bull") was a nome of Lower Egypt, with its capital at Athribis, modern Tell Atrib; Kemwer is also the oldest known name of the later city of Athribis. Keheny, whose location remains uncertain, might be the modern town of Kaha south of Athribis. The "plume-wearing chiefs" were likely rulers of Libyan origin, who usually wore a feather on their heads. Khentikhety and Khuyet were a god and goddess, respectively, at Athribis. "King Osorkon in Perbast" is Osorkon IV, the last ruler of Dynasty 23; he is mentioned earlier in the text as an ally of Herakleopolis, and he is represented in the scene at the top of the stela. The specific location of Ranofer in the vicinity of Tanis is not known. Tentremu is modern Tell el-Moqdam, the capital of the chiefdom of Leontopolis, which is known exclusively from this text.

[81]

town or the region that belonged to the man. From their titles, we see that most of them were chiefs of the Libyan tribe of the Ma.

The next portion of the text is badly preserved. It recounts a rebellion that broke out against the Kushite invader at Mesed, a town situated about nine miles northwest of Athribis and which today is called Mostai or Tell Umm el-Harb. The concluding portion, which can be read, informs us that in the end, this worrisome episode was yet another leaf in the laurel wreath of the Kushite:

> Then his majesty sent soldiers of his to see what was happening there, he being the protector of Prince Pediese. They returned to report to his majesty saying: "We have slain every man we found there." Then his majesty gave it (the town) to Prince Pediese as a gift.
>
> The Chief of the Ma, Tefnakht, heard it, and a messenger was sent to where his majesty was with cajoling words, saying: "Be gracious! I cannot see your face in the days of shame; I cannot stand before your flame; I dread your grandeur! For you are Nubti, foremost of the Southland, and Mont, the mighty bull! Whatever town you turn your face to, you will not be able to find your servant there, until I have reached the islands of the sea! For I fear your wrath on account of those fiery words which are hostile to me!
>
> "Is your majesty's heart not cooled by the things you did to me? While I am under a just reproach, you did not smite me in accordance with (my) crime. Weigh in the balance, count by weight, and multiply it against me threefold! (But) leave the seed, that you may gather it in time. Do not cut down the grove to its roots! Have mercy! Dread of you is in my body; fear of you is in my bones!
>
> "I sit not at the beer feast; the harp is not brought for me. I eat the bread of the hungry; I drink the water of the thirsty, since the day you heard my name! Illness is in my bones, my head is bald, my clothes are rags, till Neith is appeased toward me! Long is the course you led against me, and your face is against me yet! It is a year that has purged my *ka* and cleansed your servant of his fault! Let my goods be received into the treasury: gold and all precious stones, the best of the horses, and payment of every kind. Send me a messenger quickly, to drive the fear from my heart! Let me go to the temple in his presence, to cleanse myself by a divine oath!"
>
> His majesty sent the chief lector priest Pediamen-nest-tawy and the commander Purem. He (Tefnakht) presented him with silver and gold, clothing and all precious stones. He went to the temple: he praised god; he cleansed himself by a divine oath, saying: "I will not disobey the King's command. I will not thrust aside his majesty's words. I will not do wrong to a count without your knowledge. I will only do what the King said. I will not disobey what he has commanded." Then his majesty's heart was satisfied with it.
>
> One came to say to his majesty: "Hut-Sobk has opened its gate; Meten has

thrown itself on its belly. No nome is shut against his majesty, of the nomes of the south and the north. The west, the east, and the islands in the midst are on their bellies in fear of him, and are sending their goods to where his majesty is, like the subjects of the palace."

At dawn of the next day there came the two rulers of Upper Egypt and the two rulers of Lower Egypt, the uraeus wearers, to kiss the ground to the might of his majesty. Now the kings and counts of Lower Egypt who came to see his majesty's beauty, their legs were the legs of women. They could not enter the palace because they were uncircumcised and were eaters of fish, which is an abomination to the palace. But King *Namart* entered the palace because he was clean and did not eat fish. The three stood there while the one entered the palace.

Then the ships were loaded with silver, gold, copper, and clothing; everything of Lower Egypt, every product of Syria, and all plants of god's land. His majesty sailed south, his heart joyful, and all those near him shouting. West and East took up the announcement, shouting around his majesty.

This was their song of jubilation:

"O mighty ruler, O mighty ruler,
Piye, mighty ruler!
You return having taken Lower Egypt,
You made bulls into women!
Joyful is the mother who bore you,
The man who begot you!
The valley dwellers worship her,
The cow that bore the bull!
You are eternal,
Your might abides,
O ruler loved of Thebes!"[3]

In the upper portion of the stela is a scene that illustrates the text in a carefully thought-out and thoroughly didactic manner (Figure 30). Its com-

---

[3] Ibid., pp. 79–80. Nubti and Mont were gods in Upper Egypt. "(But) leave the seed, that you may gather it in time" refers to the sons of Tefnakht; from preceding portions of the text, we learn that Tefnakht had already lost one son in the fighting at the fortress "Great-of-victories" and that another had fled from the seat of Osorkon I. Neith was the goddess of Sais. Meten, modern Atfih, was the capital of the twenty-second nome of Upper Egypt; it was mentioned earlier in the text as Per-nebtepih, one of the eastern cities conquered by Tefnakhte. Circumcision and abstinence from fish were conditions of ritual purity.

For another translation of the text, along with an extensive philological commentary, see H. Goedicke, *Pi(ankh)y in Egypt: A Study of the Pi(ankh)y Stela* (Baltimore, 1998).

[83]

Figure 30. Lower Egyptian princes paying homage to the Kushite king Piye. Scene in the lunette of his large victory stela from Gebel Barkal. Egyptian Museum, Cairo.

position is striking because of its clarity and because of the perfection with which stress is apportioned and appropriate proportions are maintained with regard to its political and religious aspects. The three most important figures are represented in the middle. On his throne sits Amun-Re, "Lord of the Thrones of the Two Lands, Who Stands at the Forefront of Karnak, Resident on the Pure Mountain." Two tall feathers adorn his head; he holds a *was*-scepter in his left hand and, in his right hand, the hieroglyph for *ankh*, "life." Behind him stands his consort, the goddess Mut, "Mistress of Asheru," that is, of the temple precinct dedicated to her at Karnak. In front of the divine couple strides Piye, whose name is written in a royal cartouche. His wife, who is wearing a long gown, greets the ruler with her hand. She is accompanied by king Nimlot, who is shaking a sistrum and leading a beautiful, slender horse.

In the lower register of the scene, three kings fall on their faces before the Kushite ruler: they are Osorkon, Iuput, and Pef-tjau-(em)-aui-(en)-Bastet. Making use of a poetic metaphor known from Egyptian literature, the author of the text states that they fell on their bellies. The discrepancy between the text and the representation is comprehensible, for in the Egyptian language, one and the same word means both "belly" and "body." On the other side of the scene, five princes and counts, who are mentioned in the text, are represented in the same position.

King Piye's victory in no way meant the subjugation of Egypt. The Kushite returned to Napata with his troops and was buried with his forebears at el-Kurru. Piye was the first ruler of Kush to have a pyramid erected over his burial. In this, we can suspect a reminiscence of his stay at Memphis, where the royal tombs of the Old Kingdom must have made a strong impression on him. The Kushite pyramids differ, however, from those at Memphis: they are smaller, they incline on average at an acute angle of sixty-eight degrees, and their construction displays no formal connection to the subterranean chambers. They are merely an embellishment of the

[84]

grave. They are also not homogeneous stone constructions: hidden under their stone casings are heaps of gravel and stone held together by a mortar of clay.

Burials of horses constitute an original element of the Kushite royal tombs. This tradition was also inaugurated by Piye, who was a great lover of horses, as the text of his triumphal stela informs us. The bodies of his favorite steeds were placed vertically in special graves dug deep to accommodate their legs.

PIYE'S SUCCESSORS

Shabaka (Figures 31 and 32), Piye's brother and successor, was obliged to undertake another expedition to the north. This he did around the year 713 B.C.E. He defeated the ruler of Sais, Bocchoris (Dynasty 24), who was Tefnakhte's son, and he ascended the throne of Egypt as the first ruler of Dynasty 25. There was thus once again an authentic Lord of the Two Lands. Reliefs carved on both sides of the entrance to the temple of Luxor depict him in the embrace of Egyptian goddesses, while other scenes carved in even larger scale represent him carrying out Egyptian rituals. Finally, we see him in a relief carved on a beautiful black granite naos that he dedicated at Esna to the god Osiris. The scene decorating one of the side walls of the naos depicts him using four vessels to carry out a ritual purification of Osiris.

These reliefs enable us to observe the changes occurring in Egyptian art at the beginning of Dynasty 25. They mark the beginning of a period during which the human body was represented with greater realism than before, while at the same time, there was an imitation of archetypes from the times of the greatest periods of the past, the Old and Middle Kingdoms. There is a clear stress on the musculature of the sunken silhouette of the stocky ruler. The flat shape of the arm muscles arouses the impression that this is an atlas of anatomy, while the plastic representation of the leg muscles gives an impression of movement and is suggestive of a physiology lecture. The Kushite kings are always represented as broad-shouldered persons with short, thick necks. Their faces display African features, in particular, fleshy lips and broad, flat noses.

These traits stand out more clearly in sculpture in the round, as represented, for example, by an appealing bronze figurine now in the National Museum in Athens. It depicts Shabaka kneeling and presenting an offering. The king's name is engraved on the belt of his short kilt, which displays the same form as those worn by the pharaohs for over two millennia. Aside from the broad armlets on his upper and lower arms, the king's nude torso is adorned only by a necklace. Its ends, which hang forward on his shoul-

Figure 31. The Kushite king Shabaka purifying the god Osiris. Relief on a granite shrine from Esna. Egyptian Museum, Cairo. Photo by Andrzej Bodytko, Polish Center of Mediterranean Archaeology, Warsaw University.

ders, have the form of rams' heads with uraeus-serpents between their horns. A similar head of rather larger size is attached to the necklace above his breast and is also crowned by a sun disk. This simple piece of jewelry is an example of the rich religious symbolism that dominated the political theology of the Kushite Period. The ram, emblem of Amun, lord of Napata, bears a royal symbol on his brow, and the disk on his head identifies him

[86]

Figure 32. Detail of Figure 31. Photo by Andrzej Bodytko, Polish Center of Mediterranean Archaeology, Warsaw University.

with the sun god Re. The god Amun-Re and the king, both equally Kushite and Egyptian, thus form an organic unity.

Even more interesting is the iconography of his headdress. A broad diadem decorated with a frieze consisting of small cobras tops his tight-fitting cap. From the ruler's brow rise two uraeus-serpents whose bodies are coiled atop his head and hang loosely behind him. From the diadem, two broad ribbons hang down his back. The interpretation of this ornamentation is not as clear as in the case of the necklace, and it remains the object of Egyptological discussion. Some art historians are of the opinion that the "cap" is not a headdress but only a schematic representation of thick, closely cropped hair. They even view the rings that fill the upper suface of this hairstyle and evidently display the same form as the metal platelets on the *khepresh*-crown (the blue crown) as a stylized representation of locks of hair.

The two uraeus-serpents on the Kushite ruler's brow have engendered no less controversy. As a rule, only one serpent appeared on an Egyptian king's forehead, and two parallel elements of this sort occur only on the heads of certain goddesses and queens. A clue to the interpretation of this iconographic innovation is supplied by the fact that in the representations of the Kushites, many of the double uraei themselves wear a royal crown

[87]

on their heads. One of them appears with the white crown of Upper Egypt, and the other with the red crown of Lower Egypt. Did the rulers of Dynasty 25 need to place such ostentatious stress on the fact that they were pharaohs of the land they had reunified, that they were thus Lords of the Two Lands? Were they not rather indicating that they had accomplished something more, namely, that they had not only united a fragmented Egypt but also annexed it to their own land? Some Egyptologists are of the opinion that the symbolism of the double crown in the iconography of the Kushites assumed a new meaning, referring no longer to the two parts of Egypt but to the two lands of Egypt and Kush. Perhaps the epithet designating them as Lords of the Two Lands at that time had a broader meaning than just lords of Upper and Lower Egypt.

This hypothesis seems to be supported by the fact that in many reliefs of Dynasty 25, one of the two uraei—especially when they are decorated with crowns—was later effaced under Dynasty 26, which stemmed from the north of Egypt. Why this iconoclasm? Did it negate the Kushite rulership over the "second" land—that is, Egypt—or was it intended to erase the notion of the Kushite as a Lord of the Two Lands from the consciousness of the Egyptians? The written sources preserved to us do not permit a clear answer to these questions.

One of the portraits that later fell victim to this iconoclasm was the image of Shebitku, Shabaka's successor, in the relief on the front wall of the temple of Osiris Ruler of Eternity at Karnak. Here, the uraeus-serpent with the red crown of Lower Egypt was hacked away, leaving only the serpent wearing the white crown of Upper Egypt.

The first two rulers of Dynasty 25, Shabaka and Shebitku, were famed as royal reformers. This was especially true of the former, who was still mentioned with deep respect centuries later, in the Ptolemaic Period. Each of them reigned about twelve years, though rather more evidence has survived from Shabaka's reign than from that of his successor.

Shabaka conceived an ambition to set the already existing temples in order and to expand them with further constructions of his own. He renovated the mud brick walls that surrounded the temples and outfitted them with gateways. Among others, the temples of Karnak, Luxor, and Medinet Habu display traces of this activity. At the Fourth Pylon of the temple of Amun-Re at Karnak, Shabaka renovated the gateway, which was covered with gold leaf, and added a new portal. In front of the pylon of the Southern Harem at Luxor, which he decorated with the reliefs noted above, he constructed a propylaeum in the form of a peristyle. He built a pylon in front of the small temple of Tuthmosis III at Medinet Habu, and he decorated its walls with the classic scene of a king smiting enemies. The king is Shabaka himself, naturally, but the enemies seem to be symbolic, for the founder of Dynasty 25 is known for his policy of peace.

[88]

The seal bearing his name found at Nineveh and his seal impressions on the handle of an amphora at Megiddo clearly indicate that he maintained diplomatic and economic relations with Assyria. It was his successor who first involved himself in a coalition with Lybian princes from the delta against Sennacherib (705–689 B.C.E.) in defense of Judah, which had rebelled against the Assyrians. The only indication of military activity on Shabaka's part is to be found in a historical text carved on a scarab now in the collection of the Royal Ontario Museum in Toronto. It speaks of a massacre carried out by the Kushite ruler against rebels in Upper and Lower Egypt, thus serving as indirect evidence that Shabaka united the entire land under his scepter.

SHABAKA'S PIETY

Nearly every great religious center in Egypt bears traces of Shabaka's building activity in the form of stone blocks and various small objects with inscriptions containing his name. In the delta, he built at such places as Bubastis and Athribis, but he devoted special attention to Memphis. Like other rulers of this dynasty, he evidently felt great respect for this age-old seat of the Egyptian kings and for its god Ptah. Nothwithstanding the dominance of the cult of Amun-Re at his native Napata, Shabaka was especially concerned with the goodwill of the creator god of Memphis, in whose city he erected a chapel of limestone and donated a stela in the form of a naos.

But the best indication of his zeal for reform is the so-called Memphite Theology, which is one of the most important surviving documents for an understanding of Egyptian religion. This is a large, black granite stela on which Shabaka had a hieroglyphic copy made of a text containing the theological doctrine of the religious center at Memphis. On the stela, the Kushite ruler declares that he was compelled to this deed by the deplorable, worm-eaten condition of the papyrus on which this important document had been written. Though it was immortalized in stone, the text is unfortunately preserved in fragmentary condition, for the stela was later reused as a millstone. Nevertheless, it is an invaluable document, for it remains the only written source for our knowledge of the theology of Memphis.

Egyptological research has been able to demonstrate that the original of this liturgical text, whose principal element is a hymn to the god Ptah, must have been written toward the end of the Old Kingdom, that is, in the second half of the third millennium B.C.E. The hypothesis that this is merely an archaizing text composed in Dynasty 25 seems less probable, though theoretically it conforms to the spirit of the period with which we are dealing here. The content of the text is interesting not only for students of religion but for historians as well, for we learn from it something about the linking of Memphite beliefs with those of Heliopolis, which seem to have been dominant at the time of Dynasty 5. At the head of the pantheon is Ptah, who makes use of his heart (the seat of thought) and his tongue to create Atum and his Ennead.

Shabaka also immortalized himself at the Serapeum, where three stelae bearing his name, dated to his regnal years 12 and 14, have been found. At Thebes, we find another indication of the Kushite's dedication to the god of Memphis. On the occasion of his jubilee, Shabaka erected a gateway to the small temple of Ptah that had originally been built north of the temple of Amun-Re by Tuthmosis III. In the vicinity of the latter, he also renovated the treasury and, together with the God's Wife Amenirdis, the daughter of Kashta, he dedicated a small chapel to Osiris Lord of Life. As we can see, Osiris became an ever more frequent guest in the vicinity of the mighty Amun-Re during the Kushite Period. There was an evident change of emphasis in the theological function of this god of the afterlife, for the small temples erected to him now stressed his role in the realm of the living.

Like his predecessor, Shabaka was buried with his Kushite dynastic forebears at el-Kurru near Gebel Barkal. Over his grave rose a pyramid that is no longer preserved; its sides were thirty-six feet long, and there was a cult chapel on its east side. This, too, is evidence of the imitation of Memphite cultural prototypes from the period of the Old Kingdom.

The throne names of the Kushite rulers also exemplify their imitation of the most important pharaohs of the past. They copied royal names of Dynasties 5 and 6, such as that of Izezi (Djedkare, the name of Shebitku) and Pepi II (Neferkare, the name of Shabaka). Following the model of his predecessor, Shebitku also had a pyramid atop his grave at el-Kurru. Integral parts of the burials of both rulers were the graves in which their beloved horses were interred, just as in the case of Piye, that famous lover and connoisseur of this animal.

The Egyptians would remember the Kushite "renaissance," and especially the reign of Shabaka, as one of the finest epochs in their history. In the Late Period, one of the streets of Memphis bore Shabaka's name, and in the Ptolemaic Period, at Thebes, many of his inscriptions, which had been defaced by the iconoclasts of the Saite Period (Dynasty 26), were restored. The Greek historians also displayed great respect for Shabaka. Herodotus calls him a "great architect," and Diodorus speaks of him as a pious and righteous king. The preserved relics of his activity lead us to believe that this assessment is correct.

The "Kushite Cap"

The Kushites' special regard for the Memphite god Ptah stimulates a certain consideration of their typical, tight-fitting headdress. It has the same form as the simple cap characteristic of representations of Ptah. Did these rulers from the south, as pious as they were shrewd, wish to emulate the Memphite deity with their headdress and exploit it in their political propaganda? They wore the crowns of other Egyptian deities, such as the feathered crowns of Osiris, Amun, and Onuris—why should they exclude a comparison with Ptah? This is all the more probable in that the Ramessides had worn an identical headdress, specifically when they conducted rituals for Ptah. They are represented in many reliefs and paintings in which their partner is the leading figure of the Memphite pantheon. In this connection, we must not forget that while they sought inspiration in the traditions of the Old and Middle Kingdoms, the Kushites often enlisted the great Ramessides as models. We shall see this more clearly later in the reliefs from the reign of Taharqa, one of the sons of Piye and Shebitku's successor on the throne of Egypt.

There is a common opinion that the Kushite cap, as this headdress is often called, displaced the formerly popular *khepresh*-crown (the blue crown) from the iconography of the pharaohs. The latter had the form of a tall, arched tiara with angular edges. For the most part, it graced the head of Pharaoh in scenes depicting his coronation or his victory in battle, and it became especially popular in the Ramesside Period. Sethos I, Ramesses II, and their successors almost always wear this crown in scenes of slaughter depicting their victories over foreign peoples. This precedent was copied in the reliefs of the Third Intermediate Period.

None of the Kushite rulers of Dynasty 25 is represented wearing the *khepresh*-crown, though other crowns continued to adorn their heads. We can only suspect that this ancient Egyptian symbol was not appropriate to the Kushites because it stimulated reflection concerning their own legitimacy on the throne. Or did they perhaps avoid the crown because in Egyptian thought, it was connected with victory over other lands, including the peoples of the south?

This last consideration would supply a reason for the zeal with which the Kushites demonstrated their "Egyptian" character, especially their piety and their generosity toward the temples. Are we to see in this a reflection of the inferiority complex of nouveaux riches who came to a land from which their own culture was derived? Observing this phenomenon, we cannot help but compare it with the attitude of many Japanese today toward the age-old culture of China, though modern rulers have fewer problems with their headgear, while other articles of royal clothing fall victim to cosmopolitan trends.

[91]

Be that as it may, the blue crown fell out of use throughout the Kushite Period in Egypt (c. 712–664 B.C.E.). The hypothesis that the Kushite cap took its place, however, is probably mistaken. This conclusion is suggested by one of the reliefs carved at Gebel Barkal during the reign of Taharqa. It appears on a granite pedestal that served in antiquity as a way station for the barque containing the statue of the god during processions and which has remained in its original location in the temple of Amun down to this day. Similar pedestals were placed in all the great Egyptian temples, and their relief decoration—which was extremely important from the point of view of propaganda—followed strict rules. On the front is usually a representation of the *sema-tawy*, the motif symbolizing the union of the two parts of the land. The two parallel side walls depict the reigning monarch supporting the sky with his upraised arms. Thus, when the barque was placed temporarily on the pedestal in the course of processions, it symbolically traveled over the sky supported by the king. The king is represented four times on each side, and the *khepresh*-crown normally adorns his head. Taharqa's pedestal at Gebel Barkal is a rare exception in which the pharaoh is depicted wearing a different headdress. Here, the king supporting the sky wears the *nemes*-headcloth. Why this exception to the rule in a representation that in every other way faithfully imitates the iconography of the Ramessides? If it were really the case that the Kushite cap regularly replaced the *khepresh*-crown, we should see it on the head of Taharqa in this scene. This, however, is not the case. Is this an iconographic novelty, or does it follow some precedent not yet known to us?

The work of Polish archaeologists at Deir el-Bahri seems to provide an answer to this question. Here, the temple of Tuthmosis III of Dynasty 18, which was discovered at the beginning of the 1960s, is decorated with colorful reliefs, including depictions of just such pedestals. On each of them, the king supporting the sky appears wearing the *nemes*-headcloth, as in the case of Taharqa's relief. We may thus assume that the artists of Dynasty 25, in their search for the finest traditions of the past, also turned to examples from the early New Kingdom, even when they differed from the most common patterns.

The work of the Polish archaeologists who are reconstructing the temple of Tuthmosis III, currently under the direction of Professor Jadwiga Lipińska, will probably be helpful in solving many iconographic, religious, and historical riddles. The reliefs of this temple, preserved on the surfaces of thousands of stone blocks, still retain their original polychrome decoration, which includes a host of details omitted by the sculptors who prepared the reliefs. In most Egyptian temples and on blocks stemming from them, the painted decoration that originally covered the reliefs has been destroyed by climatic conditions, depriving us of much valuable information.

[92]

One of the most important tasks of the archaeologists working at Deir el-Bahri is the conservation of the colorful painting, which together with the reliefs constitutes a unique source for research into the iconography of Egyptian two-dimensional art.

THE REIGN OF TAHARQA

In the reign of Taharqa, Egypt again became a great power, and fear of the Kushites is connected with his name in the Hebrew Bible (2 Kings 19.9, Is. 37.9). Chosen by Shebitku "from among his brothers," Taharqa (690–664 B.C.E.) ruled in Egypt for a longer time than his two predecessors taken together. His ambition to be a restorer can be seen in his expansion and renovation of temples, as well as his founding of new ones, both in Egypt and in Nubia. The "Two Lands" of Taharqa comprised a huge empire extending from the Mediterranean to the region of modern Khartum, where graves of the period have been found. He was crowned in Memphis, where he also resided. But he was also concerned with the development of his native Napata and of the metropolis of the cult of Amun-Re, which remained Thebes.

The stelae from the Serapeum of Memphis demonstrate clearly that Taharqa reigned in person at that city. Besides the blocks from the chapels he built, a huge ashlar weighing nearly thirty tons and bearing the name of "Taharqa, beloved of Ptah" was found there. Traces of his activity in the delta have been found at places such as Athribis, where the Polish archaeological mission discovered a foundation pit containing the dedicatory foundation stones of a temple erected by Taharqa. At least one statue of this monarch was set up at Tanis, where the temple enclosure also contained one of several copies of the well-known text composed in his sixth regnal year, which serves as a sort of political-theological legitimation of the great monarch. Taharqa exploited the heavy rainfall and the good harvest in that year to take credit for even this act of divine grace. Its conclusion is simple: Taharqa was the chosen one of Amun-Re and must thus be king of Egypt. The most complete copy of this text was found at the Nubian site of Kawa, where Taharqa built another temple to Amun. A third copy of the famous text was found in Upper Egypt, at Koptos, a cult center of the ithyphallic god Min.

Evidence of the great importance attached to the level of the Nile at that time is furnished by the notations of its maximum height at Thebes in regnal years 7, 8, and 9 of Taharqa. This reformer-king built a special sanctuary for the New Year's ritual, which included a procession to the "primeval water"; only some blocks from it are preserved, reused in a chapel erected on the same spot by king Hakoris of Dynasty 29.

The temple of Amun-Re at Karnak underwent a fundamental change in the reign of Taharqa. Here, the Kushite proved to be a genuine aesthete who concerned himself with the architectural harmony of the entire layout. In all four cardinal directions, monumental colonnades were now added to the temple enclosure in front of each of the four main entrances. The most imposing of these colonnades was the western one, which leads to the face of a pylon dating to the era of the greatest Ramessides. We can easily imagine the majestic processions of priests passing through this portico in their long garments, bearing on their shoulders the barques containing the most sacred statues of the deities. From there, they would march straight to the Nile, where they boarded an even larger boat that took them to the opposite bank, the land of the west, which sheltered the tombs and mortuary temples of the great kings of the past.

Next to the temple of Amun, Taharqa erected some small chapels that were dedicated principally to Osiris. Like the temple of Osiris Ruler of Eternity, certain of these edifices were dedicated jointly by the king and the God's Wife of Amun. The office of the high priestess, who was a member of the royal family, gained in importance during Dynasty 25. Reigning in Memphis and ruling a huge territory, the king found the God's Wife to be a political tool who enabled him to control the situation in traditionally unmanageable Thebes. The role of the maiden dedicated to Amun was practically that of a royal governor. In Taharqa's reign, she was Shepenwepet II, a daughter of king Piye, who had been adopted by her predecessor, Amenirdis I. Together with her, Taharqa erected a chapel to Osiris Lord of Life and another to Osiris Lord of Eternity.

In this period, the God's Wives also dedicated sacred edifices of their own in the Theban region. A block decorated with relief from one of them has been found at Madamud, only a few miles north of Thebes and a cult center of the Theban god Montu. This relief is astonishing because of its fantastic theme, which is reminiscent of artists' sketches on ostraca from earlier periods. The scene depicts people and animals participating in the preparations for a banquet. A jolly crocodile plays a lute, while a nude female harpist stands on his back. Next to them, we see a complicated apparatus being used by two figures, one anthropomorphic and one theriomorphic, to prepare some form of beverage, probably alcoholic. This whole company is presided over by a mouse, who sits on a throne and sniffs a lotus blossom. A vertical band of hieroglyphs separates this humorous scene from a large, ritual one, of which only a fragment of a female figure remains, probably a God's Wife of Amun. Her large size leads us to infer that this relief belonged to an unidentified temple.

Previously, illustrations to animal fables had appeared on papyri and ostraca but never on the walls of temples, whose decoration was governed by strict conventions. This demonstration of artistic license testifies not only to its creator's sense of humor but also to certain new artistic trends that accompanied the Kushite domination of Egypt. They are characterized by a love of nature and an openness to fresh compositional solutions and by the stylistic finesse with which variations on the finest models from earlier periods were created. Prototypes stemming from the reigns of the greatest pharaohs became sources of inspiration, not just objects of slavish imitation.

The most interesting and also the most mysterious of all the buildings erected by Taharqa in the temple precinct of Amun-Re at Karnak is the sanctuary next to the sacred lake, which is only partially preserved. It is located near a giant scarab that, together with its tall base, was carved from a single block of granite. On its front side, its donor, Amenophis III of Dynasty 18, had a stela carved depicting him offering before Atum. The scarab was an embodiment of the rising sun, the god Kheperi.

Taharqa's edifice is unique in every respect. Part of it is aboveground and part of it is subterranean, and it is connected with the cult of Osiris and Amun-Re, and especially with the cult of the king himself. As we know, the west bank of Thebes, that is, the realm of the dead, was one of Osiris's domains. His coexistence with Amun within the walls of an edifice located on the east bank, the temple compound of Amun, was thus an astonishing display of hospitality. But it seems that this symbiosis had its ritual basis in the festival served by this edifice of Taharqa. Every ten days, the statue of Amun made a journey to the west bank of the Nile, where it visited the symbolic tomb of the primeval deities, a sort of cenotaph, which was located at Djeme, that is, at Medinet Habu, the mortuary temple of Ramesses III. There, as he visited his forebears—the god Kematef and the Ogdoad—his mystical powers as a creator god were regenerated. Kematef had the form of a serpent that, according to Egyptian belief, arose from the primeval ocean at the beginning of creation, before even the earth came into existence. His name means "he whose time (i.e., lifetime) is completed." His son Irta was supposed to have created not only the sun god but also the Ogdoad, a group of eight deities. Kematef's dwelling was a subterranean crypt at Djeme. Amun was identified with this serpent in his role of primeval god who created the other deities and humankind as well.

The renewed Amun returned from Djeme to his home at Karnak, but before the statue of the god was replaced in its sanctuary, it stopped at this mysterious edifice by the sacred lake. Here, Amun was penetrated by the spirit of the sun god Re, so that he could once again shine forth in all his splendor at dawn. He came to life again from his form of the dead Osiris, and it was thus that the latter also became a solar deity. And since the king was the unique living image of this combined divine being, his cult was ultimately predominant here. This complex religious and political symbolism made the edifice a propaganda instrument of the highest order. The rituals

[95]

conducted within it endowed the king with the religious legitimation to exercise rule on earth as successor to the gods. Pharaoh must thus have attached great importance to this edifice, and Taharqa's predecessors had probably dedicated similar sanctuaries here, of which little or nothing has survived. Certain decorated blocks reused in Taharqa's construction stem from the reign of Shabaka, who perhaps had erected an earlier building with the same purpose on this very spot.

The huge stone scarab from the reign of Amenophis III, which directly faces the sanctuary, could have been functionally connected with a similar chapel from Dynasty 18. Since the scarab-beetle was a manifestation of the sun when it renews itself in the morning, this sculpture lays stress on the cyclical rebirth of Amun-Re and thus might still have played an important religious role in the time of Taharqa. The modern inhabitants of Egypt ascribe quite a different magical power to it: young women wishing to assure themselves of fertility make several circuits around the base of the sacred scarab.

There was also construction work on the west bank of Thebes during the reign of Taharqa. The colonnade that leads into the pylon of the small temple at Medinet Habu was probably his. The reliefs decorating the intercolumnia in this construction were later usurped by Nectanebo I of Dynasty 30, but certain details suggest a work of Taharqa to the attentive investigator. First, the portico has nearly the same architectural form as the colonnades erected by Taharqa in front of the main entrances to the temple of Karnak. Second, this is the location of the crypt of Kematef, with whom the edifice of Taharqa by the sacred lake at Karnak was connected. Third, in the iconography of the king, whose cartouches were usurped by Nectanebo for his own names, there are Kushite elements such as the ribbon wrapped around the head over a tight-fitting headdress and a uraeus-serpent wearing a royal crown on its head, which is a characteristic decoration of the Kushite cap. Such an attribution seems all the more probable in that Taharqa was the king who completed the decoration of the pylon here, which had been erected by Shabaka, and to which this very portico leads.

The attribution of this portico is one of the many puzzles posed by Egyptian architecture, reliefs, and sculpture in the round, which fill the lives of Egyptologists with so much excitement that they find no time for leisure. When we look at a cartouche containing a royal name on a statue or relief, we can never be entirely certain that it does not replace the erased name of another, earlier ruler, during whose reign a sculptor created the work upon which we are gazing. Many statues, as at Tanis, bear traces of repeated alteration in periods widely separated in time. The epigrapher is not always able to make out the name that was erased by the usurper or iconoclast; for the most part, there remain only some traces of hieroglyphic signs, though sometimes the entire shapes of signs can be made out. To determine the date of such a sculpture, a thorough knowledge of Egyptian art is indispensable, for it is the style of the work that enables the investigator to determine its period of origin with a considerable degree of accuracy.

Stylistic criteria can sometimes be misleading, though. In Egyptian art, we often meet with conscious archaizing or outright copying of works from ages past. Only the expert eye of an art historian is capable of distinguishing an original from an ancient copy, and even the best experts can make mistakes regarding dating. Statues representing kings of Dynasty 25 that are uninscribed or only partially preserved have often been dated to Dynasty 12, for the austere expression to be seen on portraits of the later rulers of the Middle Kingdom displays strong resemblances to the portraits of the Kushites. The opposite error has also been made, and there have been works from the end of the Middle Kingdom that were long taken to be products of the workshops of the Kushite dynasty. Still more errors of this sort have been inspired by the art of the following period, Dynasty 26, with which we shall be concerned in the next chapter.

Taharqa was as active in his native Nubia as he was in Egypt. His predecessors Shabaka and Shebitku had left almost no traces of building activity there, and the great reformer evidently resolved to make up for this deficiency. He erected many new temples and restored old ones. Nubian art of the Kushite Period has a distinctive character that distinguishes it from the works of Dynasty 25 in Egypt itself, for the latter are more classical in their artistic expression. In Nubia, more African elements made their appearance, which when contrasted with the Egyptian iconographic canon create an impression of a certain freshness and often even an amusing naïveté.

The most splendid works of this art were discovered by archaeologists at Kawa and Gebel Barkal, though remains of temples bearing the name of this greatest of the Kushite rulers have also been found at Tabo, Semna, Faras, Qasr Ibrim, Philae, and many other Nubian sites. At Sedeinga, not far from the Third Cataract, are the remains of a pyramid from the reign of Taharqa whose sides measure over thirty-two feet in length and which is made of blocks of slate. Unfortunately, its interior was plundered before archaeologists reached it in 1963–64.

Especially interesting statues representing Taharqa stem from Kawa, a site in Upper Nubia whose ancient Egyptian name Gem(pa)aten must have been coined in the time of the "heretic" Akhenaten (= Amenophis IV, c. 1364–1347 B.C.E.) of Dynasty 18, for it contains the name of the god Aten, the sun disk who was worshiped during his reign. Taharqa developed this old center of Egyptian culture in an imposing manner. He dispatched artists from Memphis to renovate the already existing temple, which was a work

[97]

of Tutankhamun, and to erect a new temple dedicated to Amun of Gem(pa)aten. Some of the reliefs carved on its walls are authentic copies of those in the Memphite funerary temples of pharaohs of Dynasties 5 and 6, such as those of Sahure, Neuserre, and Pepy II. As at Karnak and Medinet Habu, this temple was provided with a processional way in front of its main entry.

Among the statues found there during the excavations conducted by Oxford University in 1930–36, two pairs of granite statues representing Taharqa are of special interest. The king stands between the hoofs of a huge ram, which rests sphinxlike on a pedestal. Taharqa wears the typical Egyptian *nemes*-headcloth, but the muscular build of his stocky figure, his negroid facial features, and the two *uraeus*-serpents on his brow serve to stress his Nubian origin. The ram, the sacred animal of Amun, had already appeared earlier as protector of the ruler. In front of the entrance to the temple of Amun-Re at Karnak, there remains part of an avenue consisting of two rows of similar sculptures from the reign of Ramesses II. In this respect as well, Taharqa found a model in this great pharaoh of the New Kingdom.

Also found at Kawa was a granite sphinx with the head of the pharaoh surrounded by a luxuriant lion's mane; in this case, we have an imitation of a similar sculpture from the reign of queen Hatshepsut of Dynasty 18. The latter sphinx, which is made of limestone, was found at Deir el-Bahri and is now in the Cairo Museum. The Taharqa sphinx, along with one of the four granite rams, today is in the collection of the British Museum in London. After its excavation, a second ram found a home in the Ashmolean Museum in Oxford, while the remaining two stand in all their splendor before the entrance to the Sudan National Museum in Khartum.

An especially comprehensive group of Taharqa portraits from Kawa is composed of bronze figurines representing the king either kneeling or striding. They continue common iconographic themes, and they testify to the popularity of bronze statuettes at the time of Dynasty 25. In Egypt itself, the production of bronze votive figurines developed on an unusually large scale at this time; the statuettes were placed in temples and tombs, along with a prayer for the goodwill of a deity, which is usually incised on the surface of the metal. Innumerable bronze figurines, now in nearly every museum in the world, depict the whole rich pantheon of Egypt. Their iconography is sometimes quite exceptional.

Theriomorphic representations of deities make their appearance every bit as often as anthropomorphic likenesses. In Egypt, nearly every animal— including the shrew, the pig, the crocodile, and the hippopotamus—was the manifestation or the symbol of a godhead.

The sacred animals worshiped in the various temples were mummified after death like human beings and buried in special cemeteries. Dried and

[98]

wrapped in bandages, the bodies of smaller animals were often placed in a bronze case that served as a miniature sarcophagus. Brief offering formulas, which of course included the name of the donor, were incised on the sides of these little coffins, and a bronze figurine of the sacred animal was attached to the top. Small coffins of snakes, lizards, and eels are among the most common objects. Many of these animals were associated with the Heliopolitan god Atum. The wrapped bodies of little snakes remain in some of the small chests displaying such figures. On such ex-votos, the body of the snake figure takes the form of a loop in the shape of a figure eight, with the head resting on the first coil.

More interesting still are the bronze figurines on the coffins of eels. The front part of the animal's body, represented with fins and other ichthyological details, is joined to the swollen hood of a cobra, which is itself provided with the human head of a god wearing the double crown of Upper and Lower Egypt. Such a crown was worn by the god Atum and also by the king. We can tell immediately that this is a god by the beard, whose end is curved forward. This syncretistic representation combines body parts of two sacred animals with the anthropomorphic form of the sun god. There are exceptions: figures that represent the eel with its own head, separated from the cobra's hood provided with a human head depicted in front of the fish. The most beautiful example of such a votive figure, probably dating to Dynasty 25, is to be found in the Egyptian Museum in Cairo (Figure 33).

Astonishing results were obtained by the investigation of one of the mummified "eels" in the laboratory of the Louvre in Paris. The body found in one such chest was in no way that of an eel but of another fish whose habitat is the African interior. Perhaps special, "pure" species of fish were imported into Egypt for religious purposes; we know—from the stela of king Piye, at least—that in Egypt, people who ate fish were considered unclean.

Another sacred animal of Atum known from bronzes was the mongoose, whose talent for eating snakes was highly valued. In Egyptian thought, this must certainly have been a matter of evil serpents who embodied the enemies of the sun god: good serpents, after all, were manifestations of Atum, and the god could not gulp himself down.

The seemingly defective logic in the beliefs of the Egyptians results principally from the incomplete state of our knowledge, based exclusively on the preserved sources, which do not represent all the geographical and historical aspects of this religion. The mongoose was not only an animal of Atum but of Re as well, who was also worshiped at Heliopolis, and also of the goddess Wadjit (the "green one"), whose home was the Lower Egyptian city of Buto. Finally, it was associated with Horus, the son of this goddess.

[99]

Figure 33. Figure of an eel and the hood of a cobra with the head of the god Atum on the sarcophagus of a mummified fish. Bronze. Egyptian Museum, Cairo. Photo by Waldemar Jerke, Polish Center of Mediterranean Archaeology, Warsaw University.

As the sacred animal of Atum, the mongoose was depicted running, but when it was depicted rearing up on its hind legs, it was the animal of the goddess Wadjit. Both iconographies appear in bronze figurines decorating the sarcophagi of the little animals. The back wall of one such chest served as a lid that was soldered shut after the mummy was inserted. A bronze in the Egyptian Museum in Cairo depicts a tiny priest kneeling before a disproportionately large mongoose; though there is no inscription, the fact that it is rearing on its hind legs makes it possible to identify it as an embodiment of the goddess Wadjit (Figure 34).

In ancient Egyptian belief, the mongoose formed a pair with the somewhat smaller shrew; both animals are physically capable of swelling themselves up or decreasing the volume of their bodies, each one to the size of the other. They were thus regarded as two aspects of Horus of Letopolis, a divine falcon who had both a sighted form called Mekhenty-irty and a blind form named Mekhenty-en-irty. The sighted aspect was of course the mongoose, which is distinguished by its large eyes. A further extension of these concepts made these homely animals into symbols of

Figure 34. Figurine depicting a priest kneeling before an enormous mongoose, a snake killer and an animal sacred to the goddess Wadjit. Dynasties 25–26. Egyptian Museum, Cairo. Photo by Waldemar Jerke, Polish Center of Mediterranean Archaeology, Warsaw University.

the two polar opposites of the sunlight. But as the animal of Atum, the mongoose was principally a "tracker" that hunted the evil Apophis-serpent and could attain a length of forty-six cubits, that is, nearly eighty feet. This notion was a product of fantasy, of course, but it perhaps explains the relative proportions of the animal and the priest in the bronze noted above. The mongoose as guardian of Atum was called the "protective spirit of Heliopolis."

Like Memphis and Thebes in Egypt, the Kushite capital was the object of special care from Taharqa. The style of the preserved reliefs there leads us to think that the Lord of the Two Lands perhaps sent artists to Napata from Egypt, perhaps specifically from Thebes, as suggested by the Theban prototypes of many of the scenes. Taharqa renovated the great temple of Amun at Napata, and he excavated two *speoi* (rock chapels) into the Pure Mountain. The larger of them has Hathor columns and pillars with images of Bes, the benevolent demon whose magical powers protected women in labor.

Some scholars were once of the opinion that in antiquity, the city was dominated by four colossal statues of Taharqa hewn out of the rock, perhaps on the model of the statues of Ramesses II at Abu Simbel. But the most recent archaeological work, which was conducted in 1987 by an expedition of the Boston Museum of Fine Arts under the direction of Timothy Kendall, completely changed our conceptions regarding the appearance and function of the Pure Mountain in pharaonic times. The results of their investigations were the greatest sensation of the fifth International Congress of Egyptologists, which was held in Cairo in the fall of 1988.

On the trail of a report concerning a supposedly inaccessible inscription that two other archaeologists had made out with a telescope four decades earlier, the young scholars organized a veritable Alpine expedition. The inscription was located at a height of 213 feet, just beneath the summit of the giant rock massif and not far from its southwestern corner. It faces the southeast, in the direction of the Nile. At this spot, by a lucky accident, there is a tall needle of rock in the form of a slightly bent horn directly opposite the massif. The Boston expedition climbed this very needle to investigate the inscription, and in the process, they ascertained completely unexpected facts. The inscription of Taharqa, carved in a depression that measures just over three feet by eight feet, is very badly damaged but legible enough to determine that it commemorates a victory of Taharqa over Libyans (*Tjemehu*) and Asiatics (*Mentiu Setjet*).

Why was such an important propagandistic report located at such a height that it could scarcely be made out? Further observation revealed that a row of small openings was sunk into the surface of the rock. Four of them still held bronze nails, which were used in Egypt to fasten the thin gold foil that covered bas-reliefs in the most important and especially prominent places. Directly facing the rising sun and reflecting the light from the surface of its glittering metal, this inscription was a sort of beacon that could be seen from a distance of many miles in the desert, whence many caravans journeyed to Napata.

Essentially, this dazzling billboard was a sort of chapel, complete with a divine statue that stood on a ledge of rock that the American archaeologists discovered below the inscription. How had this naos been excavated? The answer to this question was an immediate sensation. During Dynasty 25, between the needle and the massif, a complex scaffolding was erected of wooden beams stuck into hollows that are still preserved on both sides. Similar holes near the inscription and on the peak of the massif made it possible to determine that while the work was being carried out, the surface of the rock here was completely obstructed by the horizontal and vertical wooden piles that stretched across the precipice. There were even two wooden shadufs attached to the top of the mountain to serve as lifting devices for conveying the material to this height. This unique construction project and its discovery in modern times provide the key to understanding the function of the Pure Mountain in the pharaonic era.

There can be no doubt that the horn-shaped needle of rock, which was a natural geological formation, was ingeniously suited to the general architectonic concept that transformed the rock massif into a huge sacral construction. What is there is not a remnant of a gigantic likeness of Taharqa hewn out of the rock, as had been thought until recently, but rather a *uraeus*-serpent, similar in form to the cobra hood topped by the head of a god on the bronze eel figurines mentioned above, rising up at the foot of the mountain. Like the uraeus on the brow of the king, this natural cobra fulfilled a magical function with regard to the entire mountain.

On the basis of these facts, we may venture some suggestions. Since the shape of the rock needle at Gebel Barkal is reminiscent of a horn, it does not seem unlikely that the name *wepet-ta*, "Horn of the Earth," which appears as the designation of Egypt's southern boundary in texts of Tuthmosis I, early in Dynasty 18, can be identified with the holy mountain of Napata, which was at that time such a boundary. If this was so, Gebel Barkal could also have been called "horn mountain," which would have been *dju-ab* in Egyptian, and thus nearly identical to *dju-wab*, "Pure Mountain," its name in the hieroglyphic texts.

The suggestion that this otherwise incomprehensible designation had its origin in phonetic changes in a name not preserved to us is supported by the etymologies of many other ancient Egyptian toponyms. The addition of a consonant to one of the words, and perhaps a change in the vowels (which were not noted in the writing system), could have changed a specification of shape into a reference to religious function. The name "Holy Mountain" is attested as early as the reign of Tuthmosis III.

The interpretation of the needle of rock at Gebel Barkal as a giant uraeus finds its confirmation in an as yet unpublished relief at Abu Simbel from the reign of Ramesses II. It depicts Gebel Barkal, and the part of the Pure Mountain that interests us is represented as a huge uraeus-serpent wearing the white crown of Upper Egypt. It is emerging from a throne on which Amun is seated inside the mountain. There can be no doubt that the entire rock massif was regarded as a huge and unique seat of this god.

In the relief, the rock needle is represented as though seen from the southeast, the direction from which the glittering chapel on the mountain peak would also have been viewed. The white crown on the uraeus-serpent of Napata, as represented at Abu Simbel, had a special meaning. Was Napata viewed as part of Upper Egypt as early as the New Kingdom? If so, then this symbol justified the Kushite kings' rule over the south of the land as far as Thebes and even beyond. In the triumphal text of the stela of Piye, we find the further religious-political motive that served to legitimize their subjection of Lower Egypt.

While the temples of Gebel Barkal are relatively well known, the residential areas of ancient Napata remain covered with sand. We cannot expect much more than the foundations of the houses to be preserved, for in Nubia, as in Egypt, dwellings were made of dried mud bricks and were thus not durable. But the recent Italian archaeological mission under the direction of Sergio Donadoni found remnants of a temple made of stone blocks and most recently also of a palace.

The reform efforts visible everywhere in Taharqa's reign did not overlook the form of the royal burial. The ruler's ambition, before which even the peoples of Asia trembled, was evidently not satisfied with the modest appearance of the tombs of his predecessors. Taharqa moved the royal cemetery to the opposite bank of the Nile, and he was the first Kushite pharaoh to have a large stone pyramid built for himself in the place now called Nuri. We are unfortunately uncertain whether his body was ever placed inside this edifice, for the American archaeologists who excavated there in 1916–18 found no traces of a burial. Was the largest of the sixty-two pyramids at Nuri only a cenotaph, a false tomb? The subterranean portion of this pyramid imitates the architecture of the Osireion at Abydos, the cenotaph of Osiris that was built by Sethos I and in part decorated by Merneptah of Dynasty 19.

The imitation of prototypes from the New Kingdom is also to be seen in the large number of ushabtis, mummiform figurines of the king, that were found in the pyramid of Taharqa. There were more than 1,070, which is exceptional, for in Dynasty 18, the ideal number corresponded to the number of days in a year. In Dynasty 19, an overseer was added, and then a larger number of overseers—one for each ten days—and a chief of overseers. But the largest possible number seems to have been doubled in the pyramid of Taharqa. Was this to provide two huge workforces to serve the Lord of the Two Lands who ruled over such a great empire?

In contrast to the small, relatively inexpensive faience ushabtis of the Third Intermediate Period, Taharqa's next-worldly servants were as large as the similar figurines of the greatest rulers of the New Kingdom, some of them nearly twenty-four inches in height. In imitation of their prototypes, they were made of more durable material than faience and thus of various types of stone, such as serpentine, granite, limestone, calcite, alabaster, syenite, ankerite, and so forth. The iconography of the figurines is varied, though in most cases their heads are covered with one of the two royal headcloths, and their hands hold either hoes or insignia of royal authority. Baskets are slung over the shoulders of the ushabtis, which have rather the appearance of laborers.

Various types of royal portraiture find their expression in the facial features of these figurines. Some represent the style of African realism, depicting a face with thick lips, flat nose, and prominent cheekbones, while others imitate the austere, majestic physiognomies of the rulers of the Old and Middle Kingdoms. Still others display the common tendency in Egypt to idealize the royal likeness and depict the pharaoh with traits of timeless youth bearing no individual characteristics.

This imposing gallery of portraits, so varied in their expression, iconography, and materials, seems to be the product of a number of sculptors' workshops that perhaps were active in different parts of Egypt. We get the impression that throughout the land, one had announced a competition in the production of figurines of Osiris, to whom Taharqa was assimilated after his death. One common trait unites all these statuettes: each of their mummiform bodies is incised with a hieroglyphic text, a spell from chapter 6 of the Book of the Dead, supplemented by a sentence that previously had appeared only on the ushabtis of Ramesses IV of Dynasty 20. This brief text itself testifies to the nostalgia for the good old days that is so often to be encountered in the works of Taharqa. The largest collections of ushabtis from his pyramid at Nuri are in the Sudan National Museum in Khartum and the Museum of Fine Arts in Boston.

ASSYRIANS IN EGYPT

Taharqa conducted an active, even aggressive foreign policy. Perhaps he felt compelled to do so by the growing power and imperialism of Assyria.

Nevertheless, he made a mistake common to all political megalomaniacs, especially the rulers of large but heterogeneous empires: he overestimated his own power and underestimated that of his opponent. He also failed to foresee that his successor might be a figure of lesser stature, unsuited to the military challenges he would be obliged to face.

Egypt's political omnipresence in the prime of Dynasty 25 is confirmed by various objects bearing the name of Taharqa that have been found in different parts of the ancient Near East. Statues of this pharaoh were even found in the Assyrian palace at Tell Nebi Yunis near Mosul. A large ivory scarab stems from Nimrud, fragments of a vase from Assur, and a seal of Taharqa from Palmyra.

The text discussed earlier, carved high on the rock of Gebel Barkal, notes Taharqa's victory over Libyans. This report is confirmed by written sources found at Kawa, which mention "wives of the chiefs of Lower Egypt" and "children of the chiefs of (the tribes of) Tjehenu," who were pressed into service in the temple. These references might allude to a defeat of Libyan rulers in the delta.

The cause of fresh conflict with Assyria was, as always, Syria-Palestine. The two great powers, one Asiatic and the other African, had long competed for hegemony in this area. The names of Shabaka and Shebitku do not appear in the Assyrian and Hebrew sources, but certain events described in the Bible might refer to the latter, even though the ruler named as the enemy there is Taharqa.

The conflict began with the third campaign of the Assyrian ruler Sennacherib (705–681 B.C.E.), who conquered the cities of the Phoenician coast. The inhabitants of the Philistine city of Ekron expelled their king because of his collaboration with Assyria. He fled to the king of Judah, Hezekiah, who held him captive in Jerusalem and turned to Egypt with a plea for help. There was a battle, in which the Egyptian troops suffered a defeat. It seems that Sennacherib fought yet another battle with the pharaoh, which is mentioned in the Bible (2 Kings 19.8–35). The Assyrian forces were so badly weakened that their ruler was compelled to return to Nineveh, where he remained until his death.

Herodotus, ever the lover of gossip and anecdotes, describes an amusing episode in the unsuccessful Assyrian campaign against Egypt. After their troops had penetrated as far as Pelusium on the Mediterranean coast in western Sinai, they were forced to turn back, not by an epidemic, as stated in the Bible, but because of a horde of mice that ate up the quivers and the bowstrings of the invaders.

When two are in conflict, a third rejoices, and this was the case with the struggle between the Assyrians and the Kushites. At Sais in Lower Egypt, there still dwelled the descendants of Tefnakhte, who had been conquered by Piye, and those of his successor Bocchoris, who Manetho reports had been taken captive and burned alive. Efforts at Sais to regain independence had been dampened by the first Kushites but not entirely eradicated. Other local rulers of the small polities of Lower Egypt, though officially vassals of the kings of Dynasty 25, were ever ready to ally themselves with any political power that would grant them greater independence. They wagered on the Assyrians, for they reckoned that the yoke of a more distant superpower would be easier to shake off. But before that could happen, there was a struggle between Taharqa and the Assyrian king.

The hieroglyphic sources are rather sparing in their information, but the Assyrian texts, written in cuneiform on stelae and clay tablets, report on the expeditions against Egypt in all their details. Sennacherib's son and successor Esarhaddon (681–669 B.C.E.) successfully continued his father's policies. He subjected Syria and drove Taharqa south. He bragged that he succeeded five times in hitting the pharaoh with his arrows and wounding him and then in occupying his residence in Memphis, destroying it, and burning it down. He desired to rid Egypt of Kushites so thoroughly that there would be none left to pay homage to the Assyrian conqueror: he effected a personnel change in every important office, including those of the "kings," that is, the local rulers.

Esarhaddon's unexpected death made a brief return to Memphis possible for Taharqa, until the next Assyrian ruler, Assurbanipal, drove him out in 667 B.C.E. The latter must have determined that the officials named by his father had fled, making it necessary for these positions to be filled by new people. The text written on the clay cylinder found at Nineveh by Hormuzd Rassam is an inestimable source of political and geographical information regarding this event. It contains a list of the local rulers, naming all the important cities in the delta, as well as centers further south, including Herakleopolis, Hermopolis, and Asyut. The Assyrians then conquered Thebes in Upper Egypt for the first time. Taharqa fled to his native Napata, never to return.

His "son" (as the Assyrian sources call him) Tantamani, however, did not wish to relinquish the throne of Egypt. We are informed of the activities of this last Kushite pharaoh by the famous Dream Stela, whose text is dated to his first regnal year. Found with the triumphal stela of Piye at the temple of Amun at Gebel Barkal, this stela is now also in the collection of the Egyptian Museum in Cairo. It is a literary work of a propagandistic nature and of a certain historical value, similar in content and composition to the text of Taharqa reporting the high water level in the sixth year of his reign. It is also similar to the dream stelae of the New Kingdom.

The text of Tantamani reports the same events about which the Assyrian cuneiform sources provide factual information, but the nature of the report is so different that without our knowledge of the historical facts, we would place our faith in its endless string of successes on the part of the Nubian ruler. The Assyrian texts call the victor Assurbanipal, while the Egyptian source identifies him as Tantamani.

From the text of this stela, we learn that the Kushite pharaoh had a prophetic dream during his first year of rule. Two uraeus-serpents appeared before him, one to the left of the king and one to his right. This was taken to mean that if Upper Egypt already belonged to him, he should also lay claim to Lower Egypt. Since a vulture and a uraeus-serpent, symbols of the two halves of the land, were on the king's brow, no one was supposed to share the authority with him. Tantamani had thus made his appearance in this year as a new Horus, that is, the next Lord of the Two Lands.

After conducting a major festival in honor of Amun-Re at Napata, he traveled downstream to pay similar honors to Khnum at Elephantine and Amun-Re at Thebes. On his way to Memphis, he was enthusiastically hailed by throngs that gathered along the Nile; we are familiar with this literary motif from the texts of prince Osorkon and king Piye. After conquering Memphis, he made a bloody reckoning with the leaders of the rebellion that the rulers of the small princedoms of Lower Egypt had organized against him. The remaining rebels then commenced talks with the Kushite ruler, who announced to them the obvious news that his victory had been promised by the god Amun of Napata. Convinced by this irrefutable argument, the rebels made an obsequious declaration. The generous king held a reception for them and allowed them to return in peace to their hometowns to devote themselves to their agricultural tasks.

But the king of Assyria was on the alert. He could not tolerate the return of the Kushites to the delta. Preparing for a new campaign against Egypt, Assurbanipal allied himself with one who was especially burdened by the Kushite yoke: Necho, prince of Sais, who was perhaps a descendant of Tefnakhte. The Assyrian king could not send as large an army to Egypt on this occasion, for his empire was on the verge of crumbling from a threat to the east, where the kingdom of Elam was a trouble spot. Necho was one of the *novi homines* appointed by Esarhaddon to replace the disloyal vassals.

The prince of Sais, who was evidently a spirited man, at first spurned Assyria, and he was captured and taken to Nineveh; but Assurbanipal was merciful toward him, probably taking his own interests into account. He showered gifts on Necho and allowed him to return to Sais; he offered Necho's son, for whom the Assyrian evidently had more feelings than did his own father, an office at Athribis. This generosity was worthwhile for the Assyrian ruler but even more so for the princes who benefited from it.

In the year 663 B.C.E., Assurbanipal attacked Egypt, conquered Memphis, and reached Thebes, which he plundered. Upper Egypt refused to recognize Assyria and maintained the fiction of the Kushite pharaoh until 656 B.C.E. But the powerless Tantamani had fled to Kush, where he continued to rule for a time. Thus ended Dynasty 25 in Egypt.

The princes of Sais allied with Assurbanipal took advantage of a moment of Assyrian weakness to shake off their Asiatic yoke and assume the throne of the Lords of the Two Lands. Necho I, whom Manetho viewed as the third ruler of Dynasty 26, was actually its founder. In any event, it was his successor Psammetichus I who accomplished the consolidation of the Two Lands, driving out the Assyrians once and for all in 655 B.C.E.

The Saite Renaissance (Dynasty 26)

PSAMMETICHUS I

As in our own times, major political changes in ancient Egypt had little influence on the development of social conditions. To sweep away a hierarchy of high functionaries as conscious of their role in the state as the officialdom of Thebes would have bordered on a miracle. For centuries, Thebes had been a bulwark of conservatism. Whatever changes had occurred at Memphis, which had always been more open to influence, or in the delta, the Theban theocracy remained the champion of tradition. Considerable effort and utmost diplomacy were needed to persuade them of the political and cultural innovations emanating from the north. How could one speak of accepting a new king who but a short time earlier had been ruler only of Sais and a few locales in the north! Indeed, Thebes was inhabited by an army of priests of all ranks, many of them related to the Kushite rulers by blood or by marriage, and who enjoyed a degree of political sovereignty that approached pharaonic authority.

Since the reign of Taharqa, two prominent individuals had served as the spiritual and political authorities at Thebes, on the one hand as the instruments of the pharaoh who resided in Memphis, and on the other hand as the generally recognized moral authorities. In particular, there was Shepenwepet II, Taharqa's sister, who had exercised the office of God's Wife of Amun since about 700 B.C.E. Together with her, the great monarch had dedicated two small temples to Osiris in the enclosure of the temple of Amun-Re at Karnak. On her own, Shepenwepet had also erected a series of sacred edifices in the Theban area. The relief with a humorous scene depicting an animal banquet, mentioned in the previous chapter, might have stemmed from one of them. When Kushite rule over Egypt came to an end, the now

[110]

elderly maiden had already secured a successor in the service of Amun. This was Amenirdis II, a daughter of Taharqa, who often appears discreetly next to her aunt on reliefs at Thebes, as though she were coregent. Who could have suspected that the development of political events would never permit her to enjoy sole power?

At Thebes, still more authority lay in the hands of the priest Montemhet. Though he held the modest office of Fourth Prophet of Amun, he was in fact the driving force behind politics at Thebes, and the Assyrian sources designate him as the king of that city. At the time of the Assyrian attack on Thebes c. 667/666 B.C.E., his power stretched from Elephantine to Hermopolis, that is, over all of Upper Egypt. As ruler, he contented himself with the titles Prince of the City (= Thebes) and Commander of Upper Egypt, but unlike the God's Wife of Amun and the princes of Lower Egypt, he never enclosed his name in a royal cartouche.

The wife of Montemhet, this mainstay of the pharaohs of Dynasty 25 in the south of the land, was the Kushite princess Udjarenes. Her husband led the Theban opposition to Assyria. When the Assyrian rulers placed their Egyptian vassal in the delta on the throne, Thebes continued to recognize the rather theoretical overlordship of Tantamani, the last pharaoh of the Kushite line. It was Psammetichus I who at last succeeded in winning the Theban leaders' acceptance of him as Lord of the Two Lands. In fact, this king is represented in the Theban tomb of Montemhet on a lintel, in a double scene with antithetic composition, in which he is depicted once wearing the crown of Upper Egypt and once with the crown of Lower Egypt.

Montemhet's tomb is as unique in Egyptian architecture and relief sculpture as his statues are in the history of Egyptian sculpture in the round. It is located on the west bank of Thebes, not far from the temple of Hatshepsut at Deir el-Bahri, in a place that served as the cemetery of the most important Theban magnates from the period of transition from Dynasty 25 to Dynasty 26. Among all the tombs of this period, it is distinguished by its monumentality, the originality of its architectural solutions, and the beauty of its reliefs. To this day, it preserves its tall pylon of dried mud bricks leading into an area around the tomb surrounded by a wall made of the same material. The tomb itself is hewn into a limestone cliff, and its central element is a court whose walls are decorated with alternating sunken and raised reliefs. Raised reliefs depict stylized papyrus bundles between which, at regular intervals, are entrances to side rooms. On the doorjambs flanking each entrance, Montemhet is represented in sunken relief, clad in a panther skin and provided with the insignia of his priestly office. At the western end of the court is a columned portico; here, there is a shaft leading down to the burial chamber and other subterranean rooms. The reliefs decorating the interior are especially interesting, for they include scenes otherwise known from tombs and temples of the New Kingdom.

Similar copies of reliefs from centuries past appear on the walls of other officials who were contemporaries of Montemhet, such as Pabasa, Pete-menope, and Basa, whose large tombs are located near that of the Theban leader. This copying of older works is one of the characteristics of the Saite "renaissance," which began with the reign of Psammetichus I. Since we can observe the same archaizing tendency in texts of this period, Egyptologists are faced with the challenge of distinguishing the originals from the sec-ondary works of the Saite Period—that is, Dynasty 26, whose rulers stemmed from Sais. Which is an original, and which is a copy? What motifs were copied by the artists of the Saite Period? These are questions that ex-perts in this period must constantly answer.

Smoothing his way to Thebes was a delicate diplomatic task for Psam-metichus I, especially with regard to the office of God's Wife of Amun. Not only was the office held by a daughter of a great Kushite ruler, but—and this is what was problematic—her designated successor was also the daughter of a Kushite. We do not know what arguments Psammetichus used to convince the two women to adopt his own daughter, but the fact re-mains that in the ninth year of his reign, there was a ceremony that af-firmed the Saite king's rulership over Upper Egypt: his daughter Nitocris assumed the office of God's Wife, arriving at Thebes with the greatest of pomp. With what feelings did Shepenwepet II and Amenirdis II greet their successor? Were they moved by patriotic, religious, or political sentiments? We shall probably never know. They must have accepted the Saite princess into their circle and otherwise made the best of a bad situation.

The event, whose political importance and ritual setting were tanta-mount to those of a royal coronation, is described on a monument known as the Adoption Stela. As is to be expected in a literary work intended to serve as political propaganda, everyone rejoices over the new virgin priest-ess, and the Kushite princesses adopt her in a matter-of-fact manner, as though they could imagine no one else for the position. The text is carved on a stela of coarse-grained red granite that was found in 1897 by Georges Legrain in the vicinity of the small temple of Sethos II in the courtyard of the temple of Amun-Re at Karnak. This valuable document is now in the Egyptian Museum in Cairo. The upper portion of the stela, which con-tained the beginning of the text, is unfortunately not preserved. Since we are well past the prologue, we find ourselves immediately in the arena of important events.

In any case, we are spared having to wade through the thicket of royal titles that would have occupied the opening lines of the text. At the begin-ning of the preserved portion, king Psammetichus is speaking to a gather-ing we must presume consisted of courtiers and officials who had congre-gated at Sais, the capital of the new dynasty. The magnanimous king has decided to give his daughter Nitocris to the god Amun by appointing her to be God's Wife at Thebes:

"I have given to him my daughter to be God's Wife and have endowed her better than those who were before her. Surely he will be gratified with her worship and protect the land of him who gave her to him. Now then, I have heard that a king's daughter is there, (a daughter of) the Horus Lofty-of-diadems, the good god [Taharqa], justified, whom he gave to his sister to be her eldest daughter and who is there as Adorer of God. I will not do what in fact should not be done and expel an heir from his seat, seeing that I am a king who loves truth—my special abomination is mendacity—(and that I am) a son who has protected his father, taken the inheritance of Geb, and united the two portions as a youth. I will give her (my daughter) to her (Taharqa's daughter) to be her eldest daughter just as she (Taharqa's daughter) was made over to the sister of her father."

Then they pressed the forehead to the ground and gave thanks to the King of Upper and Lower Egypt Wahibre, may he live for ever; and they said: "Firmly and enduringly till the end of eternity your every command will be firm and enduring. How good is this which God has done for you! How advantageous is what your father has done for you! He put (it) in the heart of him whom he loved that he should cause his procreator to thrive upon earth, seeing that he wants your personality to be remembered and rejoices at men pronouncing your name: The Horus Great-of-heart and King of Upper and Lower Egypt Psammetichus, may he live for ever, he made as his monument for his father Amun, lord of heaven, ruler of the Ennead, the giving to him of his beloved eldest daughter Nitocris, her fair name being Shepenwepe, to be God's Wife and play the sistrum to his fair face."

Regnal year 9, first month of Akhet, day 28: Departure from the king's private apartments by his eldest daughter clad in fine linen and adorned with new turquoise. Her attendants about her were many in number, while marshals cleared her way. They set forth happily to the quay in order to head southwards for the Theban nome. The ships about her were in great numbers, the crews consisted of mighty men, all (the ships) being laden up to their gunwales with every good thing of the palace. The commander thereof was the sole friend, the nomarch of Nar-khant, generalissimo and chief of the harbour Samtowetefnakhte, messengers having sailed up-river to the South to arrange for provisions ahead of her. The sail of the mast was hoisted and the rising wind pricked his nostrils. Her supplies were obtained from each nomarch who was in charge of his (own share of) provisions and was furnished with every good thing, namely bread, beer, oxen, fowl, vegetables, dates, herbs, and every good thing; and one would give (way) to the other until she reached Thebes.

[113]

Regnal year 9, second month of Akhet, day 14: Putting to land at the quay of the city of the gods, Thebes. Her front hawser was taken, and she found Thebes with throngs of men and crowds of women standing and jubilating to meet her, surrounded by oxen, fowl, and abundant provisions, many in number. Then they said: "Let Nitocris, daughter of the King of Upper Egypt, come to the house of Amun, that he may receive her and be pleased with her. Let Shepenwepe, daughter of the King of Lower Egypt, come to Ipet-sut, that the gods who are in it may praise her." . . .

List of all the property given to her as a gift in towns and nomes of Upper and Lower Egypt. What His Majesty has given to her in seven nomes of Upper Egypt . . . [1]

The lists of endowments with which Nitocris was presented on the occasion of her entry into the line of Divine Adoratrices could make one's head spin. The enumeration of these estates occupies nearly half the preserved portion of the text. We cannot be certain how much of this list was already the property of Shepenwepet II and Amenirdis II and how much was donated by Psammetichus I. Her father's gifts undoubtedly included the estates in four nomes of Lower Egypt, which amounted to a total of 1,400 arouras (1 aroura = 0.666 acre), though the text in fact makes express mention only of a patrimony in seven nomes of Upper Egypt amounting to 1,900 arouras. Informative is the fact that the latter were all located in the northern portion of Upper Egypt; Psammetichus I evidently did not yet dare to take control over fields in the vicinity of Thebes. All the fields bestowed upon Nitocris on the occasion of her investiture with the pontificate amounted to a total of 2,230.21 acres.

---

[1] R. A. Caminos, "The Nitocritis Adoption Stela," *Journal of Egyptian Archaeology* 50 (1964): 74–75. The name of Taharqa has to be restored twice in the passage cited here because it was chiseled out by order of Psammetichus II some decades after the text was carved. "Justified" is an epithet that regularly accompanied the name of a deceased person. The phrase "a son who has protected his father" identifies the king with Horus, the protector and avenger of Osiris. Geb was the Heliopolitan earth-god. The "two portions" united by the king are the two parts of the land, Upper and Lower Egypt. Wahibre was one of the names of Psammetichus I; the two dates to "regnal year 9" refer to this king's reign. "Sole friend" is a title borne by dignitaries. Nar-khant was the twentieth nome of Upper Egypt, whose capital was Nen-nesu, that is, Herakleopolis Magna. The name Samtowetefnakhte means "the uniting of the Two Lands is his strength." "The spirits of all the living" is, in the Egyptian, "the *kas* of all the living." The "God's Wife Shepenwepe" is Shepenwepet II, the daughter of Taharqa. The term "mother" is used of the God's Wife in the sense of an adoptive mother. "Her eldest daughter Amonirdis" refers to Amenirdis II, the adopted daughter of Shepenwepet II.

In addition to these landed estates, the priestess received the assurance of regular deliveries of bread, milk, cakes, beer, cattle, geese, and other food-stuffs—all in carefully stipulated quantities from precisely defined digni-taries and temples throughout the land. The king himself assumed the obligation of donating daily deliveries of six bushels of wheat. Fifteen cen-ters in Lower Egypt were supposed to guarantee her a daily delivery of three hundred pounds of bread. We may assume that they were compelled to do so by the pharaoh. We can scarcely imagine how it could have been otherwise with regard to the considerable quantities of goods that high of-ficials at Thebes were obliged to provide to her.

Is everything accounted for in the document? How many of these en-dowments immediately became her property, and how many were to be re-tained by the priestesses of the Kushite house until they passed away? Or were some of the offerings perhaps merely a fiction? We may imagine that as young a maiden as Nitocris was, she did not pose such questions when she was sent to Thebes or much trouble herself about the material aspects of all the ceremony her father had arranged. Her tender age at this moment in history can be inferred from the fact that she died seventy years later, in the year 586 B.C.E. If she could have made her own decisions, she would probably rather have returned home and given up her career as a sacred virgin. But she probably had as little to say in the matter as the child brides in many Arab families today, where the marriage of children is above all a question of a contract between the parents. The father of the bride must know exactly what and how much he will receive from his future son-in-law. In the case of Psammetichus, it was the other way around: it was he who was obliged to endow his daughter liberally so that the god would ac-cept her as his wife. The munificence of the ruler of Sais reflected the politi-cal importance he ascribed to the sacerdotal career of his daughter. None of the earthly wives of Amun had ever had such a dowry.

With Nitocris's entry into Thebes in 656 B.C.E., Psammetichus I sealed his dominion over the entire land. He became a genuine Lord of the Two Lands.

Certain episodes from this unusual event seem to be represented in re-liefs on stone blocks found in the enclosure of the temple of Mut at Karnak. Since no inscription containing a royal name is preserved on these blocks, their dating rests entirely on iconographic and stylistic criteria. For a time, they were ascribed to the Kushite king Piye, but today, most interpret them as scenes representing the moment of Nitocris's arrival at Thebes.

One of the preserved fragments represents the Nile embankment at Kar-nak, where a ship decorated with the ram's head of Amun is docking; the daughter of Psammetichus I is evidently a passenger on the boat (Figure 35). On the riverbank, a woman wearing a short wig and a long garment stands atop a wall, greeting the new arrival with upraised hands. She is probably Shepenwepet II or her designated successor, Amenirdis II. Nearby, we see an obelisk on a tall base—probably one of the pair erected at Karnak by Sethos II, a king of Dynasty 19. It is more difficult to identify the sphinx with a king's head that is also depicted, for there were many statues of this type, and their location often changed.

Nitocris enlarged the beautiful tomb chapel that her predecessors had erected in the temple enclosure of Ramesses III at Medinet Habu. The artistic level of the bas-reliefs in the portion she added does not reach that of the dynamically modeled human forms in the reliefs depicting Amenirdis I. On the rear wall of the older chapel, the first bearer of this name is depicted twice in an antithetical composition, next to which is a series of ritual scenes accompanied on both sides by religious texts.

The gift of his daughter to the Theban Amun was only one of several shrewd steps taken by Psammetichus I with the goal of consolidating Egypt and rebuilding its power. Above all, the army had to be reorganized, for none of the boundaries was entirely secure. The Kushites, still ruled by the erstwhile pharaoh Tantamani, had in no way lost their appetite for their northern neighbor. In Libya, where they had found a haven, the princes and nobles whom the Assyrians had driven out of the delta were preparing an armed return. The temporarily weakened Assyrians might at any time resolve their internal problems and return to the northeastern border of Egypt.

The military reforms of Psammetichus I concerned his army and his navy. First, according to Greek sources, he allied himself with the Lydian king Gyges and acquired Carian and Ionian mercenaries for Egypt. We thus see Egypt making an overture to the north, a reorientation in favor of a policy directed toward the Mediterranean. Second, Psammetichus expanded his Mediterranean fleet, which was expressed most clearly in the titles of the officials in charge of shipping: instead of titles referring to shipping on the Nile, we now find titles connected with the navy. Thus, in two different ways, Psammetichus obtained precisely what he needed for campaigns to Asia.

Caught up in their struggles with Babylon and Elam, the As-

Figure 35. Arrival of a boat, perhaps with the young Nitocris on board, at the west bank of Thebes. Relief on a block from the temple of Mut at Karnak.

syrians had lost control over the coast of Syria-Palestine, and the ambitious pharaoh saw in this an opportunity to restore Egypt's empire. Feeling his way slowly and carefully in a northerly direction, he regained the southern coast of the Levant for Egypt. Then, he concluded an alliance with Assyria. For the price of military assistance against the enemies of his treaty partner, he gained the Asiatic superpower's renunciation of the western coastal area. When the enemies of Assurbanipal and his successors allied themselves with the nomadic tribes of the Scythians, Psammetichus campaigned against the latter in 620 B.C.E. Somewhat later, in 616 and 610 B.C.E., this same alliance led the ambitious pharaoh into battle against Babylon, which was now under the leadership of Nabopolassar.

On the western front, Psammetichus organized a campaign against Libya to prevent the return of the Lower Egyptian princes. He had a series of stelae set up along the route of his army's western advance. Finally, he stationed garrisons at all the important border points: Elephantine in the south, Daphnae in the northeast, and various places on the western frontier. These garrisons were manned by soldiers of many nationalities, such as Libyans, Semites (including Jews) from Asia, and Greeks.

These developments were not without consequences. Egyptian culture, once shut off but already enriched by African currents during Dynasty 25, now fell ever more under the influence of other civilizations, among which the Greek and Jewish elements became more evident with each century. Words of foreign origin began to appear more frequently in the Egyptian language, and the writing system, which for a time had assumed the character of an "abnormal hieratic"—as it is called in Egyptological jargon—was now reformed. Beginning in Dynasty 26, use of the Demotic script, a highly simplified but standardized system of notation, became widespread.

ARTISTIC DEVELOPMENTS

The reforming spirit of the times was also reflected in art. There were basic changes in the aesthetic canon, which are noticeable in the proportions of the human figure, as represented by sculptors and painters, as well as in the form of the hieroglyphs that appear on stelae, sarcophagi (Plate III), and papyri, and on the walls of tombs and temples. The human form, and the hieroglyphs as well, are taller and slimmer compared to the stocky proportions and muscular forms of Dynasty 25.

Elegance and delicacy of form often led, however, to academicism in the art, to the substitution of correctness for originality. On the walls of tombs and temples, models from the finest periods were copied—thus, at Memphis, principally Old Kingdom reliefs—but the human form is depicted with a cool beauty rather than as animated and vibrant with life. This perfection of execution seems to have been the greatest ambition of the artists of the period. Not only the sculptors' models that assisted the artists in their work, but finished bas-reliefs as well, are often provided with grids to permit the copyists a mathematical precision in the rendering of canonical forms.

These factors do not change the fact that this period saw the creation of many masterpieces of statuary and reliefs that create an impression that various artistic schools representing different stylistic directions were competing with one another. The chief centers of sculpture were in the north, and the finest artists were active at Memphis and Sais, where concepts and models originated that were gradually adopted throughout the land. The Theban workshops, as always, remained somewhat more conservative.

A naturalistic style seems to have prevailed in the sculptural schools of the north at the beginning of Dynasty 26. The most striking example of this naturalism is the representation of Psammetichus I on a basalt intercolumnium (that is, a panel occupying the space between two columns). Found at Rosetta but doubtless stemming from Sais, it depicts the king several times, kneeling and making offerings to various deities. His face is of special interest. It is a realistic portrait that stresses every detail of the uncomeliness of its subject: a pendulous double chin, furrowed cheeks and chin, a long, pointed nose, swollen eyelids. There is no trace of the conventional modeling of the eyes with geometric, lengthy eyebrows and lids made even longer by stripes of makeup. The depiction communicates truth regarding the organic structure of a visage.

We can only wonder whether the egg-shaped form of the head, with its very flat back and somewhat long neck, is also a naturalistic element or whether it is a reminiscence of the dolichocephaly that often appears in depictions of the rulers of Dynasty 25. Psammetichus I's reliefs were created, after all, in the same sculptors' workshops where only a short time earlier, artists had prepared likenesses of the Kushites in the specific style of their era; we may imagine that their creators had become accustomed to certain iconographic conventions and that they found it difficult to adjust quickly to the new aesthetic.

Another feature of Kushite inspiration in this relief of the first ruler of Sais seems to be his tight-fitting headdress, which in its present state of preservation creates the impresssion that the king is bald or has close-cropped hair. But only *one* uraeus rises from the brow of the king, and its coils are arranged in the classical manner.

We see another instance of clear Kushite influence on early Saite art in the reliefs of Montemhet at Thebes. Here, though, a continuation of Dynasty 25 traditions is more understandable than in the north of the land. The relief depicting Psammetichus on a lintel in this tomb stylistically combines elements of Theban traditionalism with the naturalism that had already made headway in Lower Egypt. Here the representation of anatomical detail is still thoroughly conservative, with the new tendencies showing through in the organic structuring of the outer surface of the body. The double chin and the furrows in the lower portion of the face display a relationship to the realistic portrait from Sais. Or were these perhaps facial features that the artist had actually seen in the physiognomy of Psammetichus?

The naturalism visible in Theban art at the transition from Dynasty 25 to Dynasty 26 also left its mark on statuary. The granite statues of Montemhet found at Karnak are counted among the masterpieces of Egyptian portraiture. The intelligent, dignified face of the Theban leader and priest bears an expression of care, even of sadness and weariness. More so than in the relief depicting the king, the age and the psyche of the subject are stressed by the naturalistic modeling of the musculature. It represents the face of a man at a specific point in his life, displaying a specific emotion and no other.

Many statues of this period were found in yet another cachette, this time not in a tomb but in the temple enclosure. This was not a cache of royal or priestly mummies but of a large number of stone statues. It was prepared in the Ptolemaic Period in one of the courts of the temple of Amun-Re at Karnak so as to rid the sacred enclosure of a superabundance of objects. About eight hundred statues of various sizes were collected, representing kings, queens, deities, and high officials, along with stelae and fragments of reliefs and another seventeen thousand objects, all of which were buried in a deep pit in front of the Seventh Pylon of the temple.

The cachette was excavated in 1903–4 by the French Egyptologist Georges Legrain, and most of the works of art he discovered there are now in the Egyptian Museum in Cairo. The statues found in the cache range in date from Dynasty 11 (Middle Kingdom) to the second century B.C.E. (Ptolemaic Period). There is every indication that such inventorying and tidying of the temple was carried out rather often, for many of the foundation pits of the sacred constructions at Karnak also contain statues from earlier periods.

PSAMMETICHUS II

Even more astonishing than those in the Saite relief of Psammetichus I are the reminiscences of Kushite art in the bas-relief of his namesake Psammetichus II, who ascended the throne some years later and ruled for only seven years (595–589 B.C.E.). While Psammetichus I evidently wished (or had) to respect the memory of his Kushite predecessors, the second pharaoh of this name set about destroying their works with an astonishing zeal. At Karnak, for instance, he had the reliefs on Taharqa's columns defaced and the cartouches containing the name of the Kushite altered into his own. It is thus all the more astonishing that the portrait of this ruler displays an iconographic detail that we explained as a Kushite influence in the case of Psammetichus I: the tight-fitting cap on his broad, egg-shaped head. Or was this relief perhaps usurped by Psammetichus II, in this case from his like-named predecessor? A recent inspection of the relief, which is now in the Museum für Kunstgeschichte in Vienna, seems to bear out this hypothesis, for it revealed that the original royal names had been altered.

The relief now bearing the name of Psammetichus II is interesting to us for yet another reason, for this archenemy of the Kushites wears the headdress that has been designated the "Kushite cap." It can scarcely be imagined how a ruler notorious for his many acts of *damnatio memoriae* against the previous dynasty would have had himself depicted with its typical accessory. Even if this relief was not an original work of the reign of Psammetichus II, but rather was created for one of his predecessors, the demonstrable popularity of this headdress in Lower Egypt at the beginning of Dynasty 26 and later confirms our hypothesis that this was no "Kushite" cap, but rather a characteristic headdress of the Memphite god Ptah, transplanted into the royal iconography. In this regard, only the color of the cap serves to distinguish the god from the king: blue in representations of the deity, yellow in those of the monarch.

There is yet another iconographic feature that the two figures share, the shape of their beards: Ptah is the only Egyptian god with a beard whose end is rectangular, like that of a king, rather than plaited and tapering to a point that curves slightly forward, as in the representations of other gods. It is striking, though logical, that royal iconography often demonstrates similarities to representations of primeval gods such as Ptah and Atum, the creator gods of the pantheons of Memphis and Heliopolis. We may recall that in the case of Atum, it was the beard that distinguished the ruler from the deity, for both wore the double crown of the Lord of the Two Lands.

The destruction of Dynasty 25 reliefs was merely one expression of Psammetichus II's aggressive policy, which was in no way directed only against Kush. Though he ruled only briefly (595–589 B.C.E.), he left many traces of an active foreign policy. He behaved as though he wanted to avenge the defensive war of his father, Necho II (610–595 B.C.E.), though he had little time to do so. It is likely that the Greek historians were correct in representing Necho II as an incompetent ruler. After prolonged struggles with Babylonia, he had been obliged to withdraw from Syria-Palestine and to fight to maintain the eastern border of the delta.

These defeats had compelled him to restructure his armed forces by developing his navy. He created a network of canals in the delta; one of them, unfortunately not completed, was to lead directly to the Red Sea, where the ruler also built up a fleet. Greek tradition ascribed a circumnavigation of Africa to Phoenician sailors in the service of this Egyptian king. We know that Necho II made use of Greek triremes. We may presume that the Egyptian navy was expanded with the intention of defeating Babylon. Relations with Greece were peaceful; the pharaoh employed Ionian soldiers and sent gifts to Greek temples. He also had the honor of burying one of the Apis bulls in the Serapeum of Memphis.

Psammetichus II decided to put an end to this passive policy. In the year 590 B.C.E., he invaded Kush, though there is no indication that Egypt's southern neighbor was behaving aggressively. It is supposed that the pharaoh penetrated as far as the capital of the land, Napata. A scant year later, we see him in the region of Palestine, where he took advantage of the temporary absence of the Babylonians to lead his troops north. He was obliged to return to Egypt without any concrete results, though upon his return, he did not fail to make a splendid celebration of his "victory." It was rather the Babylonian king Nebuchadnezzar (Nabuchodonosor) II who had achieved a lasting success in western Asia. In 597 B.C.E., he conquered Jerusalem and carried off its ruler and its people, thus putting an end to the independence of Judah.

Psammetichus II's malevolent temperament was not satisfied with the destruction of works of Dynasty 25. His *damnatio memoriae* was also directed against his own father, Necho II, whose name was hacked out in temples and even on the statues of high officials. Many officials whose names contained the name of the king were compelled to change them; on one statue, the cartouches of Necho II were replaced by those of Psammetichus II. The name Necho then fell out of use to the end of the Saite dynasty.

But his actions do not change the fact that Psammetichus II profited from the many reforms, especially the military ones, that his father and grandfather had effected. The reorganized army could be effectively deployed both to the north and to the south. Carian soldiers who immortalized their names at Abu Simbel participated in the invasion of Nubia. The western delta witnessed the development of the city of Naukratis, a colony of Greek settlers who perhaps had already migrated there during the reign of Psammetichus I. Herodotus informs us of the city's Greek milieu in the decades that followed, in the reign of Amasis. While he interprets the development of this city as a symptom of the pharaoh's philhellenism, we may suspect that it was rather a shrewd economic measure intended to liberalize the customs regulations that affected maritime trade.

[121]

Herodotus's work is a fundamental historical source for our knowledge of this period. Though he took pleasure in lurid tales, his sensation-filled account of Dynasty 26 contains a great deal of fact, as confirmed by hiero-glyphic texts, especially with regard to the details of everyday life. Its dom-inant tone, however, is that of a crime thriller. In his account of the begin-nings of the Saite dynasty, we could cite similarities to Egyptian literature, which created various legends to document the political will of the gods. In his work, the deities of Egypt bear Greek names; thus, for example, he iden-tifies the Memphite god Ptah with Hephaestus/Vulcan. This deity makes an appearance in his account of Psammetichus I:

While the twelve kings continued to observe justice in course of time, as they were sacrificing in the temple of Vulcan, and were about to offer a liba-tion on the last day of the festival, the high priest, mistaking the number, brought out eleven of the twelve golden bowls with which he used to make the libation. Whereupon he who stood last of them, Psammitichus, since he had not a bowl, having taken off his helmet, which was of brass, held it out and made the libation. All the other kings were in the habit of wearing hel-mets, and at that time had them on. Psammitichus therefore, without any sinister intention, held out his helmet: but they having taken into considera-tion what was done by Psammitichus, and the oracle that had foretold to them, "that whoever among them should offer a libation from a brazen bowl, should be sole king of Egypt;" calling to mind the oracle, they did not think it right to put him to death, since upon examination they found that he had done it by no premeditated design. But they determined to banish him to the marshes, having divested him of the greatest part of his power; and they forbade him to leave the marshes, or have any intercourse with the rest of Egypt.

This Psammitichus, who had before fled from Sabacon the Ethiopian, who had killed his father Neco—having at that time fled into Syria, the Egyptians, who belong to the Saitic district, brought back when the Ethiopian withdrew in consequence of the vision in a dream. And afterwards, having been made king, he was a second time constrained by the eleven kings to go into exile among the marshes on account of the helmet. Knowing, then, that he had been exceedingly injured by them, he entertained the design of avenging himself on his persecutors; and when he sent to the city of Buto to consult the oracle of Latona, where is the truest oracle that the Egyptians have, an answer came, "that vengeance would come from the sea, when men of brass should appear." He, however, was very incredulous that men of brass would come to assist him. But when no long time had elapsed, stress of weather com-pelled some Ionians and Carians, who had sailed out for the purpose of piracy, to bear away to Egypt; and when they had disembarked and were clad in brazen armour, an Egyptian, who had never before seen men clad in brass, went to the marshes to Psammitichus, and told him that men of brass, having arrived from the sea, were ravaging the plains. He perceiving that the oracle was accomplished, treated these Ionians and Carians in a friendly manner, and having promised them great things, persuaded them to join with him: and when he had succeeded in persuading them, he thus, with the help of such Egyptians as were well affected to him, and with these allies, overcame the other kings.

Psammitichus, having made himself master of Egypt, constructed the portico to Vulcan's temple at Memphis that faces the south wind; and he built a court for Apis, in which he is fed whenever he appears, opposite the portico, surrounded by a colonnade, and full of sculptured figures; and instead of pillars, statues twelve cubits high are placed under the piazza.[2]

Herodotus's most detailed account is that of the reigns of two great kings of Dynasty 26, Apries (589–570 B.C.E.) and Amasis (570–526 B.C.E.):

When Psammis had reigned only six years over Egypt, and made an expedition into Ethiopia, and shortly afterwards died, Apries his son succeeded to the kingdom. He, next to his grandfather Psammitichus, enjoyed greater prosperity than any of the former kings, during a reign of five and twenty years, in which period he marched an army against Sidon, and engaged the Tyrian by sea. But when it was destined for him to meet with adversity, it happened on an occasion, which I shall narrate more fully in my Libyan history, and briefly in this place. For Apries, having sent an army against the Cyrenaeans, met with a signal defeat; but the Egyptians, complaining of this, revolted from him, suspecting that Apries had designedly sent them to certain ruin, in order that they might be destroyed, and he might govern the rest of the Egyptians with greater security; both those that returned and the friends of those who perished, being very indignant at this, openly revolted against him. Apries, having heard of this, sent Amasis to appease them by persuasion. But when he, having come to them, was endeavoring to restrain them, as he was urging them to desist from their enterprise, one of the Egyptians standing behind him placed a helmet on his head, and as he put it on said, "that he put it on him to make him king." And this action was not at all disagreeable to Amasis, as he presently showed. For when the revolters had appointed him king of the Egyptians, he prepared to lead an army against Apries; but Apries being informed of this, sent to Amasis a considerable person among the Egyptians that adhered to him, whose name was Patarbemis,

---

[2] H. Cary, *Herodotus* (London, 1917), pp. 156–58 (= *Histories*, Book II, chapters 151–53).

with orders to bring Amasis alive into his presence. When Patarbemis arrived and summoned Amasis, Amasis, raising his leg, (for he happened to be on horseback,) broke wind and bade him carry that to Apries. Nevertheless, Patarbemis begged of him, since the king had sent for him, to go to him; but he answered, "that he had been some time preparing to do so, and that Apries should have no cause of complaint, for that he would not only appear himself, but would bring others with him." Patarbemis, perceiving his design from what was said, and seeing preparations being made, returned in haste, as he wished to inform the king as soon as possible of what was going on: when, however, he came to Apries without bringing Amasis, Apries, taking no time for deliberation, in a transport of passion commanded his ears and nose to be cut off. The rest of the Egyptians, who still adhered to him, seeing one of the most distinguished among them treated in so unworthy a manner, did not delay a moment, but went immediately over to the others and gave themselves to Amasis. When Apries heard of this, he armed his auxiliaries and marched against the Egyptians; but he had with him Carian and Ionian auxiliaries to the number of thirty thousand; and he had a palace in the city of Sais, that was spacious and magnificent. Now Apries' party advanced against the Egyptians, and the party of Amasis against the foreigners. They met near the city Momemphis, and prepared to engage with each other. . . .

When therefore Apries, leading his auxiliaries, and Amasis, all the Egyptians, met together at Momemphis, they came to an engagement, and the foreigners fought well, but being far inferior in numbers, were, on that account, defeated. Apries is said to have been of the opinion that not even a god could deprive him of his kingdom, so securely did he think himself established: now, however, when he came to an engagement he was beaten, and being taken prisoner, he was carried back to Sais, to that which was formerly his own palace, but which now belonged to Amasis: here he was maintained for some time in the royal palace, and Amasis treated him well. But at length the Egyptians complaining that he did not act rightly in preserving a man who was the greatest enemy both to them and to him, he thereupon delivered Apries to the Egyptians; but they strangled him, and afterwards buried him in his ancestral sepulchre; this is in the sacred precinct of Minerva, very near the temple, on the left hand as you enter. The Saitae used to bring all the kings sprung from this district within the sacred precinct; however, the tomb of Amasis is further from the temple than that of Apries and his progenitors, but even this is in the court of the sacred precinct, consisting of a large stone chamber, adorned with columns, made in imitation of palm-trees, and with other ornaments; inside this chamber are placed folding doors, and within the doors is the sepulchre. At Sais also, in the sacred precinct of Minerva, behind the chapel and joining the whole of the wall, is the tomb of one whose name I consider it impious to divulge on such an occasion. And in the enclosure stand large stone obelisks, and there is a lake near, ornamented with a

[124]

stone margin, formed in a circle, and in size, as appeared to me, much the same as that in Delos, which is called the Circular. In this lake they perform by night the representation of that person's adventures, which they call mysteries. On these matters, however, though accurately acquainted with the particulars of them, I must observe a discreet silence. And respecting the sacred rites of Ceres, which the Greeks call Thesmophoria, although I am acquainted with them, I must observe silence except so far as it is lawful for me to speak of them. The daughters of Danaus were they who introduced these ceremonies from Egypt, and taught them to the Pelasgian women: but afterwards, when almost the whole Peloponnese was depopulated by the Dorians, these rites were lost; but the Arcadians, who were the only Peloponnesians left, and not expelled, alone preserved them.

Apries being thus dethroned, Amasis, who was of the Saitic district, reigned in his stead; the name of the city from which he came was Siuph. At first the Egyptians despised, and held him in no great estimation, as having been formerly a private person, and of no illustrious family; but afterwards he conciliated them by his address, without any arrogance. He had an infinite number of other treasures, and besides a golden foot-pan, in which Amasis himself, and all his guests, were accustomed to wash their feet. Having then broken this in pieces, he had made from it the statue of a god, and placed it in the most suitable part of the city; but the Egyptians, flocking to the image, paid it the greatest reverence. But Amasis, informed of their behavior, called the Egyptians together, and explained the matter to them, saying, "that the statue was made out of the foot-pan in which the Egyptians formerly vomited, made water, and washed their feet, and which they then so greatly reverenced; now then, he proceeded to say, the same had happened to him as to the foot-pan; for though he was before but a private person, yet he was now their king"; he therefore required them to honor and respect him: by this means he won over the Egyptians, so that they thought fit to obey him. He adopted the following method of managing his affairs: early in the morning, until the time of full-market, he assiduously despatched the business brought before him; after that he drank and jested with his companions, and he talked loosely and sportively. But his friends, offended at this, admonished him, saying, "You do not, O king, control yourself properly, in making yourself too common. For it becomes you, who sit on a venerable throne, to pass the day in transacting public business; thus the Egyptians would know that they are governed by a great man, and you would be better spoken of. But now you act in a manner not at all becoming a king." But he answered them as follows: "They who have bows, when they want to use them, bend them; but when they have done using them, they unbend them; for if it were kept always bent, it would break, so that he could not use it when he had need. Such is the condition of man; if he should incessantly attend to serious business, and not give himself up sometimes to sport, he would unawares become mad or stupified. I, being well aware of this, give up a portion of my time to each." Thus he answered his friends. Amasis is said to have been, even when a private person, fond of drinking and jesting, and by no means inclined to serious business; and when the means failed him for drinking and indulging himself, he used to go about pilfering. Such persons as accused him of having their property, on his denying it, used to take him to the oracle of the place, and he was oftentimes convicted by the oracles, and oftentimes acquitted. When, therefore, he came to the throne, he acted as follows: whatever gods had absolved him from the charge of theft, of their temples he neither took any heed, nor contributed any thing towards their repair, neither did he frequent them, and offer sacrifices, considering them of no consequence at all, and as having only lying responses to give. But as many as had convicted him of the charge of theft, to them he paid the highest respect, considering them as truly gods, and delivering authentic responses. . . .

Under the reign of Amasis Egypt is said to have enjoyed the greatest prosperity, both in respect to the benefits derived from the river to the land, and from the land to the people; and it is said to have contained at that time twenty thousand inhabited cities. Amasis it was who established the law among the Egyptians, that every Egyptian should annually declare to the governor of his district, by what means he maintained himself; and if he failed to do this, or did not show that he lived by honest means, he should be punished with death. Solon the Athenian, having brought this law from Egypt, established it at Athens; and that people still continue to observe it, as being an unobjectionable regulation. Amasis, being partial to the Greeks, both bestowed other favors on various of the Greeks, and moreover gave the city of Naucratis for such as arrived in Egypt to dwell in; and to such as did not wish to settle there, but only to trade by sea, he granted places where they might erect altars and temples to the gods. Now, the most spacious of these sacred buildings, which is also the most renowned and frequented, called the Hellenium, was erected at the common charge of the following cities: of the Ionians, Chios, Teos, Phocaea, and Clazomenae; of the Dorians, Rhodes, Cnidus, Halicarnassus, Phaselis; and of the Aeolians, Mitylene alone. So that this temple belongs to them, and these cities appoint officers to preside over the mart: and whatever other cities claim a share in it, claim what does not belong to them. Besides this, the people of Aegina built a temple to Jupiter for themselves; and the Samians another to Juno, and the Milesians one to Apollo. Naucratis was anciently the only place of resort for merchants, and there was no other in Egypt: and if a man arrived at any other mouth of the Nile, he was obliged to swear "that he had come there against his will;" and having taken such an oath, he must sail in the same ship to the Canopic mouth; but if he should be prevented by contrary winds from doing so, he was forced to unload his goods, and carry them in barges round the Delta until he reached Naucratis. So great were the privileges of Naucratis. . . .

[126]

Amasis also contracted a friendship and an alliance with the Cyrenaeans; and resolved to take a wife from that country, either out of a desire of having a Grecian woman, or from some peculiar affection to the Cyrenaeans. He therefore married, as some say, the daughter of Battus; others, of Arcesilaus; though others, of Critobulus, a person of distinction among the citizens; her name was Ladice. Whenever Amasis lay with her he was unable to have connection with her, which was not the case with respect to other women: upon the continuance of this for a long time, Amasis said to this woman, who was called Ladice; "O woman, you have used charms against me, and no contrivance can prevent your perishing by the most cruel death of all women." But Ladice, finding that Amasis was not at all appeased by her denial of the fact, made a mental vow to Venus, that if Amasis should have intercourse with her that night, (for this was the only remedy left,) she would send a statue of the goddess to Cyrene. Immediately after the vow, Amasis had intercourse with her; and from that time forward, whenever he came to her, he was able to have connection; and after this he was exceedingly fond of her. But Ladice performed her vow to the goddess, for having caused a statue to be made, she sent it to Cyrene, and it was still safe in my time, facing out of the city of Cyrene. When Cambyses had conquered Egypt, and learnt who this Ladice was, he sent her back unharmed to Cyrene. Amasis also dedicated offerings in Greece. In the first place, a gilded statue of Minerva at Cyrene, and his own portrait painted; secondly, to Minerva in Lindus two stone statues and a linen corselet well worthy of notice; thirdly, to Juno at Samos two images of himself carved in wood, which stood in the large temple even in my time, behind the doors. Now he made this offering at Samos, on account of the friendship that subsisted between himself and Polycrates the son of Aeaces; but those at Lindus, not on account of any friendship, but because it is reported that the daughters of Danaus founded the temple of Minerva at Lindus, when they touched there in their flight from the sons of Egyptus: and these were the offerings that Amasis made. He was the first who conquered Cyprus and subjected it to the payment of tribute.[3]

ARCHAEOLOGY AND THE SAITE PERIOD

The Minerva (i.e., Athena) mentioned by Herodotus is of course the Egyptian goddess Neith, with whom the Greek goddess of wisdom was identified. From earliest times, Neith's cult center had been Sais, the capital of Egypt during Dynasty 26. One aspect of this goddess that recalled Athena was her warlike character. She was represented as a woman hold-

---

[3] Ibid., pp. 161–69 (= *Histories*, Book II, chapters 161–63, 169–74, 177–79, 181–82).

ing a bow and arrows in her hand, and later, in the Graeco-Roman Period, she was identified with the image of Athena wearing a helmet on her head. The temple dedicated to this goddess was the most sacred spot in Sais, and Apries and Amasis were buried in its enclosure.

Unfortunately, Sais (Plate IVa) remains one of the least explored of the ancient Egyptian cities. Where the sacred lake once lay, there is today a deep depression that at times turns into a swamp. An Arab town rises from the ruins of the ancient city on one side of the depression, while cultivated fields stretch out on the other. Only fragments of statues and sarcophagi stuck here and there in the swamp serve as reminders of the magnificence of the city in Dynasty 26 and later. In the end, Sais is best known to us through Herodotus's description and through mentions in Strabo.

Second only to the capital, Memphis played an especially important role in this period. The city of Ptah had become a cosmopolitan capital of the civilized world. To the existing Syrian, Phoenician, and Jewish colonies were now added Carian and Ionian mercenaries, whom Amasis resettled from their previous home at Daphnae. The quarters of Caricon and Hellenicon sheltered the Greeks. The kings of the Saite dynasty erected palaces and expanded the temples of the city. We know little of the palaces, for like all dwellings in Egypt, they were built of dried mud bricks and have survived to our own time in fragmentary condition. Only the most important elements of their architecture, such as door frames, columns, and the bases of thrones, were made of stone, and it is thanks to them that we know which of the brick buildings were once palaces.

At the beginning of the twentieth century, the British archaeological mission under the direction of Flinders Petrie discovered the Memphite palace of king Apries. Little remained of its living quarters, but the reliefs they discovered next to the palace, where a monumental gateway once led to the structure, became an object of considerable interest and scholarly debate. The reliefs, which depict the king during the *sed*-festival and are carved in the finest style on slabs of limestone, lay carefully embedded in a shallow depression, as though they had never been used or had been stored there after the structure was dismantled. In their theme, though not their content or form, they are reminiscent of the jubilee gateway of Osorkon II at Bubastis, which had been made of red granite. But the most striking fact is that we do not know for which king of Dynasty 26 this gateway was prepared. All the cartouches accompanying the representations of the pharaoh are empty and display no traces of alteration. Thus this is not a case of the erasure of the name of a ruler who experienced a *damnatio memoriae* after his death.

Yet more! The reliefs from Memphis are so strikingly reminiscent of well-known works of an earlier epoch that their discoverers attributed them to the Middle Kingdom ruler Sesostris I of Dynasty 12 and published them as belonging to a work of his. It was only later that study of their iconography and style made it evident that these were imitations or copies of Memphite reliefs of Old Kingdom date representing a royal jubilee. The duplicates were created in Dynasty 26, but for which ruler? Why were his names not enclosed in the cartouches? The style of the reliefs clearly shows that they were a product of the sculptors' workshops of the reign of Apries or Amasis or, in any event, from the height of Dynasty 26. We may thus assume that they were created at a time of political uncertainty, when the fate of a king weakened by war or that of a bold usurper was unforeseeable. It was evidently deemed prudent to delay including the name until the situation was cleared up. This was probably not the first, and certainly not the last, example of political opportunism on the part of artists. Fragments of these beautiful reliefs representing the jubilee of an anonymous ruler are now in various museums in cities around the world, including Cairo, Copenhagen, and New York.

Amasis added to the temple of Ptah at Memphis. One of his constructions there was a monumental granite gateway whose doorposts depict the king entering the sanctuary. Some years ago, one of these left Egypt as a gift to a city of the same name and approximately the same size as the pharaonic capital, which is also situated on a great river. This waterway flows south, however, not north, and it is called the Mississippi. Founded in 1819, the city of Memphis, Tennessee, in the United States of America is nearly five thousand years younger than its Egyptian namesake, but it has a certain Egyptological tradition whose core is this very relief of Amasis, which, once it had been received as a gift, remained completely forgotten for years. The author of this book has had personal experience of this monument and its recent history.

In 1980, while writing a monograph on the royal portraiture of the Late Period, I traveled to the United States and journeyed to Memphis in search of this as yet unpublished relief of Amasis. As it turned out, I had to follow its trail. It was no longer in the city park, where it had once stood, nor was it at the entrance to the municipal zoo, where it had been for a time. Rather, it had found a new place of honor in the middle of the lobby of the new city hall. My request to document this now barely visible relief caused a sensation. Flushed with enthusiasm, the deputy mayor informed the local press, and a reporter appeared to interview me.

Early the next morning, I left Memphis and soon forgot this little episode that had occurred in the course of my larger project. For some time, I had no news of Memphis. The reader can imagine my surprise when, five years later, at an International Congress of Egyptologists, I met a young, pleasant, rather shy woman who introduced herself as Dr. Rita Freed, director of

[129]

the Institute of Egyptian Art and Archaeology at Memphis State University. She told me that all hell had broken loose in the wake of my departure from city hall. A city councilman had come to the conclusion that if someone from Poland was willing to travel halfway around the world to see so important a monument, it was unworthy of the city not to have a museum of Egyptian art and a corresponding center at the university. Both were thus founded, and the collection of Egyptian art that had been established at the university was enriched by loans from the greatest museums in America.

When I met Dr. Freed, there were already three young, energetic Egyptologists at Memphis State University. In 1987, they organized a major exhibition, devoted to Ramesses II, of objects from the Egyptian Museum in Cairo. A colossal stone statue whose fragments had been found in the area of Memphis in Egypt was reconstructed and brought to the United States especially for this occasion. The opening of the exhibition was the occasion of an international scholarly symposium, to which I was invited as the sole representative from Eastern Europe. I gave a paper on a problem of interest to us here, namely the survival of certain Ramesside traditions in the art of the Third Intermediate Period.

The anonymous Memphite sculptor from the time of Amasis who created the relief on the doorpost of the temple of Ptah would surely have been incredulous had anyone informed him that his work would cause such confusion more than two and a half millennia later. In his day, artists did not sign their works, for it was believed that everything they produced was the creation of Ptah, the patron of artisans.

Apis, the sacred bull of Memphis, enjoyed an unusual degree of regard during Dynasty 26. At Saqqara, a new subterranean gallery was prepared for the burials of the bulls, the very Serapeum that tourists visit today. This gallery was completed by Psammetichus I in his fifty-second regnal yar. Many of the stelae dedicated to the Apis date to the reigns of Apries and Amasis. Their content and style are different from those of similar votive objects from earlier periods. The texts on the stelae of the Saite Period contain much valuable information related to chronology, for they usually state the birth and the death dates of the Apis bulls, as well as the lengths of their lives.

THEBES IN THE SAITE PERIOD

The social order in the Theban area remained unchanged, for the political storms that swept over the delta seldom reached the south of the land. A dominant role was still played by the God's Wife of Amun, who at this time was more important than the high priest of this deity. There was a chang-

[130]

ing of the guard in the position of the maiden priestess in the year 584 B.C.E., when Ankhnesneferibre, the daughter of Psammetichus II, who had been adopted by the long-lived Nitocris, mounted her throne. In an unprecedented move, the God's Wife of Amun was now also invested with the office of a high priest. Her successor, another Nitocris, a daughter of Amasis, would also inherit both roles. Ankhnesneferibre occupied her offices for an unusually long time, until the Persian invasion in 525 B.C.E. Following the model of her predecessor, she built several chapels dedicated to Osiris in the Theban region. One of them was dedicated to Osiris in his function of *neb-djefa*, "lord of provisions" (or "of nourishment"). These constructions were often cosponsored by the reigning monarchs, first Amasis and later Psammetichus III, the last two rulers of the Saite dynasty.

The administrators of the priestess' vast estates came from Sais. Those who headed her administration were at the very top of the Theban elite, and their tombs are among the largest and most beautiful on the west bank of Thebes. The most famous contemporaries of Ankhnesneferibre bore the names Shoshenq, Harsiese, and Peteneith. Every bit as splendid are the tombs of their predecessors under the pontificate of Nitocris I: Ibi, Petehorresnet, and Ankhhor. The tomb of the latter high official was recently discovered by the Austrian mission working in the Theban necropolis under the leadership of Professor Manfred Bietak.

Ankhnesneferibre herself was buried in a beautiful sarcophagus of black slate that was discovered in 1833 at Deir el-Medina on the west bank of Thebes. The sarcophagus was reused by a royal scribe of the Ptolemaic Period, but neither the inscriptions containing the name of the priestess carved on its outer surface nor her effigy were mutilated. The majestic expression of her face harmonizes here with the distinctive nose of the God's Wife, the vulture cap on her head, the uraeus-serpent on her brow, and the insignia of Osiris in her hands. The tomb chapel of the famous daughter of Psammetichus II is located in the enclosure of the mortuary temple of Ramesses III at Medinet Habu. Her successor Nitocris II, daughter of Amasis, was the last of the dynasty of God's Wives of Amun at Thebes, these maidens of royal blood each of whom had adopted her successor. The Persian rule in Egypt put an end to this office.

THE END OF THE DYNASTY

Psammetichus III, the last pharaoh of the Saite dynasty, ruled less than one full year, from 526 to 525 B.C.E. A new enemy appeared on Egypt's Asiatic border, one that would decide the future destiny of the pharaonic state. This time, it was the Persians. Under the Achaemenid dynasty, the Persian state became an imperialistic entity whose ambitions were directed chiefly toward the west. Egypt was drawn into the Persian struggle against the Greeks. Amasis had concluded a treaty with Polycrates of Samos, one that would prove fateful to the Lords of the Two Lands. The Egyptians were betrayed by Phanes of Halicarnassus, who fled to the Persian king Cambyses and provided him with information regarding Egypt's defensive system. With bedouins as his guides, Cambyses crossed the Sinai and marched into Egypt in 525 B.C.E. He took Psammetichus III prisoner and led him in chains to Susa. Part of the Egyptian aristocracy sided with the Persians, and Cambyses also found support in the Jewish garrison stationed at Elephantine. He plundered Thebes and other Egyptian cities, and he brought many statues and groups of Egyptian artisans back with him to Persia.

This last-mentioned step does not betray a snob who wished to decorate his court with the works of Egyptian artists but, rather, an aesthete demonstrating his appreciation for the sculpture produced in the studios of Memphis and the other centers of Egyptian art. And there was every reason to marvel at them, for sculpture had evolved to an unprecedented degree in Egypt during Dynasty 26. The meager quantity of reliefs from this period, which is owing to the destruction of its temples, is largely compensated for by the number of preserved stone statues depicting kings, deities, priests, and officials.

CHALLENGES TO ART HISTORIANS

The art of portraying the rulers acquired a canon of its own at this time, and it enriched the ancient tradition of idealizing portraits with elements of naturalism, in which psychological traits are joined to a concern for elegance of form. A great number of statues survive, made of granite, slate, basalt, alabaster, and other kinds of stone; unfortunately, however, most of them are in fragmentary condition.

It can happen that the head of a large statue is in a museum in America or Europe, while its torso resides in Cairo. Certain Egyptologists specialize in the art of tracking down and rejoining such *membra dispersa*, which are scattered throughout the world. The greatest success in this regard was enjoyed by Bernard V. Bothmer, who for many years was curator of the Egyptian collection at the Brooklyn Museum in New York City.

The greatest challenge to art historians is posed by statue heads that are preserved without their torsos and thus without the inscriptions that would permit the identification of their subjects. The text containing the titles of the ruler or official was usually inscribed on a vertical pillar that joined the back of the statue and formed a monolith with it. When the inscribed portion of the statue is not preserved, the head must be dated according to iconographic and stylistic criteria. This skill demands not only a thorough knowledge of the material and a great deal of experience but also an outstanding feel for style and a capacity for observation that can take in the smallest details that at first glance can seem unimportant.

A master in the dating of royal portraits of the Late Period was Hans Wolfgang Müller, long the director of the Staatliche Sammlung Ägyptischer Kunst in Munich. The author had the honor of working under his direction for many years. One of Professor Müller's achievements was the determination of the date of an outstanding black basalt portrait of Apries now in Bologna. When we read his penetrating analysis and the conclusions he draws from it, it is difficult to avoid the impression that an art historian is a detective on the trail of old masters.

Naturally, major errors are also made in this area. Aside from knowing the style of each epoch, the expert must also be aware of the phenomenon of archaizing, that is, the deliberate imitation of the artistic expression of earlier periods. In the case of the reliefs that were found near the palace of Apries at Memphis, we have seen how difficult it sometimes is to distinguish works from different periods. Years of research often go by before someone attritutes a masterpiece of Egyptian art to the king in whose reign it was created. We often do not learn the truth until the discovery of the missing part of the sculpture that bears the inscription. How great is the astonishment of art historians when it suddenly emerges that a work of art was made several centuries earlier or later than had long been supposed.

But even the presence of inscriptions does not provide a definitive answer. As noted earlier, statues found at Tanis bear traces of multiple usurpations, which mostly consisted in effacing the name of the ruler but sometimes also in sculptural retouchings whose goal was to "modernize" the work to make it resemble the style of the new era. A plausible interpretation of such works is possible only through the collaboration of a skilled epigrapher and an art historian.

A trickier problem is posed by the many forgeries that fill the storerooms of museums but are sometimes also on display, especially when they are the work of talented forgers. Many curators of Egyptian collections have been in doubt when it was time to decide the fate of an object by answering the question: original or fake? In the course of changes of opinion regarding its authenticity, many an object has passed back and forth between the storeroom and the exhibition gallery.

There have been many modern imitations of statues that display a characteristic or oft-repeated expression. Among these are the naturalistic works from the reign of the religious "heretic" Amenophis IV/Akhenaten of Dynasty 18, as well as the many likenesses of the rulers of the Late Period and the Ptolemaic era. The later art displays specific, striking traits that are easy to imitate. Their stern facial features lend a venerableness to the portraits of the Kushite rulers, while by contrast, the representations of the Saite pharaohs and their successors down through the Ptolemaic dynasty are filled with cheer. The sculptors achieved a slightly smiling facial expression by gently lifting the corners of the mouth. Puffy cheeks and a double chin are also characteristic traits of these likenesses.

Such a visage is already displayed by the sphinx that was prepared for Amasis out of a brown stone reminiscent of basalt. It evidently originated at Sais, but it was found in Rome, where it was brought at the beginning of our era to grace the capital of the Roman empire, perhaps at the behest of one of those emperors whose snobbish predilection for pharaonic antiquities sometimes awakened a full-blown Egyptomania.

Actually, this can scarcely be called a portrait. History leads us to believe that the lives of the pharaohs of the Late Period were not spent free of problems and that the troubled faces of the rulers of the end of the Middle Kingdom might rather be associated with them than the carefree countenances of the statues that were carved toward the end of the dynastic period. Already in antiquity—and to this day as well—the stiff, stylistic canon of these late works furnished a welcome source of inspiration for copyists and imitators.

The Egyptian statues taken to Persia by Cambyses remained there for nearly three hundred years. They made a triumphal return to their native land only in the reign of Ptolemy III Euergetes I, who was probably motivated by piety for the monuments of the great figures of the past, but perhaps also in an effort to bolster his own popularity in the land where he, too, was pharaoh. Those three centuries were a stormy period in the history of Egypt.

Persians and Greeks on the Throne of the Pharaohs (Dynasty 27–Ptolemaic Period)

CAMBYSES AND DARIUS

In 525 B.C.E., Egypt became a satrapy of Achaemenid Persia. It was no longer a realm composed of two parts that constituted a whole, as in Dynasty 25, but rather only one of the many provinces that comprised this huge empire. In ancient tradition, Egypt's conqueror Cambyses was a cruel man and an unbeliever. According to the Greek authors, he killed the sacred Apis bull in the sixth year of his reign, while Jewish sources accuse him of destroying all the temples of Egypt.

Archaeological discoveries, however, have rehabilitated the reputation of the Persian ruler. It has been shown that during Cambyses' lifetime, two Apis bulls died and were buried with full honors. The allegedly murdered sacred animal died in his fifth regnal year and was buried in a coffin with an inscription naming Cambyses.

His barbaric attitude toward the temples is doubtless also a product of fantasy. We know that an Egyptian named Udjahorresnet functioned as an adviser to the Persian ruler; we learn from the inscription carved on a statue of this famous Egyptian that at his recommendation, the "pharaoh" Cambyses restored some of the sanctuaries of the deities of Egypt. Toward the end of Dynasty 26, Udjahorresnet had been Admiral of the Fleet in the reigns of Amasis and Psammetichus III, yet his biography—that is, the hieroglyphic text on the statue now in the Vatican Museum—begins with the Persian invasion of Egypt.

Having been named personal physician of the Achaemenid ruler, Udjahorresnet was his constant companion and exercised various responsible functions. He drafted Cambyses' titulary as pharaoh of Egypt, and he inducted him into the rituals connected with the cult of the warlike goddess

[135]

Neith, whose principal place of worship had been Sais during Dynasty 26. Neith, represented with bow and arrows in her hand, was the chief deity of the pantheon of that city. As mother of the god Re, she was the creator of all existence. At Sais, she had a magnificent temple. At the recommendation of Udjahorresnet, Cambyses had the temple precinct cleared of the houses of squatters who had settled there. There, he also swore an oath of homage to the deities of Egypt, and he held a sumptuous banquet. Can we really imagine that this king destroyed Egyptian temples? Under the circumstances, we might rather suppose that he reduced the endowments of the priesthoods of certain sanctuaries, thus making enemies among the literate class. The text on the statue of Udjahorresnet is the only lengthy biographical text preserved to us from the Persian Period in Egypt. It is a naophoric statue, that is, it depicts the dignitary holding a small shrine.

After his conquest of Egypt, Cambyses had no further luck on the battlefield. He did not know what to do about Cyrene, and he returned unsuccessfully from an expedition to Nubia. A revolt in his own land compelled him to leave Egypt, whose administration he entrusted to the satrap Aryandes. Cambyses enjoyed the pharaonic title for only three years. His defeats evidently led him to madness. His successor Darius I (522–486 B.C.E.) quelled the rebellion, and in 517 B.C.E., he went to Egypt, where he ordered the execution of Aryandes, accusing him of disloyalty to the central authority. Pherendates was appointed to be the new satrap.

The descriptions of Darius in the classical sources draw a picture of an intelligent, just, and generous ruler whose life contrasted in every way with the dismal career of Cambyses, and historical data confirm this characterization. In the third year of his reign, Darius ordered his Egyptian satrap to convene the wisest men from among the soldiers, priests, and scribes to collect in writing all Egyptian legislation down to regnal year 44 of Amasis. The commission's efforts at codification lasted for more than ten years.

Darius's concern for Egypt can also be recognized from his economic measures. The Persian pharaoh resumed the construction of a canal connecting the Nile to the Red Sea, a project that had been begun by Necho II, one of the rulers of Dynasty 26, but had been interrupted. The opening of the canal was a great event in Egyptian history; first to sail it were twenty-four ships laden with gifts destined for Persia. A series of large stone stelae commemorating Darius's accomplishment was set up along the canal. From the preserved fragments of these monuments, it has been established that they were inscribed in four languages written in hieroglyphs and cuneiform. They are also decorated with the *sema-tawy*, the emblem symbolizing the union of Upper and Lower Egypt and thus characterizing Darius as Lord of the Two Lands, and with figures representing subject peoples and lands pledging their loyalty to the Persian king. Had it been preserved

[136]

in its entirety, this interesting geographical list would have been of great importance, but unfortunately, only fragments of it have come down to us. A great sensation was caused a quarter-century ago by the discovery of a statue of Darius whose base was inscribed with a similar representation that is wholly preserved. We shall deal with it in greater detail later in this chapter.

Darius concerned himself not only with the people of Egypt but also with their deities. After the death of the next Apis bull, the ruler sent a general named Amasis throughout the land to collect the means to finance the burial of the sacred animal. An informative detail of the inscription reporting these events is the writing of the name of the general, which is not only exactly the same as that of the great pharaoh of Dynasty 26 but is also enclosed in a cartouche, which of course was in principle a royal privilege. A similar example of megalomania—or was it perhaps just respect for a deceased ruler?—is the writing of the name of Khnemibre, another worthy of this period, for it had also been one of the names of Amasis.

These details reveal a consciousness of history and a respect for tradition in the time of Darius. And yet, many high officials with Egyptian names like Ptahhotpe and Udjahorresnet had themselves represented in Persian clothing, especially in sculpture in the round. Is this a fashion statement, or is it an expression of political conformity? Or was this outward sign of loyalty to the occupier just a cheap price to pay for independence in more important matters?

THE TEMPLE OF HIBIS

Darius erected a large temple in honor of the deities of Egypt. Located in el-Kharga Oasis, far from the great religious centers, this sanctuary is paradoxically the only great temple of the Late Period to survive nearly intact down to our own time. The sacred buildings constructed in the delta between the end of the New Kingdom and the Ptolemaic Period today lie in ruins. At Thebes, there are remains of small chapels of Dynasties 25 and 26, mostly dedicated to Osiris in his various aspects, but none of them equals the temple of Darius in size, architectural beauty, or originality of the reliefs. Evidently, the Persian ruler wished to erect a monument on the model of the temples of the New Kingdom.

The temple in el-Kharga Oasis was dedicated to Amun, but other Egyptian deities were also worshiped there. The reliefs that decorate the walls display the classical repertoire of scenes that had already been known for centuries and that served both the divine cults and the royal propaganda. In nearly every scene, Darius is depicted as pharaoh in the company of Egyptian gods and goddesses.

[137]

Figure 36. Symbolic uniting of the Two Lands. The god Harsiese ("Horus, Son of Isis") and Thoth bind the heraldic plants of Upper and Lower Egypt. Relief in the temple built by Darius I at Hibis in el-Kharga Oasis.

One of the most impressive motifs is the symbolic rendering of the uniting of Upper and Lower Egypt, with Darius seated on a throne that is elevated above the *sema-tawy* sign (Figure 36). The gods who execute the royal will are Horus, the falcon-headed son of Isis, and Thoth, the ibis-headed lord of Hermopolis. At their feet, we see two miniature Nile personifications holding bundles of the heraldic plants of Upper and Lower Egypt. The message of the scene is clear. Having united the two halves of Egypt, Darius has fulfilled the basic duty of a pharaoh, and he is thus Lord of the Two Lands.

In another scene, we see the king as a nude child standing on a potter's wheel, where his form is being modeled by the ram-headed Khnum, the patron of potters. Assisting him is Ptah, the Memphite patron god of artists and artisans, holding the equipment of a scribe in his hands. Elsewhere, we see Darius in the scene depicting the *ished*-tree, with Thoth writing the king's name on its leaves. Behind the king, the Heliopolitan god Atum, with the double crown of Upper and Lower Egypt on his head, is seated on a throne. With his left hand, he holds the hieroglyph for "life" to the mouth of the king, while his right hand sets the *khepresh*-crown on Darius's head—that blue crown which was associated with such events as pharaonic coronations and victories.

Many scenes are composed according to the symmetrical principle that predominated in the decoration of temples, with corresponding parallelism of content. This is the case with the scenes on each side of the doorways, which depict, for example, the king entering the temple wearing the crown of Upper Egypt in one case and that of Lower Egypt in the other, or the child Darius being nursed by the goddess Mut in one instance, and in the other the goddess Amaunet embracing the adult king with her somewhat overlong arm (Figure 37).

Every iconographic detail is important. In the last-mentioned representation, though Darius is shown with the lock of hair characteristic of a child and without a royal crown, he already has the uraeus-serpent of a ruler on his brow, while in his right hand, he holds insignia of the lord of Egypt: the

Figure 37. Darius protected by Egyptian goddesses. Mut nurses the king, Amaunet embraces him. Reliefs in the temple of Hibis.

ruler's crook and the *rekhyt*-bird that symbolized the people of the land. In the scene in which he is embraced, the blue crown of victory already graces Darius's head.

Aside from the traditional elements that are so visible in the composition of the scenes, the reliefs also display new and sometimes unique iconographic concepts. We see this already in the representations of the ruler himself. Though he is always depicted with the traditional garb and insignia of a pharaoh, all his crowns are provided with long ribbons that hang down his back, which had previously been almost exclusively confined to the blue crown. Perhaps we may see in this an adoption of Kushite tradition, for such ribbons were a typical element of the headdresses of the rulers of Dynasty 25.

The naturalism in the representation of Darius's face also recalls that period and, perhaps even more, early Dynasty 26. The clearly accented double chin and the organic modeling of his eyes remind us of the representations of Psammetichus I on his relief from Lower Egypt, perhaps Sais.

Since Sais, along with its deities and priests, had enjoyed the special regard of the Persian ruler under Cambyses, as we have seen, it is quite conceivable that masters of relief sculpture were brought from that very city to decorate the temple in el-Kharga Oasis. These artists had probably had no opportunity to see Darius personally; rather, they recollected the portraits of the pharaohs of the Saite dynasty on which they had worked for so many years in their studios. It is perhaps thus that we are to explain the unique style of the reliefs in Darius's temple, in which traditionalism is combined with a remarkable creative freedom.

The originality of the iconographic inventiveness found its best expression in scenes with purely mythological content, where the figure of the king seldom appears and in which, when it does, it is always accompanied by empty cartouches. Some Egyptologists are of the opinion that these scenes were added at a later date, during the reigns of the last native pharaohs or at the beginning of the Ptolemaic Period, when the decoration of the temple in el-Kharga Oasis was continued. We may suppose, however, that as in the case of many other sacred constructions from earlier periods, such iconographic and stylistic retouching was carried out on the basis of already existing reliefs.

Two places in the temple are decorated with highly unusual reliefs that have no counterpart in any other preserved sanctuary and which bewilder even the most seasoned experts in Egyptian religion. One of these is a large-scale raised relief whose colorful paint is well preserved to this day. The scene depicts a winged, falcon-headed god spearing a huge serpent with a lance (Figure 38).

The god wears the double crown of a king, and his wings spring from a falcon's body. The god's torso is adorned with the figures of two falcons

Figure 38. The god Seth slaying Apophis. Relief in the temple of Darius I at Hibis.

with their wings spread, each with a sun disk on its head. All this would seem to indicate that this is Horus, the royal ancestor, killing Seth, who murdered his father, Osiris, yet the inscription that accompanies the scene says something else entirely. It identifies the valiant god as Seth, "great of power, the great god, resident in Hibis." Hibis, the "Plow-city," where Darius's temple was located, was the capital of el-Kharga Oasis.

Seth, who generally embodied various negative characteristics, is thus represented here in his noblest aspect, namely, as the warrior who protects the sun god Re from his archenemy, the serpent Apophis. Paradoxically, the iconography here stresses the positive side of his character by investing him with attributes of Horus, who was indeed an embodiment of noble sentiments but who was also the archenemy of Seth. Is this a heretical

[141]

mockery, or is it an expression of the religious syncretism peculiar to the Late Period, which often made a unity of deities with entirely opposite qualities? Or is it perhaps just an illustration of confusion, thus stressing the most essential trait in the nature of Seth, the god of chaos?

Leaving aside the interpretation of this scene, there is every indication that such ancient Egyptian representations of a god slaying a serpent were the iconographic inspiration for the creators of early Christian depictions of Saint George battling a similar monster.

Another puzzle for historians of religion is posed by the relief decoration of the sanctuary of Darius's temple, which is located in one of the back rooms of the building and brings the temple axis to an end. The walls of this small, narrow room are completely covered with a series of mythological scenes that are small in size but rich in content. What is unusual about this "stop-action film" with its hundreds of frames lies not only in its richness but also in its iconographic originality and in the incomprehensibility of many of the motifs. As a whole, it seems to be a series of scenes illustrating abbreviated episodes selected from, or even torn out of the context of, various myths.

Nowhere in the more familiar temples of Egypt do we encounter such an accumulation of human and animal forms, along with various fantastic creatures, insignia, and symbols, though a few centuries later, the temples of the Ptolemaic and Roman eras nearly equal the temple of Darius in regard to *horror vacui*, that is, the fear of leaving even the tiniest space on any wall undecorated. The heart of the problem is that the scenes of the wall of this sanctuary display no logical connection to one another, but rather represent a selection from a huge iconographic repertoire whose models must have been found on papyri that have not been preserved to us.

Only a few of the figures represented here are familiar from other sources, and even these confirm the eclectic character of the decoration as a whole. In this kaleidoscope of deities, we behold various forms of the ram-headed Khnum or of Khnum as potter shaping a vessel on his wheel and the fetish of the Abydene Osiris in the form of a pillar crowned with two feathers. Elsewhere, we see Osiris lying on a bier, and behind him Isis the nourisher, along with a winged crocodile with a bull's head and a youthful Horus of the Two Horizons sitting on a lotus blossom.

Among the deities to whom the king offers are bellicose gods with bows and arrows and quivers. Elsewhere, he offers a figure of the goddess Maat to two theriomorphic deities, one of whom takes the form of a falcon and the other a lion with a falcon's head. This unique theological encyclopedia also displays a highly varied series of manifestations of Amun-Re crowned with two tall feathers (Figure 39). In most instances, he holds his erect phallus with one of his hands, recalling the initial act of

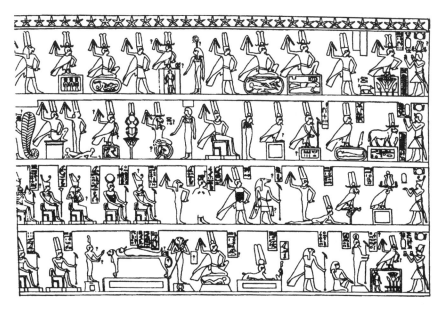

Figure 39. Various forms of the primeval god Amun-Re as he begins creation by pleasuring himself. Relief in the sanctuary of the temple of Hibis.

the creator god who engendered the succeeding generation of deities by masturbating.

These iconographic riches do little to help us set aside the question marks that Egyptian religion constantly raises in our minds, making us ever more conscious of how fragmentary our knowledge of it is. The reliefs in the sanctuary of the temple of Darius are in fact our only link between the earlier mythological representations in the temples and tombs of the New Kingdom and on the papyri and coffins of the Third Intermediate Period on the one hand and, on the other, the scenes that were later carved on the walls of the temples of the Graeco-Roman Period, or drawn on papyri, or painted on wooden coffins of that era, such as that of Isunes (Plate IVb). We encounter the development of Egyptian theological speculation in its fullest form only in its final phase, whose illustration is embodied in the reliefs of the great temples of the Ptolemaic and Roman eras. Their iconography is the product of an evolution that was consummated, during the first millennium B.C.E., in various theological motifs whose origin lay in earlier periods. The reliefs in the sanctuary of Darius's temple—the best-known link in this series of developments—are nevertheless an insufficient source for us to follow them precisely. Still, they give us a sense of how little we know.

Darius I's reverence for the deities of Egypt also found expression in works less monumental than the temple of Hibis. A small wooden naos found at Tuna el-Gebel (Plates V and VI, Figure 40), the desert cemetery of ancient Hermopolis, is decorated with colorfully painted scenes depicting him as pharaoh, with his name enclosed in the usual cartouches.

On the front wall of this little shrine, Darius is depicted twice wearing the double crown. In the symmetrically composed scene, he is depicted offering the sacred *udjat*-eye as he strides toward a closed and bolted door. We may assume that inside the naos, there once stood the statuette of a deity who was the recipient of this offering in the form of a well-known amulet. On the side walls, we see Darius kneeling, with the blue crown—the crown of victory—on his head, as he presents the same magical object to a falcon-headed god seated on a lotus blossom. The inscription identifies the deity as Harendotes, "Horus, Avenger of His Father." Let us recall that the father of Horus was Osiris, who was killed and dismembered by his brother Seth. In his struggle against Seth, Horus lost his eye, which was then healed by Thoth, the god revered in Hermopolis. This is the magic *udjat*-eye that Darius is offering to the Avenger.

The themes of these scenes lead us to surmise that the statue that once stood in the naos was that of one of the heroes of this drama: Osiris, Horus, or Thoth. The latter would be especially appropriate, for Hermopolis was the principal center of his cult. In the scene with Darius, Harendotes wears the sun disk on his head, stressing his solar aspect. The same attribute appears on the head of the goddess who stands behind the king, protectively embracing him with her wings. We recognize her as the sky goddess Nut, whose arms embraced the entire world, which in fact belonged to Darius at this moment in history.

In the scene on the back wall of the naos, two winged goddesses take the form of cobras wearing the crown of Osiris. The solar deity in the middle of the scene has a ram's head, and the presence of the king is signaled on either side by cartouches containing Darius's name. In each of these scenes, the principle of symmetrical composition is observed, with a solar god serving as the axis, and each depicts a theriomorphic deity with outstretched wings. On the front wall, there is a winged beetle with a sun disk between its front legs, and there is a corresponding, parallel figure below the scene on the back wall. Beneath the scenes on the side walls is a vulture symbolizing Upper Egypt.

We can only marvel at the masterfulness with which the artist has subsumed expressions of political propaganda to the religious content of these images without sacrificing aesthetics. The symmetry serving as the funda-

Figure 40. Darius I as pharaoh offering the magical *udjat*-eye to the Egyptian sun god. Detail of a painting on a wooden shrine from Tuna el-Gebel (see Plate VIb).

mental principle of their composition stresses Darius's role as Lord of the Two Lands, a thoroughly legitimate ruler. The solar accents recall the universality of his royal authority, which in the case of the Achaemenids took the form of an ambition to dominate the entire civilized world. Did Darius wish to suggest to the Egyptians that he played as devoted and reverent a role with regard to their land as Horus vis-à-vis Osiris? Such an interpretation cannot be excluded.

This small shrine bearing the name of Darius was reused about two centuries later in the Ptolemaic Period, as a wooden coffin for a little ape—an animal worshiped at Hermopolis as a manifestation of the god Thoth. It was discovered in the subterranean galleries excavated in the rock for the mummified animals. Since these burials were on a less monumental scale that those of the sacred bulls, there were considerably more of them.

THE STATUE OF DARIUS FROM SUSA

The statue of Darius that caused an archaeological sensation just over a quarter-century ago displays political content comparable to that of the naos from Hermopolis. It was found on Christmas Eve 1972 by the French archaeological mission excavating in the area of ancient Susa. Located in southwestern Iran at the foot of the Zagros Mountains, Susa had the honor, along with Persepolis, of being one of the two capitals of the Achaemenid state. There, around 500 B.C.E., Darius erected a palace that was later destroyed. In the course of excavating the eastern end of the palace area, geomorphological research determined the presence of an Achaemenid structure that the archaeologists decided to excavate. In a deep pit filled with stone and ceramic rubble from the Seleucid Period (312–64 B.C.E.), they hit upon a standing statue of Darius (Figure 41) that had once adorned a gateway leading into his large edifice. It was one of two effigies of the king that had been set up on either side of the entrance; its counterpart either was not preserved or has yet to be found.

The statue of the great ruler is an unusual monument in every respect, and it is of special interest to us here because of its Egyptian aspects. The head of the figure is unfortunately not preserved. Including its base, the sculpture today is about eight feet tall, and its original height would have been around ten feet. It is made of brittle gray limestone from the Zagros Mountains that was obtained to serve as a building material for the Achaemenids at Susa. The statue depicts Darius in Persian garb, standing on a tall, cube-shaped base.

On the vertical folds of the garment, inscriptions are carved in four languages written with two scripts, cuneiform and hieroglyphs (Figure 42). The cuneiform inscriptions on the right side of the garment are in Old Persian,

Figure 41. Statue of Darius I from Susa at the time of its discovery. Now in the Iran-Bastam Museum, Tehran. From *Journal Asiatique* 260 (1972), Plate IV.

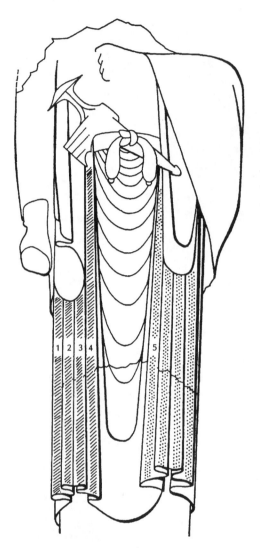

Figure 42. Inscriptions in four languages on the garment of the statue from Susa: (1) Akkadian, (2) Elamite, (3) Old Persian, (4) Old Persian, (5) hieroglyphs.

Elamite, and Akkadian. Each of them begins with the same brief formula, a repeated invocation of the god Ahuramazda, and ends by stating that the statue was prepared in Egypt, so that future generations would not forget that the Persian king had subjected the land of the pharaohs. Only the Elamite version allows the possibility of a somewhat different interpretation, namely, that the statue is "Egyptian" insofar as it was prepared in Egyptian style, but not necessarily in Egypt itself. If we lend credence to the other two versions, we must assume that the fragile limestone was taken from the Zagros Mountains to Egypt for carving and retransport to Persia. This is the first of many questions to be posed regarding this statue.

All the other inscriptions carved on the statue of Darius are in Egyptian, and we recognize the beautiful, slender forms of the hieroglyphs of the Saite Period. There are five of these inscriptions. The longest one is parallel to the cuneiform texts and thus is on the folds of the garment, in this case on the left side. Egyptian royal titles are enclosed in two rectangles that decorate the ends of the king's belt and probably represent incised metal plaques (Figure 43).

There is an informative hieroglyphic text in a rectangular field on the top of the base, at the feet of the king. At first glance, however, the attention of the beholder is drawn to the Egyptian decorations on the base. On the front and back are the familiar scene of the symbolic uniting of the Two Lands, in its classic form with two

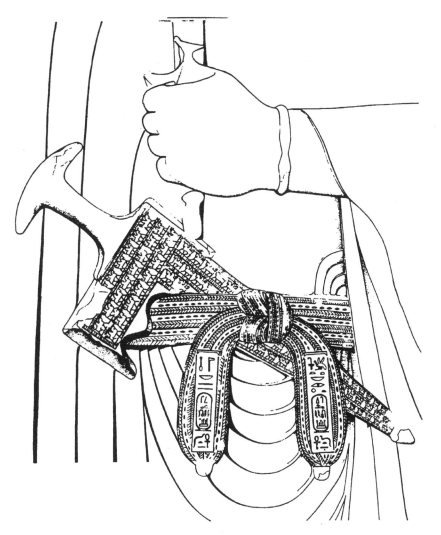

Figure 43. Belt with hieroglyphic inscription and the dagger of Darius. Detail of the statue from Susa.

personifications of the Nile. More interesting still are the reliefs on the sides of the base, each of which depicts representatives of twelve of the peoples subjected by the Persians (Figures 44 and 45).

These figures have distinctive facial features, headdresses, and clothing, and the names of the peoples are written in hieroglyphs within ovals whose serrated borders are probably supposed to represent the fortification walls of conquered cities. We thus have here a complete version of the

[149]

Figure 44. Representations and names of peoples subject to the Achaemenids. Relief on the base of the statue of Darius from Susa. From *Journal Asiatique* 260 (1972), Plate I.

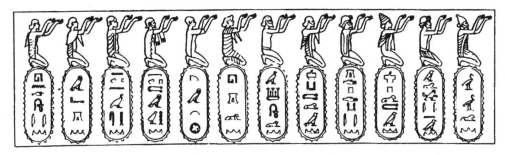

Figure 45. Representations and names of peoples subject to the Achaemenids. Relief on the base of the statue of Darius from Susa.

fragmentary list, mentioned above, carved on the stelae set up by Darius along his canal linking the Nile to the Red Sea. Of great importance as a historical document, this list of subjected peoples deserves to be cited in its entirety. On the statue base, we read the following names of lands and peoples:

To the left of the king:
(1) Persia
(2) Media
(3) Elam
(4) Aria
(5) Parthia
(6) Bactria
(7) Sogdia
(8) Arachosia
(9) Drangiana
(10) Sattagidia
(11) Chorasmia
(12) Scythians from the marshes and Scythians from the plains

To the right of the king:

(1) Babylonia

(2) Armenia

(3) Sardes (Lydia and adjoining regions)

(4) Cappadocia

(5) Scudra (Thrace)

(6) Eshur (Syria in the Demotic language)

(7) Hagar (northwestern Arabians in the Demotic language)

(8) Kemi (Egypt in the Demotic language)

(9) Land of the Tjemehu-people (Libya)

(10) Land of the Nehesi-people (Nubia)

(11) Maka

(12) Hindu

At first glance, this list of subject peoples reminds us of the decoration on the bases of a number of pharaonic statues, where we also see representatives of various peoples. In Egyptian iconographic convention, however, they are always depicted with their hands tied behind their backs: they are prisoners, and the king treads on their heads as he stands or sits on the base. In the scenes carved on Darius's statue, the foreigners have been allowed to maintain more of their dignity. Their hands are raised in a manner that can be associated with the Egyptian gesture denoting reverence. But their hands are turned palms up, just like those of the pharaoh supporting the sky, as he usually does on the pedestals intended for ritual barques, mentioned earlier, in our treatment of the iconography of the Kushite rulers. The peoples represented on the base of Darius's statue thus do not appear in the role of subjects or adorants but rather as pillars supporting the monarchy. They represent the entire world ruled by the Persian king.

The inscription at the feet of the king informs us why the statue was prepared. Here, the intent of the Persian ruler is expressed in a less brutal manner than in the cuneiform inscriptions decorating his garment. The hieroglyphic inscription would have us believe the following declaration:

The perfect god, Lord of the Two Lands, King of Upper and Lower Egypt, Darius—may he live forever! The statue, formed as a true image of the perfect god, the Lord of the Two Lands, prepared for His Majesty so that his memory might be perpetuated and to recall his person to his father Atum the Lord of the Two Lands and (to the Lord of) Heliopolis, Re-Harakhty, forever. May (they) give him all life and all dominion, all health and all joy, like Re.[1]

---

[1] J. Yoyotte, "Une statue de Darius découverte à Suse," *Journal Asiatique* 260 (1972): 255.

Here, Darius compares himself to the Heliopolitan sun god and suggests that the monument was prepared after the likeness of Atum and thus in the temple of the deity in Heliopolis. We may imagine that this statue is a replica of a similar work donated by the Persian king to the center of the solar cult in Egypt.

The equation with Atum seems to be a legitimation of this Lord of the Two Lands, for from the Old Kingdom on, every pharaoh was identified with this god. Setting up a statue of Darius at Heliopolis would thus have been as natural as decorating the temple of Ptah at Memphis with his image, as mentioned by the Greek authors Herodotus and Diodorus. According to them, Darius is supposed to have discussed the matter personally with the priests of Memphis.

An affinity of the Persian king to Heliopolis is confirmed by the fact that the above-mentioned high official named Khnemibre, who stemmed from Heliopolis and distinguished himself as a priest there through his activities from 497 to 492 B.C.E., was named Overseer of Works not only in Upper and Lower Egypt, but also "in the whole world."

More valuable information is to be found in the hieroglyphic text inscribed on the garment. This propagandistic text is a classic essay in Egyptian "political theology":

> The perfect god, who acts with his own hand, sovereign, ruler of the two crowns, who inspires fear in the hearts of humankind, august lord in the view of him who sees him, whose power conquered both of the Two Lands, who acts according to the command of the god. The son of [Re], born of Atum, living image of Re, whom he (Re) placed on his (own) throne to organize that which he had begun on earth.
>
> The perfect god, satisfied with Truth, whom Atum, lord of Heliopolis, chose to be lord of all that the sun disk encircles, for he knew that he is his son, his defender. He (Atum) commanded him (the king) to conquer each of the Two Lands, and Neith gave him the bow that is in her hand to fell all his enemies—as she had done for her son Re at the first moment (i.e., at the beginning of time), that he might be powerful, in order to repel those who rebel against him and suppress his enemies in both of the Two Lands.
>
> The mighty king, great of prestige, lord of might, who stands at the head of Letopolis, lord of (his) hand who subdued the Nine Bows (i.e., all the peoples of the world), whose decisions are splendid and whose plans are effective. Lord of a mighty arm when he enters a throng, shooting accurately—and his arrow does not miss—for his might is as great as (that of) Montu.
>
> Lord of Upper and Lower Egypt, Lord of the Two Lands, Darius—may he live forever! Great one, King of Kings, highest (lord) of this earth, [. . . son] of the god's father, Hystaspes the Achaemenid, who has appeared as King of

[152]

Upper and Lower Egypt on the Horus-throne of the living, just as Re leads the gods—forever![2]

All the divine relationships to which Darius laid claim are here combined into a unity. The pharaoh is not only the son and image of the sun god but also a protégé of the goddess Neith, who was the mother of this god in the pantheon of Sais. He is also identified with the warlike Horus, as already suggested by the naos from Tuna el-Gebel. The epithet Lord of the Two Lands is paraphrased here in a manner specific to the situation: Darius subjects "each" of the "Two" Lands, which could of course stand for any number, thus defining him as lord of a vast realm. To stress this point, the ruler's Egyptian titulary is enhanced by the Persian formula King of Kings, translated into Demotic and written in hieroglyphs.

For all its universalistic declarations, the statue has a thoroughly Egyptian character. This impression is prompted not only by the Egyptian form of the base and the hieroglyphic inscriptions but also by the pose of the ruler, who stands with one foot forward—which is characteristic of Egyptian statues—as well as by the rectangular back pillar, which distinguishes Egyptian statues from all others. The inscription on the garment, which designates Darius as "Ruler of the Two Crowns," leads us to conclude that the double crown of Upper and Lower Egypt adorned the statue's head. This hypothesis receives indirect support from the portrait of a later Persian ruler of Egypt, Artaxerxes III, on a *stater* struck in 343 B.C.E., evidently on the occasion of his reconquest of the land of the pharaohs. The Achaemenid is represented in Persian garb, but with the double crown of Egypt on his head.

Among the Persian elements of Darius's garb, special interest is afforded by the tight-fitting, laceless shoes, whose bangles end in depictions of cows' horns, and the dagger in a case decorated with a frieze of winged oxen. This could be either a Persian or an Elamite dagger.

This is the earliest known large statue representing an Achaemenid ruler, and it is so well preserved that it is possible to learn the details of Persian dress. It was doubtless made by an Egyptian artist, as can be ascertained from both its general concept and its iconographic details. The execution of the hieroglyphic inscriptions betrays the hand of a master sculptor who was not carving an inscription of this sort for the first time. Both of these specialists could have found a place at Darius's court, for the Persian ruler surrounded himself not only with Egyptian physicians but

---

[2] Ibid. Horus was the god worshiped at Letopolis; the modern name of the site, which was called Khem in the ancient Egyptian language, is Ausim. "God's father" was the title of a dignitary whose son became king.

also with artists from the land of the Nile. Sculptors traveling between Egypt and Susa are mentioned in a letter from Arsames, the satrap of Egypt, and the tablets from the treasure of Persepolis mention an Egyptian who worked in wood, though not in stone. In an inscription, Darius himself affirms that the people who decorated the walls at Susa were Medes and Egyptians.

The activity of Egyptian artists left many traces in the iconography of the Achaemenid reliefs. Lintels of entrances were decorated with winged sun disks, and in the course of time, even Ahuramazda—an embodiment of good—assumed the form of a bearded man emerging from a winged disk of this sort. The "manager" who dispatched the Egyptian artists to Persia might have been the above-mentioned Khnemibre of Heliopolis, in his capacity of Overseer of Great Artisans and Overseer of Works "in the whole world" and responsible, moreover, for the procurement of stone in every foreign land. It cannot be excluded that he played a role at Darius's side similar to that once played by Amenhotpe, son of Hapu at the court of Amenophis III.

Consideration of certain essential details makes it easy to date the creation of Darius's statue fairly accurately. Thrace and Libya are included among the subject lands on the base, and these did not become part of the empire until after 513 B.C.E. The statue must have been created after Darius' campaign to Egypt, which occurred between 513/512 and 493/492 B.C.E. Darius's name is written on the statue in a manner characteristic of the later years of his reign. Thus all indications are that the statue was made at the beginning of the fifth century B.C.E. and is likely to be a copy of one set up at Heliopolis but no longer preserved or not yet found. The quadrilingual stelae hailing Darius as creator of the canal were evidently prepared at that time as well. The inscriptions and the layout of these monuments display a similar content and form, and they serve the same propagandistic goal.

While Darius's Egyptomania might have been caused by his reverence for age-old pharaonic tradition, both cultures—the Persian and the Egyptian—contained similar ideological elements that could easily be compared. The relationship between the ruler and the divine was the same in both religions: just as the pharaoh was the chosen one and the image of Atum, so the Persian king was the incarnation of Ahuramazda. The Egyptian love of order and truth, concepts personified by the goddess Maat, had its counterpart in the Persian opposition of truth (*arte*) and falsehood (*drauga*). The bow, the attribute of the Egyptian goddess Neith, was the preferred weapon of the Persians. It is no wonder, then, that there were no great obstacles to the mutual assimilation of the two cultures, which could also find expression in the art.

The identification of the king with the Heliopolitan god Atum is an especially interesting theme in Egyptian political theology. The surprisingly small number of statues of the latter—he was, after all, one of the most important Egyptian gods—among the almost inexhaustible quantity of statuary representing other deities, and kings as well, invites some consideration. Given the nearly total identity of Atum and the living Lord of the Two Lands, one cannot help hypothesizing that statues of the ruler were also considered to be likenesses of Atum, at least those representing him wearing the double crown.

The author of this book had occasion to speak of this at the thirty-first Congress of Orientalists, which was held in Tokyo and Kyoto in 1983. I gave the paper in a panel discussion on the topic "Monarchy and Socioreligious Traditions in the Ancient Near East." The panel was organized by the only living brother of Emperor Hirohito, Prince Takahito Mikasa, who is a historian well known in scholarly circles and president of the Center for Near Eastern Culture in Japan. On the day before my paper, I asked the secretary of His Royal Highness, Dr. Hisa Tottori, if I might have the use of two slide projectors. She called to a diminutive gentleman standing not far from us in the crowd. He turned out to be the emperor's brother, and he responded that it would be possible. Since my paper was the first after the lunch break, I returned a half hour early to prepare to show my slides. In the empty corridor, I was astonished to see the unimposing figure of the prince carrying a projector under his arm and then personally closing the curtains in the conference room. Despite his position, the brother of the former "god" had managed to free himself from the psychological burden that his family position might have entailed.

The defeat of the Persians at Marathon in 490 B.C.E. was not without repercussions in Egypt, for it aroused hopes of throwing off the Persian yoke. In 486 B.C.E., Egypt achieved a short-lived independence, but Darius's son Xerxes I, who came to the throne in that year, suppressed the rebellion. Darius's Achaemenid successors ruled Egypt for another eighty years, yet they left no traces whatsoever of building activity. While Xerxes (486–465 B.C.E.) was never personally in Egypt, he was remembered there as a cruel tyrant. In the Ptolemaic Period, his name was written with a determinative depicting a bound and beheaded captive! (A determinative is a hieroglyph, written at the end of a word, that was not read aloud but helped to indicate the meaning of the word.)

To prevent further uprisings in Egypt, Xerxes replaced the satrap Pherendates with his own brother Achaemenes. But he was unable to pacify the Egyptians for long, for the defeat of the Persian fleet at Salamis in 480 B.C.E. activated freedom forces who allied themselves with Greece. Xerxes was blamed for having statues stolen from Egypt and transported to Persia. If we are to lend credence to the ancients, he was, briefly put, a thief and a bandit.

After Xerxes, the first of the three Artaxerxes with whom the history of Egypt was connected ruled for forty years (465–424 B.C.E.). We know him above all from the Aramaic papyri found at Elephantine, where there was a border garrison consisting of an entirely Jewish colony. But these Jewish soldiers were not the only persons in Egypt who used the Aramaic language, nor was the island in the Nile at the southern border of the land the only Jewish community.

The Aramaeans were a nomadic people speaking a northwest Semitic language who were apparently present in upper Mesopotamia as early as the twenty-third century B.C.E. Their administrative center was most likely in the Damascus region, where distant echoes of their language may be heard to this day in the town of Malula. In Egypt, Aramaic inscriptions already began to appear under the Saite dynasty. Spread by Assyrian caravans in the eighth century B.C.E., this tongue became the lingua franca of the entire Persian empire. In Egypt, too, Aramaic attained the status of official language of the Achaemenid administration. The Jews, who sympathized with the Persians, adopted the language for their own needs. The Aramaic-speaking military colonies had their origin in the compulsory conscriptions that the Assyrians in the east, and later the Saites in Egypt, had carried out among the mass of refugees from the Babylonian state. In the end, these colonies were supporters of the Persians in Egypt.

One of our oldest Aramaic documents, found at Saqqara, is a plea for help in the struggle against the Babylonian troops. Among the later ones, special interest is afforded by private letters of Darius dating to the fourteenth year of his reign (512 B.C.E.), which were written on leather and sent to Egypt. A cache of letters written in a colloquial style by two soldiers has been found at Hermopolis. But the largest collection of texts in the Aramaic language comes from Elephantine. At the beginning of the twentieth century, one public and two private archives were discovered there, along with an archive of ostraca belonging to Jews who lived there in the sixth and fifth centuries B.C.E.

These documents are mostly private in nature, but there are also administrative and legal documents, such as marriage contracts, divorces, adoptions, sales of real estate, lawsuits, and so forth. From them, we learn of the daily life of the Jewish community and of the historical data and events connected with the religion of this population group. Mixed marriages testify to the mutual interpenetration of the Egyptian and Jewish cultures at the southern boundary of Egypt.

They also acquaint us with the eclectic law of this colony, in which Egyptian elements appear side by side with northwest Semitic features and especially with elements from the Mesopotamian codices. We encounter these again later in Egyptian documents written in Demotic and later still in the Ptolemaic Period. Many of these documents bear a double date: the Egyptian and the Babylonian-Persian (i.e., Jewish). Legal texts from the middle of the fifth century B.C.E., in particular, are dated in this manner. The documents from the beginning and end of this century display only the Egyptian date, while official petitions are always dated according to the Jewish calendar. In each of these systems, the date is precise and consistent. Toward the end of the fifth century B.C.E., formulae of Greek origin begin to appear in juridical texts.

The Jews of Elephantine erected a temple to their god around the middle of the seventh century B.C.E. In its size, it was not to rival the Solomonic temple in Jerusalem. It was spared by Cambyses, the conqueror of Egypt. From the Aramaic documents found at Elephantine, we learn that the Sabbath was celebrated and offerings made there. A royal edict introduced the festival of unleavened bread, evidently to standardize or even sanction the Jewish religion.

Since the Jews stood firmly on the side of the Persians, the xenophobia of the Egyptians was directed against them. Taking advantage of the absence of the satrap Arsames (Arsham), who administered Egypt in the reign of Darius II, the priests of the native Egyptian god Khnum bribed the local authorities and destroyed the Jewish temple in 410 B.C.E. The severe punishments dealt out to the venal officials could not change the facts, and the Jewish community at Elephantine began to disintegrate, though permission was granted some years later for the rebuilding of the temple, after many efforts and thanks to the recommendation of the satraps of Judea and Samaria.

Offerings of meal and incense were also renewed. A collection for the Jewish god, on the modest scale of two shekels per person, was organized in the year 400 B.C.E., which is the last firm date in the Aramaic documents from Elephantine. In 399 B.C.E., a letter was sent from Memphis reporting the coronation of Nepherites, a ruler of Dynasty 29. Letters and accounts written in Aramaic in the fourth century B.C.E., most of them badly preserved, already contain exclusively Egyptian names. Greek names, and even Greek words, appear in the Aramaic texts of the third century B.C.E. Around 250 B.C.E., the now modernized Jewish script became far less common than Greek.

A second people who left many written traces in Egypt were the Carians. These inhabitants of southwestern Asia Minor are mentioned already in the *Iliad* by Homer, who called them *barbarophonoi* because their language was incomprehensible to the Greeks. Their history is known to us only from the time they became part of the Achaemenid empire. They are called *Karka* in the Old Persian language, and they appear as *Keres* and *Geres* in hieroglyphic inscriptions. The history of the Carians in Egypt can be reconstructed by comparing the epigraphic sources with the traditions of the ancient Greek historians.

From Herodotus, we learn that Carians and Ionians helped Psammetichus I to assume power. They made their appearance as mercenaries in Egypt in the seventh century B.C.E., and they evidently felt at home on the Nile. They first settled in the eastern delta, northeast of Bubastis. In the middle of the sixth century B.C.E., Amasis recruited his bodyguard from among the Carians, whom he resettled in Memphis; one of this city's quarters bore the name Caricon, while its inhabitants were called Caromemphites. Many texts written in the Carian language have been found in the Memphite cemetery near modern Saqqara, where Caromemphites were buried.

Carian inscriptions have been found in other places in Egypt as well, such as Sais, Abydos, Thebes, Abu Simbel, and even in the Nubian fortress at Buhen. The texts preserved in Egypt are among the oldest known Carian inscriptions, and ironically, because of conditions affecting the preservation of the sources, they are more numerous and varied than those preserved in the Carian homeland.

The Carian writing system has not been widely investigated. It is clear, though, that it is an alphabetic script similar to Greek, and also to Lydian and Lycian, though with more letters. The Carian language remains a mystery to scholars, though there is a prevailing agreement that together with Lydian and Lycian, it belongs to a group of small western Anatolian languages descended from the Hittite and especially the Luwian languages of the second millennium B.C.E.

Among the monuments bearing Carian inscriptions found in Egypt, special interest is afforded by the many stelae and by the so-called false doors in Egyptian style from the Memphite cemetery of the sixth century B.C.E., as well as by the inscriptions on bronze votive objects from Sais, such as the base of a figurine of the goddess Neith and on a reliquary containing mummified reptiles, and finally by the graffiti on the walls of temples and tombs and on rock surfaces. The Carian inscriptions in Egypt date from the seventh to the third centuries B.C.E.

STRUGGLES FOR INDEPENDENCE

The multinational empire of the Achaemenids began to fall apart after the defeats suffered by the Persians in their struggle with the Greeks. Egypt profited from this situation. Artaxerxes I (465–424 B.C.E.), who was caught up in a web of intrigue in his own court, was unable to mount an expedition when the puppet ruler Inaros had himself proclaimed pharaoh and subordinated the delta to himself. At first, Memphis and Upper Egypt remained in Persian hands. With the help of the Athenian fleet, Inaros emerged victorious over the satrap Achaemenes, who was killed in battle at Papremis. Artaxerxes angrily dispatched his general Megabyses into a decisive struggle for Memphis, the seat of the Persian administration in Egypt. Inaros was defeated in this battle and taken into captivity. In Persia, he experienced the martyrdom of a patriot and hero: he was crucified.

Pacified, Egypt now experienced a quarter-century of relative peace. After the death of Achaemenes, Arsames (454–404 B.C.E.) was named satrap. It was while he was in office that Herodotus of Halicarnassus, to whom we owe the fullest description of this period, made his journey to Egypt. Since we can scarcely accuse the Greek historian of sympathy for the Persians, other sources that can help provide a more objective picture of Egypt during Dynasty 27 constitute a valuable complement to his account. The Aramaic papyri from Elephantine are among the most important historical documents of this sort.

Egyptian hopes of regaining independence were tied to alliance with Greece. Supported by Sparta, Amyrtaios was embroiled in constant conflict with the Persians from 414 to 405 B.C.E., annexing the delta to his realm, and a series of battles to shake off the Persian yoke was eventually crowned with success. When Artaxerxes II ascended the throne in 404 B.C.E., an armed rebellion led by his younger brother Cyrus broke out in Persia. Under the circumstances, a campaign to Egypt was impossible, and Amyrtaios took advantage of the situation to free the entire land from Persian rule.

Though the Jews at Elephantine continued to recognize the Persian ruler until 400 B.C.E., as shown by the Aramaic papyri, Egypt now had its own Lord of the Two Lands. After 120 years of bondage, Egypt was once again independent, though this was to last for only sixty years. Amyrtaios was the only king of this new Dynasty 28. He stemmed from Sais and reigned only six years (404–398 B.C.E.). His name is not found in any hieroglyphic inscriptions, though it appears in two Aramaic papyri from Elephantine, as well as in a Demotic chronicle that also makes it clear that the assumption of power by the following dynasty, Dynasty 29, was not one of the most peaceful periods in the history of Egypt.

RITUAL CONFIRMATION OF ROYAL POWER

History and historiography have a decided preference for paradoxes. One of them is related to the period with which we are concerned here. It should be viewed as an irony of history that it is precisely from a phase of absence of genuine Egyptian rulers, as in the case of the last pharaohs of Dynasty 27, or of the rulership of ephemeral kings, as in Dynasties 28 and 29, that we have a unique document whose politico-religious content con-

[159]

cerns the confirmation of royal power. Dated to the end of the fifth or the beginning of the fourth century B.C.E., this hieratic papyrus contains instructions of a liturgical sort concerning the celebrations conducted annually to mark the anniversary of a king's assumption of power. The prayers and the instructions for the priests that it contains enable us to reconstruct the entire ceremony and even the layout of the buildings between which the procession moved. The frequent references to the god Atum allow us to conclude that the ceremony took place in Heliopolis, the principal center of his cult. This is not surprising, for Pharaoh was identified with no other god as completely as with the Lord of the Two Lands at Heliopolis.

The ceremonies began at dawn, as soon as Pharaoh awoke from sleep. The ruler evidently was ritually purified in the palace itself and then dressed. When the master of ceremonies made his appearance, the "ceremony of the royal house of the morning" was read. A procession was formed, and it made its way to the temple. A priest of the king seated himself in the royal palanquin, which was ceremonially borne to the Chapel of the Great Seat, where the priestly stand-in for the king received a talisman and magical jewels and then was anointed. The accompanying prayers were chiefly intended to pacify the goddess Sakhmet, who symbolized the dangers that lay in wait for humankind toward the end of the year. The priest playing the role of Pharaoh was also invested with royal insignia and anointed with nine different oils as liturgical songs were sung.

When this ceremony was completed, the act of the "approach of the earth to the *benben*-palace" was carried out. To all indications, this entailed bringing a container of sand from the primeval mound located in the temple of Re-Harakhty at Heliopolis. The sand in the container was sprinkled around the royal stand-in, so that the latter would be placed under the protection of the "intimates of Atum." A protective zone of purity and holiness was thus created around the symbolic ruler. After various deities were worshiped in their chapels, the participants turned in the direction of the sanctuary, which was in all likelihood entered by the king himself to perform the ceremonies provided for in the ritual in front of Horus and the deities responsible for the crowns.

Returning to the procession, the king marched, inter alia, past flags decorated with representations of deities. The procession then approached the "pavilion of the House of Life that is in the Great Seat." Before they set foot on its threshold, the priest playing the role of the king was obliged to secure the goodwill of the divine by making a food offering. They then entered the court of the House of Life, where the ruler himself had to make an offering to the deities who resided there. With that, the first part of the cultic ceremonies reached its conclusion.

In the course of the second, no less exhaustive ritual, the king finally received satisfaction for his efforts. In the "pavilion of the transfer of the inheritance," there occurred the ceremonial transfer of power to the first of all the kings, Horus, with whom the pharaoh identified himself. The king spent several days here, occupied with an uninterrupted series of ceremonies. Many of these were magical in nature and served to strengthen the safety of the ruler for the entire year to come. In addition to various amulets, the pharaoh received four wooden seals, inscribed with divine names, that confirmed he was the heir of Horus. Two of them bore the name of Geb and the two others the name of the warlike goddess Neith and that of the goddess Maat, the personification of truth. Finally, the mystery of death and rebirth was enacted. The king lay down with the four seals under his head, and he was supposed to fall asleep in this position. After this symbolic death, he awakened with his power to rule renewed. With the new year already begun, Pharaoh's powers were regenerated and his authority confirmed.

But this was not yet the end of the ceremony. The king still had a long road to travel, one that began with his enthronement bearing the royal insignia. All the deities, especially Horus, now had to be informed of the confirmation of his power. The master of ceremonies fetched two birds, one of which was a messenger to Horus, and the other to all the rest. At this moment, curses were uttered against all the enemies of Horus. They were also rendered harmless symbolically by destroying seven rolls of papyrus, evidently by burning them, and by cutting off the blossoms of seven marsh plants. To stave off the dangers to which the king might be exposed through the coming year, exorcisms were performed on the fifth day of the new year. As precisely specified, the king was dressed in a linen garment that was red, the color of victory, along with sandals that were white, the color of purity; in his hand, he held the ceremonial "staff of the foreign lands" that symbolized his rulership over subject peoples.

In the course of this ceremony, the king was invested with various amulets whose magical powers were supposed to assure his safety. An indispensable requisite in this regard was the "barque of Seth," a god who symbolized chaos and whom the Horus-king had to drive off with a stalk of papyrus. At the close of the exorcisms, the priests of the House of Life sang a hymn. The procession again assembled around the king and left the "place of the transfer of the inheritance." At a place that is not precisely specified, offerings were made to the ancestors, that is, to the deceased kings and to the deities who accompanied them in the afterlife.

The concluding ceremony saw a return to the House of Life, where nine live birds were presented. This began with a prayer to the sun god Re, "who is in his disk." As they were brought in, the heads of the birds were anointed with sacred balsam, and their wings were spread protectively over the king. While the birds were being presented, three jewels were brought from the treasury to adorn the neck of the royal stand-in. One was in the form of a golden falcon, the second a vulture of faience, and the third a turquoise blue cat. Something different was done with each of the avian messengers. The first of them was a live falcon that was censed and then anointed with olibanum oil. Then the birdcatcher turned the falcon's head to one side and took a tear from its left eye. This tear of Horus was then used to anoint the eye of the falcon-shaped jewel, made of gold, that was hanging from the neck of the king. This symbolized the transfer of power and Pharaoh's consecration for the coming year. Other birds that played a role in the ceremony were a vulture, a hawk, and a Nile goose. They were set free so that they might serve as both emissaries and protectors of the king. The ceremony ended with a prayer to these "birds of Re," who granted life and health to the king for the coming year. Once the prayer was said, the pharaoh could take a well-deserved rest.

These were busy days for the king, whose thoughts often strayed into the sphere of politics, war, and court intrigues, especially in this stormy period of history. It would be interesting to know how many rulers of the last Egyptian dynasties allowed themselves the luxury of an annual celebration as extensive as that described in the papyrus, which is now in the collection of the Brooklyn Museum in New York. We may imagine that the complete version of this anniversary liturgy, which was probably copied from older papyri, was not always carried out in its entirety.

THE FINAL DECADES OF INDEPENDENCE

Pharaonic Egypt's final decades of independence were a period of intense rivalry between the princely families of various cities in the delta. We do not know the circumstances under which Amyrtaios, who stemmed from Sais, made way for other rulers who came from Mendes, an important administrative and religious center in the northeastern delta. In Greek historiography, they constituted Dynasty 29, which ruled for only twenty years. Two of the four kings of this dynasty sat on the throne for only several months. The first and last monarchs of the Mendesian dynasty bore the name Nepherites. The first of these reigned for four years, the second scarcely four months.

An interesting interpretation of the political successes and failures of the rulers of Egypt in the period following the expulsion of the Persians is to be found in the so-called Demotic Chronicle, a Demotic text recorded on a papyrus from the end of the third century B.C.E. now in the Bibliothèque Nationale in Paris. The work has the character of a moralistic political essay composed in the form of prophecies relating to the individual rulers. The prophecies were made to king Nectanebo I (378–360 B.C.E.), one of the two last native pharaohs, and they were based on historical facts well known to the author of the text, for the work was composed a good century and a half later.

In a biblical manner, the Demotic Chronicle links political success to the piety and honesty of the ruler. If he had a brief reign, that meant he had broken the law or had a bad character. The interpreter of the dreams is evidently a priest from Herakleopolis, another ambitious political center at the end of the dynastic period, so we can hardly expect objectivity from the moral evaluations of this oracle. Nine rulers are judged, of whom Hakoris probably comes off best: he ruled for thirteen years (390–378 B.C.E.) because he was "generous toward the temples." In the end, however, he too broke the law, neglecting his family, and so he was deposed.

The author of the Demotic Chronicle is in fact not satisfied with any of the kings, so he divides them into those with whom he is more or less dissatisfied. In this work, historical fact is almost entirely subordinated to propaganda serving the political interests of Herakleopolis. Fictive genealogies are formed, with Nepherites I, the first king of Dynasty 29, appearing as the father of Nectanebo I, the founder of Dynasty 30.

A similar legend made Nectanebo II, the last pharaoh of Egyptian descent, the father of Alexander the Great. This fiction was of great political importance, for it asserted a native ancestry of the Greek rulers of Egypt. Nevertheless, it also served as a judgment on the kings from Sebennytos who comprised Dynasty 30. It is against the latter that the prophecies of the Demotic Chronicle are particularly directed. The last ruler of this dynasty, Nectanebo II, is called a "woman," and the fall of his dynasty is attributed to his cowardice. The prophet predicts the appearance of Alexander the Great and the rule of the Ptolemies, of course, but they were supposed to be succeeded by a native dynasty that would this time stem from Herakleopolis. This last prophecy leaves no doubt in whose interests this chronicle was written.

Because the Egyptian sources are sparse, our knowledge is based chiefly on Greek writers, such as Diodorus and Xenophon. We know that during the last three dynasties–Dynasties 28–30—Egypt conducted a philhellenic policy focused entirely on cooperation with Greece. This is scarcely a wonder, for the two lands had a common enemy: Persia. Finding itself always in a state of preparedness for political and military action, the pharaonic state sought an ally on the other side of the Mediterranean. The Persians gathered a mighty army in Phoenicia, one that awaited only the appropriate order to march against Egypt.

Cyrus, however, involved himself in a war against Sparta, which had set out in 400 B.C.E. to defend the Greek cities of Asia Minor. This war, which lasted for ten years, left Egypt in peace. In 396 B.C.E., Sparta concluded a treaty with Egypt, and Nepherites I was supposed to support king Agesi-laus with a large quantity of grain and equipment, but by the time the Spartan ships carrying the Egyptian cargo reached Rhodes, the island had already been taken by the Persians, and the grain fell into the hands of their admiral, the Athenian Conon. Since the alliance with Sparta had proved unhelpful, Hakoris, who took the throne after the one-year reign of Psam-muthis, found another partner. This was Evagoras, the king of the Cypriot city of Salamis. This alliance once again brought Egypt closer to Athens, for Evagoras was on friendly terms with Conon.

Exhausted by the war, the two parties—Persia and Sparta—concluded a peace known as the Peace of Antalcidas in 386 B.C.E., which accepted the hegemony of Persia over the Greek cities of Asia Minor and in return recognized the autonomy of all the other Hellenic states. This was a threat to Hakoris and Evagoras, who saw themselves directly exposed to Artaxerxes II. The Persian ruler began by attacking Egypt. But in the meanwhile, this land had taken advantage of its decade of peace to strengthen its forces, and the Egyptian army had acquired the outstanding Athenian general Chabrias. We do not know much about this war, which dragged on until at least 383 B.C.E., if not longer. It is mentioned with contempt by the Athenian orator Isocrates, a disciple of the Sophists.

Evagoras proved to be a thoroughly effective ally, conquering Tyre and other Phoenician cities. Unfortunately, after losing a battle at sea, he was besieged in his own city of Salamis. After having put up a resistance for more than a decade, he was finally obliged to capitulate, and in 380 B.C.E., he concluded an agreement with the Persians on terms that were favorable to himself. This spelled the beginning of the end for Hakoris. The weakened dynasty was not saved by his son Nepherites II, who ruled for only a few months. Authority over Egypt then fell into the hands of a general from Sebennytos. The Demotic Chronicle explains the fall of Dynasty 29 as an unavoidable fate that Egypt had to suffer for the sins of its last rulers.

While the seat—and probably also the necropolis—of the kings of Dynasty 29 was located at Mendes in the north of the land, the most interesting object from this period has been preserved to our own times at Thebes, in front of the temple of Amun-Re at Karnak. Here, the second king of the dynasty, Psammuthis, founded a small temple; since its construction and decoration were completed by Hakoris, it is today known as the Hakoris Chapel. This interesting building is the first one encountered by tourists approaching the temple area from the direction of the Nile.

Though it stands in the shadow of the huge pylons and monumental temples erected in earlier periods, the chapel is worth a closer look, for it is the only construction of the late dynastic period still standing to this day. It replaced an earlier shrine of Taharqa of Dynasty 25, and it was intended for the temporary storage of the sacred barque of Amun-Re, in which the statue of the deity completed its journeys on major religious festivals. Mounted on two poles, the portable barque was borne from one station to another by bald-headed priests. It remained for a time in each of these, while various ceremonies were carried out around it. On such festival days, one of the most important tasks of the god was the giving of oracles, that is, answers to the various questions of the faithful. The Hakoris Chapel was erected to serve as such a barque station, and so the reliefs decorating its walls depict both the king and this most sacred object. The chapel itself was recently reconstructed, consolidated, and described in a publication by the Franco-Egyptian mission active at Karnak.

A highly interesting though fragmentary relief of Hakoris was found at Tod, a site located south of Karnak. It depicts the king and a baboon, both making the same reverential gesture (Figure 46). They are undoubtedly worshiping the sun god, whose likeness is not preserved. The king is evidently performing the function of a priest of the sun god, in the process identifying himself as the child of this deity. This function resembles the role of the baboons who worship the rising sun at dawn, and this comparison in no way belittles the king, but rather honors him, for the baboon personified one of Egypt's most important gods, Thoth, the patron of scribes. The ape thus sometimes forms part of a statue, sitting on the shoulders of a

Figure 46. Hakoris as sun priest and a baboon worshiping the rising sun. Relief from a temple at Tod. Photo by Andrzej Bodytko, Polish Center of Mediterranean Archaeology, Warsaw University.

[165]

scribe and embracing his head. We may recall that the cult place of the divine ape was Hermopolis in Middle Egypt. It is to just this god that Nectanebo I (378–360 B.C.E.) offers a figurine of Maat—symbol of truth and order—in a scene on a wall of a granite naos from Abydos.

Nectanebo erected or restored temples to Thoth and other deities worshiped at Hermopolis (Figure 47), as he states in the hieroglyphic text of a large limestone stela found there in May 1939 by a German archaeological mission. The document contains a series of interesting technical details about the appearance of the temple and the entire temple compound at Hermopolis, but it is also a monument in the florid style of royal propaganda. The text immortalized on the stela concerns the period between the fourth and the eighth regnal years of the king, when large-scale building projects were being carried out at Hermopolis. But before that happened, and even before Nectanebo became king, he stopped at the city of Thoth while still a general to suppress a revolt by the local population.

Perhaps the success of this pacification effort paved the way to the throne for him, which would explain the unusual attention he paid to the deities of Hermopolis. From the text of the document, we gather that the local priesthood was well disposed toward the general and later king. In this inscription, Nectanebo's assumption of the throne is attributed to the Hermopolitan goddess Nehmetawai, to whom the grateful king erected a temple in the first year of his reign. The author of the text also identifies her with the uraeus on the brow of the king. The goddess assumed her place in the new temple to the great joy of the inhabitants of Hermopolis, and the king heaped rich rewards on the priesthood there. Then Nectanebo thought of other deities:

> He rebuilt what he found in ruins (using) fine stone, the door leaves of cedar covered with bronze, (the building being) 60 cubits long and 30 cubits wide (i.e., about 100′ × 50′). The place of rest of his mother Wosret-Nehmetawai, "House of Khmun, House of the Golden One"—so it is called. In it are eight sistrums of Hathor-Nehmetawai. . . .
>
> They came and said to his majesty, "The house of your mother, Wosret-Nehmetawai is prepared, lasting and enduring like the sky. Columns of beautiful white stone are in front of this house, each of them (topped) by the four faces of a sistrum, covered with gold, and the ceiling—a beautiful sight—is of genuine stone. The Great Seat (i.e., the holy of holies) is inside it, covered with gold within, its door leaves being of gold engraved with the great name(s) of his majesty. Nothing (like this) has been made since primeval times." His majesty provided it (i.e., the Great Seat) with vessels of gold, silver, and every sort of genuine stone, and (with) all kinds of beautiful

Figure 47. Head of a limestone statue representing a pharaoh of the Late Period, possibly Nectanebo I. From Hermopolis, now in the Mallawi Antiquities Museum. Photo by the author.

things. Her majesty (i.e., the goddess) was more pleased with this than with what had been here previously.[3]

But above all, it was necessary to enlarge the temple of Thoth, who stood at the head of the local pantheon:

> Year 4, third month of Winter: his majesty founded the house of his father Thoth, the twice great, lord of Khmun, the great god, who came out of the nose of Re, who created his beauty, (the house—i.e., the temple—being of) beautiful white stone, its floor of *kis*-stone, 220 cubits long and 110 cubits wide (i.e., about 380′ x 190′), an excellent work for all eternity. Never has (anything) like it been made since primeval times.
>
> His majesty concerned himself every day and every night with the work in it. He completed it successfully and saw his father Thoth enter it, while his majesty was (endowed) with life, stability, and dominion forever. He made greater offerings than had been (made) there previously. His majesty rewarded the prophets and priests at the conclusion of all the work that he did in Her-set.[4]

Dynasty 30, the last dynasty of pharaonic Egypt, actually had two important kings who bore the name Nectanebo. Ancient Greek historians separate their reigns by the brief (two years at most) rule of Teos, who was a son of Nectanebo I and uncle of Nectanebo II.

The dynasty from Sebennytos prolonged the independent existence of pharaonic Egypt by thirty-seven years (378–341 B.C.E.), after which the throne of this land fell once again to the Persians. Sebennytos became the capital of the dynasty and an important cult center as well. It was in the reign of Nectanebo I that Isis, the goddess worshiped there, began the worldwide career that she was to enjoy in the decades and centuries that followed.

Nectanebo I, son of the commander in chief Djedhor (the Egyptian prototype of the Greek name Taho/Tachos/Theos), secured a sixteen-year period of peace and prosperity for Egypt. The idyll came to an end in 373

---

[3] G. Roeder, "Zwei hieroglyphische Inschriften aus Hermopolis (Ober-Ägypten): Der Denkstein des Königs Nacht-nebôf," *Annales du Service des Antiquités Égyptiennes* 52 (1952): 403. Nehmetawai was a goddess worshiped at Hermopolis as partner of Thoth; her theological importance grew during the Late Period. Khmun, which means "city of the eight gods" (i.e., the Ogdoad), was one of the names of Hermopolis. The eight sistra were probably columns whose capitals took the form of a sistrum, a musical instrument decorated with the head of Hathor. Each side of the square capital would have been carved in the form of a sistrum with the face of Hathor.

[4] Ibid., pp. 410–11. *Kis*-stone has been identified as a hard limestone. *Her-set* was a designation of Hermopolis, probably referring specifically to the temple area in that city.

B.C.E. with Artaxerxes II's campaign against Egypt, in which Greek mercenaries participated under the command of the satrap of Syria. The Persians, however, did not even reach Memphis; the high Nile water level prevented them from entering the capital.

From 366 B.C.E. on, Nectanebo I again sought an alliance with Sparta and Athens, at the prompting, so it seems, of his son Teos, who evidently became coregent with his father in 365 B.C.E. The politically active son, who soon became sole ruler, supported a revolt of the satraps against Artaxerxes II and even attempted the subjection of Syria. At the instigation of the Athenian general Chabrias, he instituted a harsh system of taxation. He also had coins struck to pay his Greek mercenaries.

The great campaign to Syria in 360 B.C.E. under the command of Teos with Greek mercenaries headed by Agesilaus, the aging king of Sparta, and a fleet commanded by Chabrias, ended tragically for the ambitious pharaoh. His brother, who was supposed to fulfill the duties of regent in Egypt for the duration of the war, took advantage of his absence. Playing on the displeasure of the Egyptians with the tax burdens Teos had placed on them, he decided to place his son, who was with the Egyptian army in Syria, on the throne. He had him return to Egypt, where he proclaimed him king. Agesilaus and most of the soldiers declared in favor of the young prince. Teos was left with no choice other than to flee to the court of the Persian king. Thus commenced the eighteen-year reign of the usurper Nectanebo II (359–341 B.C.E.), the last pharaoh of dynastic Egypt.

This last pharaoh was the son of a general. At the beginning of his reign, he had to contend with a pretender to the throne who stemmed from Mendes and was supported by a part of the population. With the help of Agesilaus and his Spartans, he was able to suppress the revolt. In the winter of 351/350 B.C.E., he was obliged to withstand a Persian attack led by Artaxerxes III Ochus. The attack ended in defeat, but the Persians did not allow themselves to be discouraged. In 343 B.C.E., they were again poised on the border of Egypt, this time with forces that substantially exceeded those of Egypt. Nectanebo II saved himself by fleeing to Upper Egypt, where he remained in power for two more years after the withdrawal of the Persians. We do not know what became of him; we know only that Egypt fell again into the hands of the Persians, whose rule over the land of the Nile would last another eleven years.

THE ART AND ARCHITECTURE OF DYNASTY 30

Nectanebo I and II, the two great kings of Dynasty 30, unleashed an enormously active building campaign that would have done honor to the most renowned monarchs of centuries past. Traces of their activity have been found in nearly all the important religious centers, in the form of ruined temples, stone blocks with carved reliefs, naoi, stelae, statues, inscribed ritual implements, and the like.

The first of these rulers is known for his new and renovated temples not only at Hermopolis but also at Tanis, Heliopolis, Memphis, Letopolis, Koptos, Karnak, el-Kab, Philae, and many other places. In recent years, traces of his work have been found at Mendes, el-Moalla, and Elephantine. At the temple of Luxor, he added an avenue of sphinxes, provided with his own visage, that is mostly preserved to this day (Figure 48).

A similar avenue was situated in front of the Serapeum at Memphis, whose surroundings were completely renovated. Individual sphinxes were also set up by Nectanebo I at other temples. Naoi dedicated by this king, made of hard stone and decorated with reliefs, have been found in the delta.

The most famous of these is a large granite naos from Saft el-Hinna in the eastern delta, now in the Egyptian Museum in Cairo. Its abundance of mythological scenes and figures reminds us of the sanctuary of the temple of Darius described earlier in this chapter. This naos was dedicated to

Figure 48. Sandstone sphinx with the head of Nectanebo I in the avenue of sphinxes leading to the temple of Luxor. Photo by the author.

Sopdu, and it constitutes an essential source for the study of the role of this god in Egyptian religion.

A beautiful black granite stela from the first regnal year of Nectanebo I bears a hieroglyphic text informing us of his coronation and his donations to the temple of the goddess Neith at Sais. The goddess was to receive a tenth of all the income from tariffs and from taxes imposed on the production of artisans. In the upper portion of the stela, the ruler is depicted offering a large necklace to the goddess.

While we may suspect artistic influence from the period of the Saite rulers of Dynasty 26 on the statues and reliefs of this period, some of the likenesses of Nectanebo I from the delta surprise us with the originality of their treatment of the ruler's physiognomy. The features of the king in the reliefs on basalt slabs now in Bologna and London are practically a caricature. The large, pointed nose and the double chin are the dominating features of the full face. A tight-fitting cap reminiscent of the "Kushite" headgear adorns the head, with its clearly noticeable dolichocephaly. Or are we to view these portraits as imitations of Dynasty 26 originals, such as the naturalistic portraits of Psammetichus I and Psammetichus II? Doubtless, though, these representations resemble the actual features of the last pharaohs more closely than the much more numerous depictions in the classical style.

Nectanebo II in every way equaled his like-named predecessor in the honor he displayed toward the deities of Egypt. Was this a symptom of increasing piety in a time of political uncertainty, or was it need for self-promotion employing the most effective means of propaganda, which at that time was theology? It is difficult today to supply an answer to this question.

However that may be, the preserved monuments bearing his name would suggest, at least, that the last pharaoh was one of the most religious rulers of Egypt. He erected and renovated temples nearly everywhere, and their priesthoods received donations even larger than those made by Nectanebo I. In the Memphite cemetery, he added relief decoration to the eastern and western Apis temples that bordered the dromos leading to the Serapeum.

He also did not neglect Buchis, the sacred bull worshiped in Upper Egypt. From the beginning of Dynasty 30 on, the bulls bearing this name were buried at Hermonthis, about twelve miles south of Thebes, in a tomb similar to the Serapeum. Now known as Armant, the site was regarded as the "southern Heliopolis" in antiquity. It is scant wonder, then, that the necropolis of the Buchis bulls was called the Bucheum, or "House of Atum." Buchis was believed to be the incarnation of the warrior god Montu, and burials in the Bucheum continued until the time of Diocletian (284–305 C.E.).

[171]

In the Bucheum, the name of Nectanebo II appears not only on stone blocks from a temple dedicated by this last of the pharaohs but also on a stela from his third regnal year containing information about the birth, enthronement, and death of a Buchis bull and on an elegant green faience vase now in the Egyptian Museum in Cairo. There are many traces of Nectanebo II's building activity in the delta at Heliopólis, Athribis, Bubastis, and other sites. From Bubastis, we have a fragment of a red granite naos representing the king kneeling before a deity to whom he is offering a figurine of the goddess Maat. Here, the king wears the *khepresh-*crown, the blue crown symbolizing victory (Figure 49).

But the most magnificent structures of this dynasty were erected at Sebennytos, the hometown of the last pharaohs. Located in the northern delta, this city now attained the status of one of the most important centers of culture and religion, one that it continued to retain in the Ptolemaic Period. A monumental temple was erected of huge blocks of red, black, and

Figure 49. Nectanebo II offering a figurine of the goddess Maat to a deity. Fragment of a red granite naos from Bubastis. Egyptian Museum, Cairo. Photo by Andrzej Bodytko, Polish Center of Mediterranean Archaeology, Warsaw University.

[172]

gray granite and diorite, and it would be enlarged and further decorated by the Ptolemies. A large number of its reliefs are now in museums in Europe and America.

At Behbeit el-Hagar (Figure 50), the modern name of the site, a heap of ashlars bearing the remains of reliefs of the Ptolemaic Period lies in the midst of cultivated fields not far from an Arab town. Luxuriantly growing grass creates a natural ambience of past greatness, and the holes between the blocks are home to snakes. Absolute quiet prevails around the ruins. Is the rest only silence? This question has yet to be answered by archaeologists.

In antiquity, the city teemed with dignitaries, artisans, and travelers from everywhere in the civilized world. The temple of Isis loomed over the other buildings of Sebennytos, though the most important deity worshiped there was the god Onuris, a hunter and warrior whom the Greeks identified with Ares. The Egyptians mostly combined him into a syncretistic unity with Shu, god of the air. In the Heliopolitan Ennead, Shu and Tefnut were the first divine couple of the group of nine deities, and they were spat out by the primeval god Atum after he swallowed his own semen.

It was to this Onuris-Shu that Nectanebo II dedicated an impressive diorite naos, a fragment of which was found in one of the temples of ancient Sebennytos and can now be admired in the Egyptian Museum in Cairo. The king, of course with the crown of victory on his head, is depicted here holding two spherical vessels containing an offering of wine for the god. Onuris is seated on a throne, his head decorated with a four-feathered crown whose height is greater than that of the god's entire torso. A cat-headed goddess stands behind him; she is Bastet, who reigned in nearby Bubastis.

The reliefs decorating the temples at Sebennytos were the work of the finest Egyptian artists, who had perhaps been brought there from the most inspired sculptors' workshops throughout the delta. During the reign of Nectanebo II, they worked out a specific style that would leave a distinctive mark on the relief sculpture of the Ptolemaic Period. We find its reflection in the decoration of the greatest temples of that period and even in some of the sacred constructions of the Roman Period that were erected during the first centuries of our own era.

This style is connected with the aesthetic canon of Dynasty 26 of Sais, as is especially evident in the shape of the face, with its full cheeks and double chin, while a cheerful expression is stressed by the smiling mouth with up-turned corners. We can immediately recognize these likenesses by the specific manner in which the eyes are modeled: the almond-shaped eyeball is accompanied by a geometric treatment of the carved lines that serve to stress the eyebrows and to lengthen the eyelid with a cosmetic stripe. Carved only a few decades later, the reliefs depicting Alexander the Great,

Figure 50. Head of Hathor atop a hieroglyph for "gold," along with a uraeus-serpent wearing the crown of Upper Egypt. Fragment of a granite block at Behbeit el-Hagar near Sebennytos. Photo by the author.

Philip Arrhidaeus, and even the early Ptolemies emulate this model with almost no change.

Still, this was a period when great importance was accorded to the question of style. This is shown at the very least by the many changes and retouchings carried out on reliefs of the pharaonic era in the time of Alexander the Great and his successors. Alexander, for instance, did not just content himself with erecting a sanctuary of his own in the innermost part of the temple of Amenophis III at Luxor (Figure 51), but he also had the re-

Figure 51. The god Montu extends the sign of life to Alexander the Great as he conducts the king to Amun-Re. Relief in the sanctuary of Alexander the Great at Luxor. Photo by Zbigniew Doliński, Polish Center of Mediterranean Archaeology, Cairo.

[175]

liefs decorating one of the chapels in Tuthmosis III's jubilee temple at Karnak reworked. This "cosmetic" sculptural intervention retained the original scenes, of course, but the style was changed, endowing the figures and the hieroglyphs with more rounded forms. On this occasion, the names of Tuthmosis were hacked out and replaced with those of Alexander—though not everywhere, of course, for Alexander's people were not barbarians. On the front wall of this room and in certain scenes decorating its interior, the name of the great pharaoh was retained. This entire activity must have been confidently deemed a "restoration" of the neglected sanctuary. Alexander's people possessed a sufficient sense of history, or rather political cunning, and his Egyptian sculptors sufficient experience, to know how to carry on propaganda, so that the wolf was sated while the sheep remained safe.

Later, one of the Ptolemies altered the reliefs of Ramesses II in an especially prestigious location, the entrance of the Second Pylon at Karnak. The scenes carved in this much visited place had special propagandistic meaning. Ramesses II's sunk relief was now altered into raised relief, and the name of the Dynasty 19 pharaoh was replaced with that of Ptolemy VI. Only here and there does a tiny cartouche of the great Ramesses, left in its sunk relief, recall who had actually donated this magnificent decoration. Stylistic retouchings in the service of politics—not for the first time and not for the last.

In the reign of Nectanebo II, preoccupation with style went hand in hand with an excessive sense of self-interest. This ruler's donations to the gods and goddesses were not made out of sheer altruism. The art from his reign bears witness to a feverish search for a religious legitimation of his authority. He was not the first usurper to sit on the Egyptian throne, and he was no less inclined to employ the devices of artistic expression to affirm the legality of his rule.

Many rulers of earlier periods had already been represented in the shadow of animals who incarnated great deities. There are statues of a small pharaoh under the head of a huge Hathor cow or protected by a gigantic cobra whose hood is inflated behind the king's body as it rests its head on his crown. The artists of the last ruler of this dynasty took advantage of these precedents, and they produced similar small statues depicting Nectanebo II as a diminutive figure standing between the feet of a much larger falcon. This animal, which embodied Horus, the progenitor of the pharaohs, was the ultimate guarantor of their authority. The most beautiful and best preserved of these statues, made of a gray stone, is in the collection of the Metropolitan Museum of Art in New York City (Figure 52). It stems from Heliopolis, a religious center where pharaonic authority received the confirmation of the solar creator god.

The Second Persian Occupation

But the protection of Horus and the other deities was of little help to the final ruler of Dynasty 30. The ambition of this political upstart, so patent everywhere, might have enabled him to endow Egypt with a period of cultural ascendancy and to lead Egyptian civilization down rather different paths of further development, had the Persians not foiled his plans. Artaxerxes III Ochus occupied the land of the pharaohs in 343 B.C.E. This conqueror has a terrible reputation in the works of the Greek historians, and he is even accorded the sobriquet "donkey." He is supposed to have killed the sacred ram worshiped in Mendes. This was a crime of the highest order, like the murder of the Apis bull by Cambyses. It seems that when Greek tradition wished to paint

Figure 52. Nectanebo II protected by the Horus falcon. Statue from Heliopolis. Graywacke. Metropolitan Museum of Art, New York. Photo by the author.

the enemy as the worst possible barbarian, it accused him of having murdered one of the sacred animals of Egypt.

The second Persian rule over Egypt lasted little more than ten years. Coinage spread through the land of the Nile under the satrap Pherendates, and certain products of the local mints were imitations of Attic coins with the addition of a Demotic inscription. Unlike the rulers of Dynasty 27, the Persian kings of this decade had no concern to join in the flow of Egyptian life; instead, they treated the land rather harshly. Bagoas, who poisoned Artaxerxes and placed the latter's son Arses (338–336 B.C.E.) on the Persian throne, was evidently an Egyptian. In Egypt, there was an uprising under the leadership of Chababash, a delta prince with whose help Nectanebo II made a vain attempt to regain his throne. Chababash held out at Memphis for a time, but he was unable to shake off the foreign rule permanently.

[177]

ALEXANDER'S CONQUEST

It was Alexander the Great who played the role of liberator, defeating Darius III Codomanus (336–332 B.C.E.) in the battle of Issus in 333 B.C.E. and crossing the border of Egypt near Pelusium on the Sinai peninsula in December 332 B.C.E. Days later, he stood at the gates of Memphis, where the new satrap Masaces surrendered the land without a fight. Alexander the Great became Lord of the Two Lands. Proceeding northwest along the western branch of the Nile, he reached the Mediterranean, where he founded a city, later named Alexandria after him, at the site of the village of Rhakotis.

The campaign continued west along the seacoast, via Paraetonium (Marsa Matruh), and to Siwa Oasis, where the age-old oracle of Amun was supposed to decide the further destiny of the Macedonian king. As could easily be expected, the oracle confirmed that Alexander was the god's son and thus had the right to rule the entire world. Nothing remained but to appoint a governor to administer Egypt before continuing to conquer the earth. The finances of the land were entrusted to Cleomenes of Naukratis, and in the spring of 331 B.C.E., Alexander moved on to the Euphrates. Eight years later, he returned to Egypt in a coffin. Ptolemy I placed his body in a splendid mausoleum built especially for him in the middle of Alexandria; to this day, no trace of the structure has been found.

After Alexander's death, his somewhat feebleminded stepbrother Philip Arrhidaeus (323–317 B.C.E.) was proclaimed king by the Macedonian army. Philip never made an appearance in Egypt, though a splendid granite barque chapel was erected on his behalf at Thebes, in the temple of Amun-Re at Karnak. This chapel is preserved in excellent condition, perhaps confirming the paradox that the less important a king was, the better known his works are. Its walls are decorated with vivid reliefs depicting Philip as pharaoh, and ironically enough, there is even a cycle of scenes illustrating the individual episodes of his coronation.

The style of these reliefs shows them to be faithful copies of the models worked out by the artists of Sebennytos during Dynasty 30. Or were they perhaps the very sculptors who had worked for Nectanebo II in the north of the land only twenty years earlier? Though they might have been only apprentices at that time, the artists working for Philip reproduced well-known themes without troubling themselves about historical authenticity in depicting the physiognomy of the king.

While Philip Arrhidaeus is designated Lord of the Two Lands in the inscriptions carved on the walls of this chapel, the situation underwent a complete reversal. He did not rule over the Two Lands, but rather, Egypt became a "land with two lords," both of them absent. The other person named king was the son of Alexander and Roxane, who was born after the

[178]

death of his father. He, too, never visited Egypt, though on the island of Elephantine, at the very south of the land, a monumental gateway was erected for him; its reliefs, which depict him as pharaoh, are inscribed with his name. Like his father, he bore the name Alexander, and he is designated Alexander IV in modern history books.

Did this messy situation have much influence on the broader destiny of Egypt? It did not, of course, for the land was in any case controlled by someone else entirely. First there was Perdiccas, then Antipater from 321 B.C.E. on, and then, beginning in 319 B.C.E., Polyperchon. Cassander, son of Antipater, allied himself with Philip Arrhidaeus against the last-named regent and against Olympias, the mother of Alexander the Great. They were defeated, however, and Philip fell into the hands of Olympias, who had him killed. After that, Alexander IV was sole monarch, though he enjoyed full authority for no more than a year. In 316 B.C.E., he became dependent on Cassander, who had him and his mother done away with five years later.

THE PTOLEMAIC DYNASTY

In Egypt, years continued to be dated to the reign of this no longer living king until 305 B.C.E., when Ptolemy I Soter had himself proclaimed king. The latter was a son of Lagos, and it is for this reason that the Ptolemaic dynasty that ruled Egypt until 30 B.C.E. is sometimes called the Lagide dynasty. After the death of Alexander the Great, Ptolemy was at first the satrap of Egypt. He had himself proclaimed king in order to resist attempts to revive Alexander's empire, so that he might rule an independent land.

He achieved this goal, and the twelve successive Ptolemies were Greek "pharaohs" of Egypt. While the reliefs decorating the walls of the many temples erected during their reigns depict these rulers in the garb of a pharaoh, they resided in Alexandria, where they dressed in Greek clothing and spoke the Greek language.

Their attitude toward the culture of pharaonic Egypt, however, was filled with respect. They acknowledged the age-old gods and goddesses, and they erected monumental temples to them, many of which remain well preserved to our own day. One cannot visit Egypt today without seeing the Ptolemaic temple of Horus at Edfu, or that of Hathor at Dendara, or the temple complex dedicated to the goddess Isis on the island of Philae, not far from Aswan (Plate VII, Figures 53 and 54). Paradoxically, these are sometimes our only sources for many important aspects of ancient Egyptian religion. This is especially true of cult ritual, for their reliefs contain many texts and scenes not to be found in older temples, though it is in the

[179]

Figure 53. Philae. Colonnade reconstructed on the island of Agilkia. Photo by the author.

latter that we must actually seek the models used by the theologians and artists of the Graeco-Roman Period.

During the third century B.C.E., Alexandria developed into the leading metropolis of the Hellenistic world, a status it would maintain for centuries. But the new capital functioned as it were *ad Aegyptum*, "next to Egypt," and it remained in principle a center of Greek culture, notwithstanding the fact that it was also adorned with ancient Egyptian monuments brought there from various cities in the delta, such as Heliopolis, Memphis, Sais, and Bubastis. This presence of pharaonic civilization in the city was only symbolic, however, and we can qualify it as Egyptomania rather than Egyptophilia, for it entailed no meaningful knowledge of Egypt.

Traditional Egyptian culture continued to develop in the great cult centers of the age-old deities. The Ptolemies supported the Egyptian priesthoods, and many texts speak of generous donations of land and the according of privileges to deities and to their temples and servants. The coronation of certain Ptolemies—so Ptolemy V and probably also Ptolemy II—was carried out according to ancient Egyptian ritual in the temple of Ptah at Memphis. The annual priestly synods convened in various cities were occasions for practical dialogue between the Alexandrian court and

[180]

Figure 54. Columns in the form of a Hathor sistrum. Small Hathor chapel on the roof of the temple of Dendara. Photo by the author.

the intellectual elite of Egypt. In return for their generosity, the Ptolemies received various titles and honors that sanctioned their rule over the Egyptian people.

The decrees proclaimed by the priestly synods were recorded on stone stelae, usually in several copies set up in various temples throughout the land. Since these were multilingual documents written in at least two different scripts, they played an important role in the decipherment of the hieroglyphs in modern times. The most famous of these is the Rosetta Stone, which contains Egyptian-language inscriptions in the hieroglyphic and Demotic writing systems and an inscription in the Greek language and alphabet. These inscriptions record the decisions made by the synod at Memphis on March 27, 196 B.C.E., during the reign of Ptolemy V Epiphanes.

Two other decrees from the reign of this king are preserved, inscribed on the wall of one of the temples on the island of Philae. Both are written in hieroglyphs and Demotic. Another well-known document of this sort is the so-called Canopus Decree, which is earlier in date, for it was composed by the priests who gathered at Canopus in the ninth regnal year of Ptolemy III

[181]

Euergetes, that is, in 238 B.C.E. Two complete and three fragmentary copies of this document are preserved to us. Like that of the Rosetta Stone, its text is recorded in three writing systems.

Two great religious centers of this period merit special interest. Isis, a goddess who would soon have an international career, was worshiped in both of them. One of them is the aforementioned Sebennytos (modern Behbeit el-Hagar, Plate VIIIa) in the north of the land, already a center of religion and culture in Dynasty 30. Here, the Ptolemies enlarged the temple complex founded by Nectanebo I and II.

Manetho, the famous priest to whom we owe a genuine history of pharaonic Egypt, was active in this very city in the reigns of Ptolemy I and II. Unfortunately, his work is known exclusively from later copies containing only a portion of the content of the original. Nevertheless, his division of Egyptian history into dynasties, which is also confirmed by ancient Egyptian sources, serves as our basis for chronology to this very day. It is also thought that Manetho was one of the creators of the cult of Sarapis, the Hellenized form of the Egyptian god Osiris-Apis. The cult of Sarapis played an important role in the cultural rapprochement of Egyptians and Greeks throughout Egypt, after which it spread far beyond the borders of Egypt.

The other important center of the cult of Isis was Philae, an island in the Nile located at the southern boundary of Egypt. In the Graeco-Roman Period, the modest building dedicated there by Nectanebo I was joined by majestic temples and porticos among which crowds of pilgrims from all over the civilized world bustled. Culturally and linguistically, it must have been a veritable Babel. Adherents of Isis came here even from distant Meroe to the south of Egypt. As heirs to the Kushite state, the Meroites developed a culture whose roots were Egyptian but which displayed many African features, as can best be discerned in the reliefs of their temples (Figure 55). Their language, written with an alphabet derived from the Egyptian hieroglyphs, continues to puzzle philologists.

In our own time, the temple complex of Philae experienced an unexpected journey in connection with the construction of the High Dam at Aswan and the creation of the huge artificial lake south of the island. To save the priceless architectural and artistic monuments from damage by the waters of the lake, UNESCO organized an international rescue campaign aimed at dismantling all the preserved buildings and moving them 875 yards to the island of Agilkia. This effort took eight years, from 1972 to 1980. Rebuilt according to their original layout, the temples of Philae are today one of Egypt's greatest tourist attractions.

These two centers of the Isis cult, one in the north of the land and one in the south, were like religious brackets around the pharaonic land ruled by the Greeks and then by the Romans. We may view them as a symbol of the special task now fulfilled by the deities of Egypt. Identified with Greek

[182]

gods and goddesses, they served to bring the Egyptians and the Greeks closer together. These divine personages were the bearers of a syncretistic culture that included the Two Lands and prepared to conquer the Hellenized world. No lesser figures than Isis, Sarapis, and Harpokrates were now the true Lords of the Two Lands, the spiritual representatives of ancient Egyptian civilization in the world of classical culture.

The twin-track nature of Egyptian culture in the last centuries B.C.E. found its expression not only in sacral but also in sepulchral art, which of course also displayed a largely sacral character.

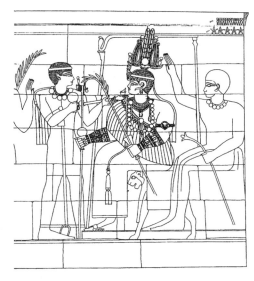

Figure 55. Enthroned queen from Meroe. Relief from pyramid N 6.

An especially well-known example of Egyptohellenic eclecticism from the end of the fourth century B.C.E. is a chapel that served as the tomb of Petosiris, one of the most important Egyptian dignitaries of the period. His Greek name is a Hellenized version of the Egyptian Pa-di-Usir, which means "gift of Osiris." Petosiris was the high priest of the god Thoth at Hermopolis, and his beautiful tomb is located in the necropolis—today called Tuna el-Gebel—of that ancient city (Plate VIIIb). From the biographical inscription carved on the walls of the tomb, we learn that one contribution of the deceased had been the restoration of temples and cults in times of political confusion. This information leads us to date the tomb to the period of transition from the Persians to the Greeks.

Such a date is confirmed by the iconography and the style of the scenes that accompany these texts. While their themes are connected to the decoration of the monuments of the pharaonic period, the artistic concept is Greek, an impression that is in no way diminished by the fact that the scenes are accompanied by hieroglyphic texts. Though the bodies of the Egyptians are depicted here according to the rigid rules of the Egyptian relief canon, the peasants and artisans for the most part wear Greek tunics. The representation of the naked bodies of the men working in the vineyard seems to be a faithful copy of many of the figures known to us from Greek vase painting.

The scenes of daily life are rich in details that do not appear in Egyptian reliefs but are characteristic of the Greek depiction of the environment. In the procession of traditionally depicted men making typical Egyptian offerings, we suddenly notice a boy sitting on his father's arms and nestling his head against him, while another child in its mother's arms turns backward with interest toward the birds being carried by the next person. These details betray an attitude toward surrounding reality on the part of the artist that is no longer wholly Egyptian but rather more personal and open. A new aesthetic makes its appearance here, one whose preference for natural modeling breaks with the earlier canon of the representation of the human figure.

Fresh spirit shines forth even from the religious scene depicting the birth of Osiris-Khepri as a scarab with the feather-crown on its head, protected by the wings of the goddesses Wadjet and Nekhbet, who symbolize Lower and Upper Egypt. Some Egyptologists are even of the opinion that this scene already illustrates an *interpretatio graeca* of the Egyptian myth. The scenes we see in the tomb chapel of Petosiris leave no doubt whatsoever that the deities of Egypt had now become the common property of Egyptians and Greeks and thus embodiments of the Lords of the Two Lands.

The Divine "Lords of the Two Lands": The Last Thousand Years of Pharaonic Egypt; Polish Archaeology on the Nile

Where is the tomb of Alexander the Great? This question arouses the curiosity of millions and continues to inspire archaeological excavations at various places in Egypt. Sensational news concerning each alleged discovery of the tomb, however, always proves wrong. Such was the case in 1995 with a hypogeum unearthed in Siwa Oasis and interpreted as the tomb of the great Macedonian. Alexander did in fact visit the famous oracle of Zeus-Ammon located in that oasis in 332 B.C.E., where the local priests recognized him as a "son" of this god. But even if the great conqueror had expressed a wish to be buried there, it seems almost unthinkable that the king-god who liberated Egypt from the Persian yoke would have been interred anywhere other than in a royal necropolis, and the ancient sources do not indicate otherwise. According to the ancient writers, his corpse was first buried at Memphis, the capital of pharaonic Egypt, and then was transferred to Alexandria, where a magnificent mausoleum was built for him. This monument became the nucleus of a royal necropolis in which the Ptolemies, Egyptian rulers of Macedonian blood, subsequently had their tombs as well. No one knows how long the holy corpse rested in the ancient cemetery of the pharaohs. The locations of both the Memphite and the Alexandrian sepulchre remain unknown.

Unfortunately, there is not much chance of discovering the tomb of the great Macedonian in Alexandria. The ancient buildings of the splendid city founded by Alexander and developed by the Ptolemies served for centuries as a stone quarry and eventually disappeared under the modern town. Only a few places are still left for archaeological investigation. One of them is Kom el-Dik in the very center of modern Alexandria, where remains of monumental architecture dating from the Ptolemaic Period, lying deep under constructions of Roman and Byzantine Periods, have recently been discovered by the Polish archaeological mission exploring this site.

Archaeological strata containing remains of Ptolemaic Alexandria today lie under water, the level of which has risen since ancient times as a result of geological and tectonic changes that have occurred during the last two millennia. French archaeologists have discovered remains of the ancient royal quarter at the bottom of the bay near the modern seashore of the city. One of the submerged buildings is believed to be the palace of the famous queen Cleopatra VII. But the royal necropolis that developed around the tomb of Alexander the Great thus far remains undiscovered.

There might be a greater chance of identifying the location of his first sepulchre. As king and god, Alexander was certainly buried in the royal necropolis of Memphis and not in the city itself. But where? The field of pyramids and mastabas, that is, the Memphite cemetery extending on a high rocky plateau westward from the city, is enormous. A diagnostic monument may, however, be found at Saqqara, in the oldest part of the gigantic necropolis. It was here that pharaohs and noblemen found their eternal rest at the dawn of Egyptian history. The oldest pyramid in the world, built here by the famous architect Imhotep for king Djoser (ca. 2650 B.C.E.), still stands today.

Admiring this earliest achievement of monumental stone architecture, tourists seldom notice a much smaller construction found near the road leading from Djoser's pyramid to the Serapeum, the subterranean gallery of the mummified, sacred Apis bulls. Unearthed in the mid-nineteenth century, this construction, called the "Ptolemaic *exedra*," has the shape of a hemicycle, a semicircular podium on which more than ten large stone statues are displayed. What surprises the keen observer is that the statues do not represent Egyptian gods, kings, or other celebrities of pharaonic times but rather some of the greatest Greek poets and philosophers. Archaeologists easily recognize Pindar, Hesiod, Homer, Protagoras, Thales, and Plato among them. Other statues represent the Greek god Dionysus riding various animals, such as the lion, panther, peacock, and griffin.

What are such figures doing here? Some of the statues in this group, such as those of sirens and sphinxes, point to a funerary connotation of the monument. This showcase of Greek civilization, with its Dionysiac and mortuary accents, set between royal pyramids and hypogea of sacred bulls, makes sense only if we connect it with the tomb of an exceptionally important personality of Greek origin. Considering the most plausible date of the "Ptolemaic *exedra*," the third century B.C.E., we can propose only one candidate: Alexander the Great.

It would be difficult to imagine a better place for the tomb of the divinized king who liberated Egypt from the Persians. It was here that the last indigeneous pharaohs, Nectanebo I and Nectanebo II of Dynasty 30, built a long paved road leading from the edge of the rocky plateau to the Serapeum and decorated it with sphinxes and temples. The *exedra* added to this complex at the beginning of the Ptolemaic Period seems to have adorned or commemorated the first tomb of Alexander, from which the corpse, the holiest relic of the Ptolemies, was eventually transferred to Alexandria.

A possible confirmation of this hypothesis seems to result from recent Polish-Egyptian excavations on the western side of the pyramid of Djoser (Plate IX), some hundreds of yards south of the mysterious *exedra*. Here, in 1997, the archaeologists discovered the tomb of an important, although heretofore unknown, nobleman of the late Old Kingdom, the rock-hewn mastaba of vizier Meref-nebef; the reliefs and paintings decorating its funerary chapel remain unparalleled. But as surprising as the existence of the mastaba at this place was the content of the thick layer of sand that accumulated during the centuries over the Old Kingdom necropolis. The upper stratum of our excavations turned out to be a necropolis of the Ptolemaic and Roman Periods. Mummies and skeletons lying on mats or directly in the sand, as well as wooden and ceramic coffins containing beautifully painted cartonnage mummy wrappings (Plate Xa), appeared one after another, sometimes almost directly under the surface and sometimes inserted into holes inside or underneath ancient mud brick walls. Some of the bodies are surrounded by reused bricks or stones that originally belonged to much earlier tombs, and some are covered by partly destroyed "false doors" from tombs of the Old Kingdom. An intact cartonnage of a young girl (Plates Xb and XI) has a gilded face, the jaw of which is framed by a winged solar disk. It was found lying inside an anthropoidal cavity hewn in the rocky platform that constitutes the court of the vizier's tomb.

But the most unusual thing about this discovery is that there are no traces of any human activity at this place during the long period extending from the Old Kingdom to the Ptolemaic Period. Unlike other parts of Saqqara, where subsequent periods of Egyptian history had left some traces, most frequently new burials disturbing the integrity of earlier tombs, this place had remained intact for almost two thousand years. Why did it suddenly become fashionable again shortly after the death of Alexander the Great? If the corpse of the king-god was ever buried in this area, even for a brief period, the amazing "resurrection" of this part of the Memphite necropolis would be a natural consequence. The west of the royal cemetery at Saqqara, extending between the "Ptolemaic *exedra*" in the north and the tomb of Meref-nebef in the south, may still prove to be a theater of sensational discoveries.

The Ptolemaic dynasty ruled Egypt until 30 B.C.E., when the famous Cleopatra VII took her own life with the bite of an asp. Daughter of Ptolemy XII and Cleopatra V, she had been queen of Egypt since 51 B.C.E., and she had held the title Queen of Kings since 34 B.C.E. Egypt became a province of Rome and remained one for three centuries.

But this was not the Romans' first encounter with the culture of the land of the pharaohs. The cult of Isis had already been introduced in Rome at the beginning of the first century B.C.E. Mentions of the first "college" of her adherents date back to the time of Sulla, about 80 B.C.E. A temple was built to the goddess on the Capitoline Hill, the most prestigious of locations. Though the Senate immediately ordered it torn down, unknown hands quickly built it anew. The temple was destroyed again on several occasions, in 58, 53, 50, and 48 B.C.E.

The persistence of Isis's devotees in repeatedly rebuilding her temple demonstrates how deeply rooted the cult of the Egyptian goddess had already become at Rome. Though Caesar had forbidden the Collegia Isiaca to enter Rome, the triumvirate allowed the construction of a common sanctuary for the deities of Egypt as early as 43 B.C.E.; this was probably the Iseum Campense on the Campus Martius, which would become the center of the Egyptian cults in Rome.

In the reign of Tiberius, c. 19 C.E., a scandal resulted in the destruction of the temple, and its statues were cast into the Tiber. It was not rebuilt until the reign of Caligula, around 40 C.E. Under Titus, in 80 C.E., this temple to the Egyptian deities fell victim to a conflagration, but it was restored by Domitian (81–96 C.E.) just a few years later. Alexander Severus (222–35 C.E.) embellished the entire complex of temples and outbuildings, which covered an area of 220 by 76 yards.

There were other temples to Egyptian deities at Rome. Smaller Isea (as they were called) dedicated to the goddess Isis were erected at three other locations in the city. In yet another temple, the Egyptian goddess was worshiped together with Sarapis, and in the reign of Caracalla (211–17 C.E.), a Serapeum was erected, a splendid construction that was later dismantled by Justinian (527–65 C.E.).

To decorate their city, the emperors of Rome imported many statues, obelisks, and reliefs that had been created in pharaonic times. Works in Egyptian and Egyptianizing style were also executed at Rome itself. Egyptomania reached its zenith in the reign of Hadrian, whose favorite, Antinous, drowned in the Nile, evidently in the region of the later Antinoopolis.

Emperors visited Egypt not just to suppress local revolts or to make a proverbial *acte de présence* but also for purposes of tourism. The famed Colossi of Memnon on the west bank of Thebes were one of their favorite destinations. In Roman times, one of these huge statues of Amenophis III was believed to be the image of Memnon, the mythic son of Eos, goddess of the dawn, who was believed to have been killed by Achilles during the Trojan War. In 27 C.E., an earthquake evidently caused the statue to crack. At night, the cracks filled with moisture, which in conjunction with the rising sun would cause them to emit a sound that visitors interpreted as Memnon's groans.

Notwithstanding their sentimentality and their snobbish interest in things Egyptian, the Romans unscrupulously plundered the land of the pharaohs, imposing burdensome taxes on the local population. In the temples they built in Egypt, the emperors had themselves depicted as pharaohs decked out with all the classical attributes of their authority. Of the reliefs preserved to us from this period, the scenes carved on the intercolumnia of the mammisi (birth house) at Dendara are among the loveliest. This temple of the god Horus was built immediately adjacent to the temple of the goddess Hathor in the reign of the emperor Augustus. The decoration of the intercolumnia, which is more than a hundred years later than the building itself, depicts the emperor Trajan as pharaoh, offering to Isis as she nurses the child Horus. The youthful god Ihy is seated behind the divine mother.

The cosmopolitan city of Alexandria served as a conduit of Graeco-Egyptian culture to the entire civilized world. But the most effective intermediaries were deities, especially Isis, Sarapis, Anubis, Harpokrates, Osiris, and Apis. Sanctuaries dedicated to them, along with various cult objects, have been found everywhere the Roman army penetrated, from Spain to the borders of Mesopotamia and from the northern coast of Africa to the middle of England. The investigation of these cults is today an area of specialized research that has already seen the publication of a large number of Egyptological studies. While the Romans were spreading the cults of these ancient deities, a threat to the latter appeared in Egypt itself: Christianity. After the Roman Empire was split into an eastern and a western portion in 323 C.E., Egypt found itself in the Byzantine sphere of influence, where Christianity became the official religion. The patriarchs of Alexandria, successors to the evangelist Mark (40–63 C.E.), who had founded a Christian community in that city, now played a leading role—including a political one—in the land of the Nile.

The worship of the ancient deities of Egypt was forbidden by an edict of the emperor Theodosius I in 392 C.E. Nevertheless, the cult center of Isis on the island of Philae continued to function for yet another century. In 451/452 C.E., when the Byzantine general Maximius concluded a treaty with the Blemmyes and the Nobatae, the southern neighbors of Egypt, he was obliged to guarantee them free access to the temple of Isis and even to agree to their "borrowing" the statue of this goddess from time to time for the performing of oracles in Nubia. The final blow to the faithful and their steadfast priests occurred in the years 535–37 C.E., when Justinian compelled the closing of the temples of Philae. Shortly thereafter, four churches were founded in the precinct of the temple of Isis.

But Christianity could not extirpate the cultural and religious heritage of millennia past. In the early centuries of the present era, Christian thought, and even more so art, made use of achievements of the eclectic ancient culture, in which Egyptian elements were mixed with foreign ones, mostly Greek and Jewish. At Alexandria and in other Egyptian cities as well, outstanding personalities of various nationalities and religions continued to thrive and create.

The binding element was their common tongue, Greek, the language of the intellectual elite and of the administration, although the latter also made use of the Demotic language and script, especially in the provinces. This language was the penultimate stage in the evolution of ancient Egyptian, while the Demotic script had developed from hieratic. Undergoing still further development during the first centuries of our own era, the Demotic language evolved into Coptic, whose written form was to serve the needs of Christian Egyptians, known as Copts. For practical reasons, this language was written using the Greek alphabet, with the addition of a few characters to indicate sounds not found in Greek. The designation of the Copts and their language stems from the Greek word *Aigyptioi*, which is the Hellenized form of the ancient Egyptian name of the chief temple of Memphis, *Hut-ka-Ptah*, "*ka*-house (= temple) of Ptah."

In Egypt, the Byzantine era lasted a little more than three centuries (323–641 C.E.), and it ended with the conquest of the land by the troops of the caliph Omar under the command of Amr Ibn el-As. From that time until today, Islam has been the predominant religion of Egypt.

During the period when it was dependent on Byzantium, Egypt was politically, militarily, and economically weak. Religious life, in contrast, thrived. Ancient temples were turned into churches, and of course, new sacred buildings were erected. For fear of persecution or to facilitate deeper contemplation, many Christians chose a hermit's life, in the process popularizing the new faith outside the Nile valley. In the desert, monasteries were founded, and modest dwellings were excavated in the rock cliffs; rock-cut tombs of earlier periods were also adapted to the latter purpose. The lives of the cenobites and the eremites contrasted with the lifestyle of the church hierarchy, which sometimes led to conflict and schism.

After the Arab conquest, Christianity continued to develop unhindered to the south of Egypt, in Nubia. The population of northern Sudan was almost entirely Christian down to the fourteenth century C.E. Notwithstanding various difficulties, the Copts have retained their religion in Egypt as well. The religious texts written in their language served, along with the multilingual texts of the Ptolemaic Period, as a starting point for the decipherment and study of the language of pharaonic Egypt.

The final millennium of ancient Egypt, comprising the Ptolemaic, Roman, and Byzantine Periods—that is, from the end of the fourth century B.C.E. to the early seventh century C.E.—is a highly interesting era. The native population, which used Demotic and later Coptic, lived in symbiosis with the ethnic Greek element, whose culture enriched the age-old civilization. The Greek language functioned on an equal basis with Egyptian, and the Greek alphabet, adapted for writing the native language, ended by serving the survival of the latter.

We find the same manifestations reflected in art. Egyptian and Greek elements were blended in the works of the sculptors and painters of the Graeco-Roman era, and they passed in this form into the repertoire of early Coptic art, which had no traditions of its own.

POLISH ARCHAEOLOGY IN EGYPT

This millennium of encounter between two great cultures is the foremost research specialty of Polish archaeologists in Egypt. I shall therefore conclude this discussion with a survey of their efforts and an account of my own excavations at Athribis.

An example of ancient Egyptian sacred architecture in which the pharaonic era meets the Graeco-Roman and Byzantine Periods is the temple of queen Hatshepsut at Deir el-Bahri on the west bank of Thebes. Located at the foot of a cliff-bound inlet, this age-old cult place of the goddess Hathor remained a destination of pilgrims in search of divine assistance down into the Roman Period. In the Ptolemaic Period, a portion of the temple was modified, and a small sanctuary was created to function in the dual capacity of sanatorium and oracle. In it were worshiped two important Egyptian saints, famed architects and sages who were also regarded as physicians equipped with magical powers.

The first of these was Imhotep, who built the first stone pyramid, the Step Pyramid of king Djoser of Dynasty 3 at Saqqara, at the outset of the Old Kingdom. The second lived a thousand years later. He came from Athribis in Lower Egypt, and at Thebes he served Amenophis III, one of the most famous rulers of Dynasty 18. His name was Amenhotpe son of Hapu. Among his accomplishments was the king's mortuary temple, of which the two statues later styled the Colossi of Memnon still remain.

In the Graeco-Roman Period, the first of these two men was identified with Asclepius, while the second received the name Amenothes and was thought to be the son of Apis. Both of them were thus considered gods, and

Ptolemy VIII Euergetes II dedicated the chapel at Deir el-Bahri, where they are represented in relief. The hieroglyphic texts and the scenes on the walls of this sanctuary were the object of study by Dr. Ewa Laskowska-Kusztal, who prepared an *editio princeps* of them. This specialist was subsequently invited to work on the decorated elements of the temple architecture of this period excavated by the German Archaeological Institute at Elephantine.

Notwithstanding the fragmentary state of their preservation, which did not lighten the burden of the epigrapher, these inscriptions proved to be quite interesting. From them, it appeared that Dr. Laskowska was on the trail of a House of Life, a structure that was of fundamental importance for the ritual renewal of the king's power, as we learned from the liturgical text discussed in the preceding chapter.

The inclusion of a Ptolemaic sanctuary in the temple of Hatshepsut entailed walling up one of the niches of the original construction. In 1982, this niche was excavated by the Polish-Egyptian archaeological mission in the course of the excavation and conservation work they were carrying out at Deir el-Bahri. Among the objects found in it was a coin of Ptolemy VI Philometor with a representation of a bearded Zeus-Ammon on the obverse and an eagle standing on a lightning bolt on the reverse.

On a wall of the niche is a Demotic text that was translated by Professor Edda Bresciani of the University of Pisa. Written in black ink on the white limestone wall, this text is the first known Demotic inscription from the first regnal year of Ptolemy I Soter, who—as we know—had been satrap of Egypt from the death of Alexander the Great until he had himself proclaimed king. It is also thus far the only Demotic text in which the name of Berenike I, the wife of this ruler, accompanies that of her husband. Other Demotic texts left behind by pilgrims on the walls of the temple of Hatshepsut form the subject of research by Professor Krzysztof Winnicki. The documentation and reading of the numerous Greek graffiti left by the faithful in the Ptolemaic and Roman Periods has been pursued by Dr. Adam Łajtar. Many of them contain interesting information concerning the customs of the pilgrims; they even lead us to conclude that pilgrims would spend the night in the temple, evidently in anticipation of a prophetic dream.

In the Byzantine Period, the temple of Hatshepsut was converted into a monastery, while many other temples became churches. The monastery of St. Phoibammon at Deir el-Bahri was studied by Professor Wlodzimierz Godlewski, who published his results in the form of a monograph.

In the Ptolemaic Period, and even earlier, Egyptian deities received Greek names. We may recall, for example, that the warlike goddess Neith, represented with a bow in her hand and especially revered at Sais, was identified with Athena. Aphrodite was an incarnation of Isis and Hathor. Certain Egyptian names were Hellenized; thus Osiris-Apis became Sarapis, and *Hor-pa-chered* ("Horus the Child") became Harpokrates. Festivals that entailed the drinking of wine and the lighting of torches and oil lamps were celebrated in their honor. The participants in these assemblages were obliged to bring or to pay for these necessary items. Indications of such contributions, written in Greek on sherds from large clay amphorae, were found in the Dynasty 19 mortuary temple of Sethos I on the west bank of Thebes by a team of excavators from the German Archaeological Institute in Cairo. These ostraca were deciphered by the eminent Polish papyrologist Professor Zbigniew Borkowski—who unfortunately died at an early age—and dated to the second century C.E., that is, to the Roman Period.

These scholars also worked on the Greek inscriptions of the Byzantine Period from the theater excavated by Polish archaeologists at Kom el-Dik in Alexandria. They bear interesting witness to the conflicts between groups with different beliefs on the soil of early Christian Alexandria.

The Polish excavations at Alexandria, which began in 1958 and have continued to the present day, were crowned by the discovery of two monumental constructions in the center of the Roman and Byzantine city, as well as residential areas from these periods. Professor Kazimierz Michalowski led the excavation of the above-mentioned theater, which served as an odeum, as well as of a complex of public baths. Both constructions experienced multiple renovations. Dr. Wojciech Kolataj, an engineer, was occupied for many years with reconstructing the baths and interpreting the individual phases of their use. He published his results in a fundamental monograph, and today he directs the work at Kom el-Dik.

Though the entire world eagerly anticipates that archaeologists concerned with ancient Alexandria will answer the question of where the tomb of Alexander the Great is located, there are grounds to doubt whether this curiosity will be satisfied. The modern city developed so rapidly during the nineteenth and twentieth centuries that archaeologists were unable to investigate all the remains of ancient structures. At Kom el-Dik, the site of the present-day Polish excavations, the water table seldom permits examination of strata deeper than those of the Roman Period. Another obstacle to such investigations is the preserved buildings of the Roman and Byzantine Periods, which would have to be dismantled to provide archaeologists access to the Ptolemaic levels. Perhaps the discovery of the tomb of Alexander the Great is reserved for future archaeologists with even more modern technology at their disposal than those of today.

Polish investigation of the last millennium of ancient Egypt has not been confined to the two above-mentioned sites. Remains of a town and its cemetery have been uncovered about six miles west of Alexandria, in the area of the Marina El-Alamein on the Mediterranean coast. Among those concerned with excavating and conserving the site are a group of specialists under the direction of Professor Andrzej W. Daszewski.

[193]

Yet another Polish mission is conducting very interesting excavations at the site of Naqlun in the Faiyum. An early Christian monastery, which was identified by Professor Ewa Wipszycka-Bravo with the help of an obscure Greek papyrus, proved to be the site of sensational discoveries just a few years ago. Next to a ruined building, archaeologists working under the direction of Professor Wlodzimierz Godlewski found an ancient rubbish pit that turned out to be an inexhaustible source of Greek, Coptic, and Arabic papyri, some of them in an excellent state of preservation. The greatest surprise to scholars was the discovery of fragments of a Latin literary text whose author could be identified. No less interesting was the discovery of a large number of hermits' caves hewn out of the rock by settlers in the vicinity of the monastery.

The stormy history of early Christianity in what is now northern Sudan has been a traditional area of study for the Polish school of archaeology. Professor Kazimierz Michalowski began these investigations more than thirty years ago with his sensational discoveries at Faras. The early Christian wall paintings that were found there and rescued from the flooding of Lake Nasser now enrich the collections of the Sudan National Museum in Khartoum and the National Museum in Warsaw. The many inscriptions in the Coptic, Greek, and Nubian languages shed new light on the history of Egypt's southern neighbor in Christian times.

The great international campaign organized by UNESCO at the end of the 1950s to save as much as possible of the archaeological sites in Nubia, which were to disappear under the waters of Lake Nasser, was an unprecedented archaeological project. In recognition of their tremendous efforts, many countries have received antiquities of unique value from both the Egyptian and the Sudanese governments. Among these there are even some temples, such as the temple of Dendur (Figure 56), now standing in the Metropolitan Museum of Art, New York, and the temple of Debod (Figure 57), which now graces the very center of Madrid.

Polish archaeological activity in Nubia did not end at Faras. For several years, an archaeological mission under the direction of Dr. Stefan Jakobielski has worked at Dongola, another important administrative and religious center in northern Sudan in the first millennium of the present era.

Burials from the Graeco-Roman and Early Christian Periods were found in an unusual archaeological context in the necropolis of Minshat Abu Omar, a site located in the eastern delta. Some years ago, the necropolis, which was discovered by Egyptologists from Munich under the leadership of Professor Dietrich Wildung, was the site of excavations in which Polish scholars participated actively. Professor Lech Kryzyżaniak of the Archeological Museum in Poznań was one of the directors of the fieldwork of this mission. The stratigraphic peculiarity of the cemetery at Minshat lies in the fact that at one and the same level, early dynastic graves of the third mil-

Figure 56. Temple of Dendur in Nubia, constructed for the cult of the deified brothers Peteese and Pahor during the reign of the emperor Augustus. Reconstructed in the Metropolitan Museum, New York, after the salvage campaign in Nubia. Photo by the author.

lennium B.C.E. occur side by side with burials of the final centuries of antiquity, that is, of the first centuries of our own era. The two types of graves, which serve as brackets enclosing the beginning and the end of antiquity in this area, are in an excellent state of preservation, making them an important archaeological source for our understanding of the history of the eastern delta.

ATHRIBIS

Among the sites under excavation by the Polish Center for Mediterranean Archaeology of Warsaw University, Tell Atrib (Plates XII and XIII) can be viewed as a genuine cross section of Egypt's history in the last millennium of antiquity. This site, which lies thirty miles north of Cairo and is today a suburb of the city of Benha, was the first site investigated by Polish archaeologists in Egypt following World War II. Professor Kazimierz Michalowski began the excavations in 1957. For many years, they were led by Dr. Barbara Ruszczyc in collaboration with the Coptic Committee in

Figure 57. Temple of Amun from Debod in Nubia. Ptolemaic or Roman Period. Reconstructed in Madrid after the salvage campaign in Nubia. Photo by the author.

Cairo. Salvage work was undertaken in 1985 under the direction of the author of this book, and it continues today with the participation of the Supreme Council of Antiquities. The goal of this work is to conduct a comprehensive investigation of the area around Kom Sidi Yusuf, which is slated for modern construction work in the foreseeable future. In this area, a residential quarter of the Ptolemaic Period lies side by side with ruins of the Roman city, with remains of the Byzantine settlement to either side of them. All three phases of late antiquity in Egypt thus make their appearance here.

The Arabic name Tell Atrib stems from Coptic Athrebi or Atrepe, which in turn is derived from Greek Athribis. The latter is a Hellenized form of the ancient Egyptian name *Hut-ta-hery-ib(t)*; in pharaonic times, this was the designation of the capital of the tenth nome of Lower Egypt, which comprised this very area. In the Egyptian language, this name was a simple phrase meaning "city in the middle," indicating that Athribis lay in the middle of the delta.

In this phrase, the expression *hery-ib* can have yet another meaning, namely, "on the heart" or "that which is on the heart." In this case, we would have to do with a "city on the heart." This interpretation has its basis in the local theology of Athribis. It was believed that a major relic was kept in this city, namely the heart of Osiris, who had been dismembered by his brother Seth. Other parts of his body were conserved in various religious centers throughout Egypt. But the heart, which the Egyptians believed to be the seat of the mind, was an especially important organ. There thus developed a myth about this heart and its association with Athribis. The heart of Osiris was supposed to be in the care of the goddess Khuit, whose principal task was the wrapping of the deceased god, and especially his heart.

All the deities associated with Osiris were included in the local pantheon, of course, but especially Horus-the-Child, Isis, Nephthys, and Hathor. The local embodiment of Horus was identified with the god Khentekhtai, who could assume the form of a crocodile, a falcon, or a bull. The last-mentioned animal enjoyed special worship at Athribis. Its sacred bull, called Kem-wer, even became a heraldic figure in the emblem that designated the tenth Lower Egyptian nome.

Thus far, Athribis is best known to the reader of this book from the text portraying the Dynasty 25 Kushite king Piye's triumphal march through the north of Egypt. The Kushite Period brought no glory to the city, though one of the later kings dedicated a temple there. Athribis became especially famous as the hometown of Amenhotpe son of Hapu, the deified architect and sage who lived in the time of Amenophis III. Already in his own lifetime, he was accorded a nearly royal status, for he had a mortuary temple of his own in the row of similar structures on the west bank of Thebes otherwise reserved only for pharaohs.

All indications are that the creator of the Colossi of Memnon was also concerned with the development of his hometown, for the archaeological material unearthed at Athribis is filled with indications of the importance of the city from the reign of Amenophis III on, that is, beginning in the fourteenth century B.C.E. In particular, there are stone blocks carved with reliefs stemming from monumental constructions, as well as magnificent statues made of various kinds of stone.

The most famous of these is a statue of a healer and priest named Djed-Hor (the Egyptian prototype of the Greek name Taho or Theos), who lived toward the end of the fourth century B.C.E. As indicated in the inscription carved on the base of the statue, his contribution was the erection of a sanctuary containing twelve chapels for the mummification of the falcons, the sacred animals of the god Khentekhtai. The statue, which is made of black granite, depicts the priest in the pose typical of a cuboid "block statue," that is, squatting, with his legs drawn up to his chest and his hands resting on his knees. Leaning against his legs is a magical stela whose form is characteristic of the period. It depicts Horus as a youth, standing on crocodiles and holding various dangerous animals in his hands. At the top of the stela

[197]

is the head of Bes, a god with caricaturelike features who had especially beneficent magical powers. All these figures are carved in raised relief. Except for the face, the hands, and the feet, the entire statue of Djed-Hor is covered with magical inscriptions. An oval container for water is carved into the base of the statue in front of the squatting figure; water entered it after coming into contact with the hieroglyphic inscriptions, which endowed it with magical power to protect people from illness. Prophylactic qualities were thus ascribed to this statue, which can today be admired in the Egyptian Museum in Cairo. Of an identical, parallel statue that was probably set up on the other side of the entrance to one of the temples of Athribis, only the base is preserved today.

One of the most important bits of historical information conveyed in the text carved on the base of the statue is the mention of foreigners who had settled in the courtyard of the temple of Horus-Khentekhtai. They were evicted, and they then moved several hundred yards further to the east. These were doubtless soldiers from the army of Alexander the Great. When we consider the place where the temple of Horus lay, as determined by archaeological data, we can conclude with a fair amount of certainty that the portion of the city excavated by our mission about a third of a mile east of that spot was the very suburb of Ptolemaic Athribis where many soldiers of the Macedonian army found their permanent homes toward the end of the fourth century B.C.E. While the army was ethnically mixed, it was mostly characterized by its Greek element. These points are demonstrated not only by the predominantly Greek iconography of the many objects we found there (though there are certain Near Eastern elements as well), but also by the fact that this sector was first inhabited in the second half of the fourth century B.C.E. and thus not during the late dynastic period.

Our test drillings, which reached several yards below the earliest excavated levels, revealed no traces of usage of this area before the last dynasty of native pharaohs. Only some limestone blocks with traces of carved cartouches of Nectanebo II (361–343 B.C.E.) point to the existence of a monumental temple of this ruler at Athribis, but this need not have been in the immediate vicinity of the residential sector that we studied. The blocks could have been transported from elsewhere to be reworked into vessels or other objects, or even to be turned into lime, as suggested by the presence of limekilns in the late Ptolemaic levels we excavated.

These limestone blocks lying near a late Ptolemaic lime oven are preserved in fragmentary condition and are decorated with hieroglyphic inscriptions in sunk relief. Among them, during our 1995 season, we found two fragments that we could piece together to reveal a cartouche with the throne name of Alexander the Great, *Setepenre-meryamun*. Since this throne name was also borne by Philip Arrhidaeus and Ptolemy I Soter, Alexander's successors, this find shows that an important temple was erected or at least enlarged at the beginning of the Ptolemaic Period, perhaps not far from the residential sector that we excavated.

The deepest stratum of our excavation, which corresponds to the late fourth century B.C.E., contained many objects that clearly confirm the identification of this portion of the city as a Greek settlement. Two terra-cotta figurines found side by side depict a Macedonian horseman trampling—in accordance with ancient Egyptian prototypes—a prisoner of war. In the level just above, we excavated a limestone head of a ruler; it was probably a sculptor's model, and it depicts one of the early Ptolemies, evidently Ptolemy II Philadelphos. This dating is supported by several bronze coins and two silver ones from the same level, which date to his reign, or perhaps to that of his father, Ptolemy I Soter. Especially interesting in this connection are the coins depicting Soter that were struck in the reign of his son, and not at Alexandria, but at Ptolemais (modern Akko) on the Mediterranean coast of Asia.

We know from written sources that there was not only a Greek but also a Jewish colony at Ptolemaic Athribis. Conditions were thus suitable for the flourishing of a Hellenistic koine—a local version of the syncretistic culture that embraced the entire world under the influence of Mediterranean civilization. Various native traditions now thrived in a symbiosis with Greek culture, and the language and mythology of the Greeks became the common denominator of communication for the many nationalities.

In the Hellenistic era, Egypt played a highly creative role in the Mediterranean basin. Our excavations at Tell Atrib confirm the growing impression that inventive contributions were not restricted to Alexandria, the seat of the Ptolemies and the new capital of the land, but also involved the Chora, that is, the provinces. In this periphery, there existed age-old traditions that the Greek "pharaohs" of Macedonian origin were obliged to take into account. More than all others, it was the priests of Memphis, the old capital of the pharaonic state at the southern edge of the delta, who guarded the sacred flame of the ancient Egyptian cults. The Ptolemies were able to exercise authority over Egypt and maintain a relative, though by no means stable, peace in the provinces only at the price of many concessions, and not just of a spiritual nature, to the Memphite priesthood.

Situated between the old and the new capitals of the land, and with long-standing ties to Memphis—especially as the domain of crown princes—Athribis now found itself the focus of both the rivalry and the mutual influence of the two centers. The city had the opportunity to play an important role in shaping Hellenistic culture in Egypt. The Polish-Egyptian excavations that have been systematically conducted at Tell Atrib since 1985 have shown that this was a center of outstanding artists and artisans who were able to combine ancient Egyptian traditions with elements of Greek culture and also with strong influences from the east,

[199]

especially Achaemenid Persia, which had already paved the way for Alexander's conquest of Egypt.

ARTISANS' WORKSHOPS

In the very first season of these excavations, which were preceded by geophysical surveys, it was evident that we were dealing with a stratigraphy of levels that were not intermingled and that, if they were disturbed here and there, this was owing to the activity of treasure hunters who, as we learn from the accounts of travelers, had come to prize the ruins of ancient Athribis as early as the Middle Ages. The remains, which took the form of several extensive mounds, were known as a mine of gold and silver objects, undoubtedly because of the presence of goldsmiths' workshops (Plate XIVa) in the area in ancient times.

In one of our first trial pits, we found a group of fragmentarily preserved marble statuettes, most of them representing Aphrodite (Plate XIVb-c), a scant four inches below the surface. This was no surprise, for the Greek goddess of love—identified with Isis and Hathor, the most important goddesses in the Egyptian pantheon—was extremely popular in the land of the Nile in Hellenistic times. Certain Egyptian cities received the name Aphroditopolis.

We were amazed, however, by the presence of polychromy on the surface of certain statues. In the moist environment of the delta, where the ground is systematically watered by canals, this was quite an event. The garment of a seminude Aphrodite had retained its blue color, while the hair on the pretty little head of another statue was graced by a layer of red ocher.

Even more surprising was that the limestone fragments were found in a context of coins and stamped amphora handles whose dates pointed unequivocally to an undisturbed archaeological stratum of the third century B.C.E. Had we hit upon copies or imitations of the famous statue of Aphrodite sculpted by Praxiteles, whose sons, according to written sources, visited Egypt at the beginning of the Hellenistic era?

After our first season, we were still uncertain whether we were dealing with the remains of a sculptor's workshop that specialized in depictions of this goddess or whether this was simply one of her many cult-places. It was difficult to draw any conclusions from what remained of the architecture, for the walls of the room in which the statues were found were built of mud brick, a highly unstable building material.

It was only in the course of the campaigns subsequently conducted on an annual basis by the Polish Center for Mediterranean Archaeology of Warsaw University in conjunction with the Egyptian Antiquities Service that it emerged that we had discovered a large complex of workshops where artists and craftsmen of various specializations were active for several centuries. The largest group were potters, who left behind not only thousands of vessels of all types and with all sorts of decoration but also kilns, deposits of unbaked wares, molds for stamping three-dimensional decoration, and pigments for preparing paint. The latter also served the native coroplasts, whose creations have survived to us in the form of innumerable terra-cotta figurines (Plate XIVd) with rich and often highly original iconography. Their origin in local workshops is shown by fragments of modeled but unbaked figurines or small, misfired terra-cottas or parts thereof. Oil lamps were made of the same raw material as the vessels and figurines.

The sculptors left behind not only fragments of marble figurines in the Greek style but also limestone models of various objects; unlike marble, which had to be imported, the latter raw material was native to Egypt. The head of Ptolemy II mentioned earlier seems to have functioned as one of these models. Here, stonemasons also reworked fragments of monumental architecture from earlier periods, such as stumps and bases of granite columns or bases of statues and sarcophagi, into stone vessels.

The many faience objects found in the same context probably also stemmed from local workshops. Many of the faience vessels are decorated in Greek or Graeco-Persian style reliefs, while amulets representing various deities of pharaonic Egypt were produced for the needs of the traditional Egyptian cults, along with figurines for burial purposes, the so-called shawabtis. Also made of faience were many votive figurines in a syncretistic style that is typically Hellenistic. Finding traces of the activity of *toreutai* (gold- and silversmiths) in the local workshops, however, is a circumstantial process, for the ruins of the ancient city were "cleansed" of their gold and silver objects over the centuries and in a manner that has nothing to do with archaeology.

From a scholarly standpoint, it is important that we can date the objects we found precisely, because they occur in undisturbed strata. The presence of many well-preserved coins enables us to date the successive strata not only to individual phases of the Ptolemaic Period but sometimes even with exactitude to the reign of a specific ruler. This is especially true of the contexts corresponding chronologically to the first half of the Ptolemaic epoch, that is, the third century and the first half of the second century B.C.E., down to the reign of Ptolemy VI Philometor. Thanks to these circumstances, certain categories of artifacts that have heretofore been dated vaguely to the Graeco-Roman Period, and sometimes erroneously to the Roman Period, can now receive a precise chronological specification that is supported by the stratigraphy.

Above and beyond these chronological determinations, the materials from the workshops of Ptolemaic Athribis also provide new insights into the mutual interpenetration of Egyptian and Greek traditions in the Egyptian provinces, not only on the artistic but also on the religious and political levels. This is especially true of art in the service of political theology, that is, the dynastic propaganda, which clothed itself in mythological garb.

A Public Bath

The attention of the investigators was aroused by the fact that a large number of the terra-cotta figurines from Athribis were erotic in character. Many of them, representing Isis-Aphrodite *anasyromene*—that is, as a woman obscenely exposing her womb by lifting her skirt—are accompanied by representations of naked women who can also be associated with mythological figures. Among these are a type of figure generally designated "concubine"—a woman lying with her arms alongside her body whose only "clothing" is her sumptuous headgear—or the type of a woman who squats with her legs spread as her hand points to her swollen womb. She wears boots, and in addition to her luxurious headdress, she is adorned with two chains that cross each other between her breasts. Her gesture and her enlarged genital area show clearly that such ex-votos were connected with the erotic aspects of fertility.

Along with the terra-cottas depicting unclothed women, there were phallic figurines at Athribis representing men with an exaggeratedly large member. These are representations of mythological figures, including the Egyptian Bes and Harpokrates, as well as male figures from outside the pantheon, often wearing Greek clothing. Even theriomorphic personifications were similarly represented. One such figurine depicts a battle between a frog wearing armor and an animal carrying a shield. Although the head of the latter is not preserved, we may presume it was a mouse, so that the entire scene is to be interpreted as a three-dimensional representation of a *batrachomyomachia*, that is, a battle between frogs and mice, a Hellenistic parody of Homer's *Iliad* otherwise attested only in literary sources. It is striking that each of the theriomorphic warriors is brandishing a huge phallus.

The excavators of these interesting groups of terra-cottas were surprised that most of the figures of an erotic nature were found in and around a public bath that had been unearthed in the vicinity of the workshops, just to their north. This unusual building, which consisted of small water basins of various shapes arranged along a narrow corridor, must have been constructed in the reign of Ptolemy VI, for the numismatic material from the stratum that covered its floor consisted only of coins of this ruler. Under-

[202]

neath the floor, however, there was a coin from the reign of his father, Ptolemy V.

Under the floor of this solid construction of fired bricks covered with a thick layer of waterproof, red-painted plaster, there was a tidy drainage system for channeling water away, though it was for the most part not connected to the water basins. The used water from the basins must have flowed onto the floor, whose slope would have ensured its drainage into the system of pipes below. Fresh water was collected and brought to the bath in hemispherical, thick-walled earthenware vessels fired gray and covered with bright black glaze. Their surfaces were engraved with reliefs that clearly imitated metal vessels. Even the large handles of these containers had a purely decorative function, for they were modeled in raised relief.

One of the terra-cotta figurines found near the bathhouse illustrates how the water basins were used. It represents a naked woman sitting on the raised back of an oval water basin, pouring water on herself from a small bowl whose edge is turned inward. Hundreds of such bowls, made in the local ceramic workshops, filled the layer of earth immediately above the ruins of Ptolemaic Athribis. Even deposits of unfired vessels consisted mostly of this type of bowl.

An original terra-cotta that served as a flagon depicts another regular at the bathhouse. Its tall neck emerges from the head of the figure of a nude, squatting youth whose locks hang down over his back. A folded garment is draped over his left arm, evidently a *himation*, a mantlelike wrap, and an object in the form of a scraper leans against his right leg. This figurine, which was found near a kiln dating to the end of the third century B.C.E., not far from the bathhouse, is distinguished by its archaizing features. We find a similar composition and modeling of individual details in the statuettes of *komastai*—youths who were noted for their dancing during ritual processions.

Such figurines occur in the art of archaic Greece. A flagon of similar size found by American archaeologists digging in the Athenian agora has the form of a kneeling athlete tying a ribbon around his head. Our figurine, however, is made of Nile clay fired dark gray. Both the material and the firing technique point to the same local workshop that produced the above-mentioned imitations of metal vessels for containing water in the baths.

A PRIVATE BATH

We often find imitation of the style of Greek artists of past eras in the works of the coroplasts (i.e., the artists who made terra-cottas) of Athribis in the Hellenistic Period. We can recognize reminiscences of archaic *kouroi* in the form of one of the terra-cotta figurines that we found inside a large pot dating to the beginning of the third century B.C.E. All depict so-called concubines, nude women with their arms hanging down alongside their bodies. But their styles vary, and with its masculine proportions and form, one of them reminds us more of the statues of athletic youths from two centuries earlier than of the sensuous curves of Hellenistic depictions of women.

This group of terra-cottas deserves attention for yet another reason. They belong to a deposit of ceramics that lay directly on top of the floor of a private bathroom from the beginning of the Ptolemaic Period. The discovery of this little bath in a precisely dated stratum underneath the remains of the workshops was a complete surprise. This little bathroom, whose lower portion is completely preserved, had three small basins of different shapes, along with a little stove. Its floor was a thick layer of cement laid directly on the ground without first leveling the latter's surface. The floor sloped toward the wall opposite the basins, permitting the water to flow into a drainage system consisting of ceramic pipes and then directly into a large cylindrical container set into the ground.

Since we found fragments of many smashed ceramic tubs in the immediate neighborhood of this bathroom, we may conclude that there was already a complex of baths in this area in the first decades after Alexander the Great. Its function was cultic as well as hygienic, as shown by the presence of votive figurines in addition to the vessels found in the bath. Ablutions, or simply a sprinkling of water, for magical purposes had been a long-standing practice in Egypt. In this context, we may recall the statue of Djed-Hor-the-Savior, whose function was to bestow magical power on the water that flowed down the statue and was collected in the little basin sunk into its base. The statue stems from a period only a little earlier than that of the baths we excavated. Discoveries made by earlier Polish excavations near the Ptolemaic baths revealed that this part of ancient Athribis became a popular resort during the Roman Period, when much larger, monumental public baths were built. Some of the fragmentary statues (Plate XV) found in this area might depict gymnasiarchs, that is, high officials responsible for a gymnasium at Athribis.

THE CULTIC ASPECT OF BATHS

In the public baths from the reign of Ptolemy VI, in addition to the erotic statuettes, we found a number of terra cottas representing various figures from the Dionysiac *thiasos* (procession). Among the companions of Dionysus, we recognize Priapus and the satyr Silenus. The figurines representing the latter are especially beautiful and iconographically varied. An oil lamp made at Athribis has the form of a naked Silenus with somewhat thinning hair, whose phallus functioned as the spout of the lamp. The erotic play between a Silenus and a Pan is represented in relief on an appliqué from a black-varnished hydria that reached Athribis from an Alexandrian workshop, or perhaps even a foreign one. We see Dionysus himself in certain figurines that are fragmentarily preserved, most of them headless. It seems that it is the god of wine, dressed in female clothing and accompanied by a young woman playing a triangular harp, a characteristic instrument in scenes with Dionysiac content. The female element in Dionysus's nature has a mythological basis with special fertility cult associations. A naked man with a huge phallus, accompanied by a youth with goat's legs, is probably another representation of Dionysus. This unusual depiction can be viewed as an *interpretatio aegyptiaca* of the figure of Dionysus, perhaps even an original iconographic invention of one of the coroplasts at Athribis.

We can also acquaint ourselves with the nature of the local cults from the little terra-cotta representations of the young god Harpokrates (Figure 58). Some of them wear ivy leaves in addition to their Egyptian headdress, such as the double crown of the pharaohs, thus displaying a symbiosis of the mythological circle of Osiris with the Dionysiac element. Osiris himself, accompanied by

Figure 58. Phallic Harpokrates ("Horus the Child") wearing the Egyptian double crown and Greek attire. Terra-cotta figurine from Ptolemaic Athribis. Photo by Waldemar Jerke, Polish Center of Mediterranean Archaeology, Warsaw University.

Isis, appears in a relief decorating one of the miniature stelae we found at the site of the baths and their surroundings. These stelae mostly take the form of a simple naos inside of which a nude goddess stands with her arms hanging down. The frontal rendering of these representations seems to imitate depictions of the Asiatic fertility goddess Cybele, whose cult was popular in Egypt. But the fact that the goddess on one of the stelae wears the crown of Isis allows us to connect this type of votive object with the cult of the ancient Egyptian goddess, who was associated with Aphrodite in Ptolemaic Egypt. In the vicinity of this piece, we also found a fragment of a small magical stela with a representation of "Horus on the crocodiles," topped by the head of the tutelary god Bes.

The nature of the votive objects found in the area of the baths confirms the hypothesis that the latter had a cultic function. It is doubtless to be connected with the cult of Dionysus, who was evidently associated here with Osiris. Further evidence for his worship is supplied by the many terra-cottas alluding to the theatrical aspects of Dionysiac celebrations: small votive masks representing figures from the New Comedy of Athens, figurines of actors, portraits of old, drunken priestesses of Dionysus, and grotesque caricatures depicting representatives of various social groups offer a broad spectrum of the local Dionysiac traditions.

This picture is enhanced by the many vessels intended for drinking wine, including *lagynoi*, that is, flasks distinguished by a squat, broad-shouldered body and a tall, narrow neck with a vertical handle. The Lagynophoria, a drinking festival in honor of Dionysus, derives its name from this type of vessel. Certain smaller flasks that were also made in the local workshops are more exceptional in form. Prepared in a mold like the terra-cotta figurines, they are shaped like grapes. One of the molds used to produce such vessels was found in a stratum that we dated through its coins to the reign of Ptolemy IV Philopator.

A deposit of still more drinking vessels at the bathhouse was found in a side room whose construction and function were distinctly different from those of the bathing section itself. The room is distinguished by its especially thick mud brick walls, which are covered with colored plaster divided into a series of square panels. It contains no water basins, but rather small amphoras with painted decoration, and cups of various sorts. Fragments of phallic votive objects were also found in the room. All this seems to show that Bacchic gatherings occurred here, which would also confirm our hypothesis that the bathhouse was a place that served the devotees of Dionysus. In its function, the installation is reminiscent of a *stibadion* (little nest), an idyllic spot connected with the erotic aspect of the cult of Dionysus. Small buildings of this type, which can be recognized by the presence of many phallic figurines and bas-reliefs, are known from Delos and other centers of Hellenistic culture.

Among our finds in the area around the bathhouse, the terracotta figurine of an elephant decorated with original reliefs merits attention. Atop the Indian elephant, there must originally have sat a god who symbolized the victory of Dionysus, alluding also to the triumphs of Alexander the Great in the east. Perhaps it was Harpokrates, or perhaps the youthful Dionysus—we cannot be certain, for the upper part of the terra-cotta is not preserved. But the reliefs that decorate the body of the elephant and thus far have no analogy among works of the Hellenistic Period depict two parallel scenes whose contents

Figure 59. Bes dancing between two roosters. Relief on a figurine representing an Indian elephant ridden by the young Dionysos or Harpokrates (now missing). Photo by Waldemar Jerke, Polish Center of Mediterranean Archaeology, Warsaw University.

form a unity. On one side of the elephant, the jolly Bes is depicted dancing between two cocks (Figure 59), while on the other, we see two naked dancers whose phalluses hang down to the ground. Since a rooster was a typical lover's gift in the context of homoerotic relationships in ancient Greece, we can easily guess that the piece alludes to "Greek love" as one of the many aspects of Dionysiac eros.

POLITICAL SYMBOLISM

Aside from its erotic and theatrical aspects, the cult of Dionysus also had a clearly political character in Ptolemaic Egypt. As prototype of the Ptolemies, this god was the dominant figure in the political theology promulgated by the court at Alexandria. The dynastic propaganda exploited these associations in a great many ways, and the artists who worked at Athribis were in no position to keep their work free of these influences. Their ideas regarding the connection between myth and politics sometimes assumed original forms. Thus, for example, in a relief projecting from the side of a terra-cotta rhyton, we see a youthful god wearing a radial crown and holding a *thyrsos* (wand), an attribute of Dionysus, in his hand. This solar deity is clearly identified with one of the Ptolemies, for he is standing on a bolt of lightning between two eagles with their wings spread. These typical elements of royal heraldry were borrowed from representations that appear again and again on Ptolemaic coins, the most popular instrument of dynastic propaganda. On

[207]

either side of the god, we see a horseman carrying a lance; these are un-doubtedly the Dioscuri, that is, Castor and Pollux, whose cult was very pop-ular in Egypt, while above the scene, there is a row of winged female figures who are to be identified with Nike, the goddess of victory.

This accumulation of symbols of triumph and glory undoubtedly makes a political statement. To solve the riddle, it remains only to answer the question of which Ptolemy is in question here. The archaeological stratum in which the fragment was found corresponds chronologically to the end of the third century B.C.E.; the most likely ascription of the work is thus to the reign of Ptolemy IV Philopator. It is scarcely a coincidence that the popu-larity of the cult of Dionysus in the Egyptian provinces began in the reign of this very ruler. Philopator's victory over Antiochus III at Raphia in 217 B.C.E.—made possible only by the precedent-setting step of conscripting twenty thousand Egyptians to strengthen the army—brought the Alexan-drian court closer to the Egyptian *Chora*. It is entirely possible that the sym-bols of victory assembled in relief on the rhyton from Athribis refer to the triumph of this very ruler.

It is worth mentioning that a contemporary papyrus contains a com-mand that the persons responsible for the cult of Dionysus in the provinces be summoned to Alexandria for an "examination." At the royal court, they were to affirm their competence by indicating from whom they had re-ceived their instruction through the last three generations. Even if this was basically a question of taxes not mentioned in the decree, as some scholars think, the Ptolemies were concerned with preserving the unity and perhaps even the orthodoxy of this dynastic cult.

A mythological embodiment of one of the Ptolemies is probably to be seen in the beautiful figure of Dionysus on the protome (i.e., the head and shoulders of a figure or figures decorating a vessel) of another rhyton found at Athribis. Here, the bearded god forms a pair with a goddess who leans on his arm (perhaps Ariadne, his companion, or Selene, his mother), who was doubtless identified with one of the Ptolemaic queens. Unfortu-nately, only the hair on the goddess' head is preserved, so we can only con-jecture as to her identification.

The two deities are accompanied by an eagle with outspread wings, a heraldic symbol that assures us they embody a Ptolemaic royal couple. To judge from the stratigraphic context in which the fragments of this beauti-ful rhyton were found, they are most likely Ptolemy VI and his famous mother, Cleopatra I, or Cleopatra II, his wife and sister.

This group forms the front of the rhyton; its outer surface is decorated with friezes of relief. The central motif is an erotic scene depicting a couple engag-ing in *coitus a tergo* on a bed. They are accompanied by mythological figures, including a female whose iconography indicates that she is Isis playing a lyre. A frieze of cupids riding dolphins represented in another register of this rich decoration also emphasizes the Dionysiac aspects of the entire vase. This extemely thin-walled vase, which is made of an unusually brittle type of clay, was probably a model used by a master craftsman in fashioning a similar vase in more precious material, such as gold or silver. The vessel, which was undoubtedly intended for ritual purposes, might have been used during festivals honoring Dionysus.

This fascinating object is interesting not only because of its exceptional decoration but also because of its form. At its bottom, the rhyton has an elongated, oval base that is characteristic of orientalizing rhytons that continued to be made under the influence of Persian traditions. Egypt's stormy history during the final centuries B.C.E. was thus reflected in the arts and crafts of the Egyptian provinces.

Through the tangle of cultural influences we have discovered in the work of the artists at Athribis, there runs a proverbial Ariadne's thread leading to Alexandria. It is possible that some of the local masters were commissioned by the Ptolemaic court. Even if this was not the case, the artistic quality of their work was not inferior to that of the court, and in its iconographic originality, it sometimes surpasses the Alexandrian art that has survived to us. And it is entirely certain that this art served the dynastic propaganda

Figure 60. Terra-cotta figurine from Athribis probably representing Cleopatra I associated with Isis and accompanied by her sons, the future kings of Egypt Ptolemy VI and Ptolemy VIII. Photo by Waldemar Jerke, Polish Center of Mediterranean Archaeology, Warsaw University.

of the Ptolemies. To all indications, we must often conclude that representations of Dionysus are portraits of Alexandrian rulers, while many of

the representations of Isis and Aphrodite must be likenesses of their royal wives.

This is probably the case with regard to a small terra-cotta figurine from Athribis depicting a woman with the garb and the hairstyle of Isis (Figure 60). The coroplast depicted her with two children, the younger at her breast and the older at her side. The latter, doubtless a son, has a heart-shaped amulet, a symbol of Harpokrates, hanging from his neck. Since this figure differs from all other known representations of Isis and her priestesses, as well as from those of nurses and tutors—women who were also depicted with children—this figure is most likely to be interpreted as a Ptolemaic queen identified with Isis. Such an identification was not unusual at the Alexandrian court. If we take into consideration that the figurine was found in an archaeological stratum that can be dated by numismatic finds to the reigns of Ptolemy V Epiphanes and Ptolemy VI Philometor, we can only see her as Cleopatra I, who—as the widow of the murdered Epiphanes—served as regent for approximately five years. She was at that time the mother of two minor sons, each of whom later ascended the throne of Egypt, one as Ptolemy VI Philometor and the other as Ptolemy VIII Euergetes II.

Figure 61. Head of a youth wearing the Egyptian double crown. Possibly a portrait of Ptolemy VI. Fragment of a terra-cotta figurine from Athribis. Photo by Waldemar Jerke, Polish Center of Mediterranean Archaeology, Warsaw University.

From the standpoint of Egyptian theology, each of these boys could be viewed as a young Horus, as a Harpokrates, who had been regarded as the original ancestor of the rulers of Egypt since pharaonic times (Figure 61). Of the coins found in the vicinity of

[210]

Figure 62. Representation of the goddess Isis or queen Cleopatra I on a bronze coin from Athribis. First half of second century B.C.E. Photo by Waldemar Jerke, Polish Center of Mediterranean Archaeology, Warsaw University.

the figurine, two are the best preserved. One of them, evidently struck during the brief regency of Cleopatra I, depicts Isis with the locks that are typical of her (Figure 62). Many scholars are of the opinion that this is a representation of the queen herself as an Egyptian goddess. The other coin stems from the reign of her older son Ptolemy VI and shows a bearded Heracles with a lion's pelt on his head. The Ptolemaic rulers often identified themselves with this god, as they did with Dionysus. But on the coins of the Ptolemies, we most often see Zeus-Ammon, the god who symbolized the union of the two great civilizations, the Egyptian and the Greek, a union whose legacy has exercised an influence down to our own day.

[211]

Bibliography

Abd el-Raziq, Mahmud. *Die Darstellungen und die Texte des Sanktuars Alexanders des Grossen im Tempel von Luxor*. Archäologische Veröffentlichungen des Deutschen Archäologischen Instituts Kairo 16. Mainz, 1984.

Africa in Antiquity: The Arts of Ancient Nubia and the Sudan, vol. 1: *The Essays*. New York, 1978.

Arnold, Dieter. *Temples of the Last Pharaohs*. Oxford University Press, 1999.

Arslan, Ermanno A., Francesco Tiradritti, Monica Abbiati Brida, and Alessandra Magni, eds., *Iside: Il mito, il mistero, la magia*. Milan, 1997.

Assmann, Jan. *Ägypten: Eine Sinngeschichte*. Munich, 1996.

——. *Das Grab des Basa (Nr. 389) in der thebanischen Nekropole*. Grabungen im Asasif 1963–1970, vol. 2. Archäologische Veröffentlichungen des Deutschen Archäologischen Instituts Kairo 6. Mainz, 1973.

——. *Das Grab der Mutirdis*. Grabungen im Asasif 1963–1970, vol.6. Archäologische Veröffentlichungen des Deutschen Archäologischen Instituts Kairo 13. Mainz, 1977.

Badawy, Alexander. "Das Grab des Kronprinzen Scheschonk, Sohnes Osorkon's II. und Hohenpriesters von Memphis." *Annales du Service des Antiquités Égyptiennes* 54 (1956): 153–77.

Baines, John, and Jaromír Málek. *Atlas of Ancient Egypt*. Oxford, 1980.

Bietak, Manfred, and Elfriede Reiser-Halauer. *Das Grab des Anch-Hor, Obersthofmeister der Gottesgemahlin Nitokris*, Part 1: *Textband und Schuber mit Plänen für Teil 1 und 2*. Untersuchungen der Zweigstelle Kairo des Österreichischen Archäologischen Instituts 4. Vienna, 1978.

Bonhôme, Marie-Ange. *Les noms royaux dans l'Égypte de la Troisième Période Intermédiaire*. Cairo, 1987.

Bothmer, Bernard V. *Egyptian Sculpture of the Late Period: 700 B.C. to A.D. 100*. Catalog of the exhibition Brooklyn Museum, October 18, 1960 to January 9, 1961. New York, 1960.

Bowman, Alan K. *Egypt after the Pharaohs, 332 B.C.-A.D. 642: From Alexander to the Arab Conquest*. London, 1986.

Bresciani, Edda, Sergio Pernigotti, and Maria Paola Giangeri Silvis. *La tomba di Cien-*

nehebu, capo della flotta del Re, Biblioteca degli studi classici e orientali 7. Serie egittologica. Tombe d'età saitica a Saqqara 1. Pisa, 1977.

Burkhard, Günter. *Spätzeitliche Osiris-Liturgien im Corpus der Asasif-Papyri: Übersetzung, Kommentar, formale und inhaltliche Analyse.* Wiesbaden, 1995.

Chevereau, Pierre-Marie. *Prosopographie des cadres militaires égyptiens de la Basse Époque: Carrières militaires et carrières sacerdotales en Égypte du XIe au IIe siècle avant J.-C.* Paris, 1985.

Clayton, Peter A. *Chronicle of the Pharaohs: The Reign-by-Reign Record of the Rulers and Dynasties of Ancient Egypt.* London, 1994.

Cleopatra's Egypt: Age of the Ptolemies. Catalogue of the exhibition, Brooklyn Museum, October 7, 1988, to January 2, 1989. New York, 1988.

Corcoran, Lorelei H. *Portrait Mummies from Roman Egypt (I-IVth centuries A.D.): With a Catalog of Portrait Mummies in Egyptian Museums.* Chicago, 1995.

Daumas, François. *Les mammisis des temples égyptiens.* Annales de l'Université de Lyon, sér. 3, lettr. 32. Paris, 1958.

Davies, Norman de Garis. *The Temple of Hibis in El Khargeh Oasis*, vol. 3: *The Decoration.* Publications of the Metropolitan Museum of Art, Egyptian Expedition 17. New York, 1953.

Derchain, Philippe. *Zwei Kapellen des Ptolemäus I. Soter in Hildesheim.* Zeitschrift des Museums zu Hildesheim, Neue Folge 13, Wissenschaftliche Veröffentlichungen 5. Hildesheim, 1961.

Dunand, Françoise. *Le culte d'Isis dans le bassin oriental de la Méditerranée*, 3 vols. Études préliminaires aux religions orientales dans l'empire romain 26. Leiden, 1973.

Dunham, Dows. *The Royal Cemeteries of Kush*, vol. 1: *El-Kurru* (Cambridge, 1950); vol. 2: *Nuri*; vol. 4: *Royal Tombs at Meroe and Barkal*; vol. 5: *The West and South Cemeteries at Meroe.* Boston, 1955, 1957, 1963.

Epigraphic Survey. *The Bubastide Portal.* Reliefs and Inscriptions at Karnak 3. Oriental Institute Publications 74. Chicago, 1954.

Epigraphic Survey. *The Temple of Khonsu*, vol. 1: *Scenes of King Herihor in the Court*; vol. 2: *Scenes and Inscriptions in the Court and the First Hypostyle Hall.* Oriental Institute Publications 100, 103. Chicago, 1979, 1981.

Favard-Meeks, Christine. *Le temple de Behbeit el-Hagara: Essai de reconstruction et d'interprétation.* Studien zur Altägyptischen Kultur, Beiheft 6. Hamburg, 1991.

Friedman, Florence Dunn, ed. *Gifts of the Nile: Ancient Egyptian Faience.* London, 1998.

La Gloire d'Alexandrie. Catalog of the exhibition, Petit Palais Paris, May 7–July 26, 1998. Paris, 1998.

Goddio, Franck. *À la recherche de Cléopâtre: Alexandrie engloutie depuis quinze siècles, la ville de la reine mythique se dévoile enfin.* Paris, 1996.

Goddio, Franck, André Bernand, Étienne Bernand, Ibrahim Darwish, Zsolt Kiss, and Jean Yoyotte. *Alexandria: The Submerged Royal Quarters.* London, 1998.

Gomaà, Farouk. *Die libyschen Fürstentümer des Deltas vom Tod Osorkons II. bis zur Wiedervereinigung Ägyptens durch Psametik I.* Wiesbaden, 1974.

Goyon, Jean-Claude. *Confirmation du pouvoir royal au Nouvel An (Brooklyn Museum Papyrus 47.218.50).* Bibliothèque d'Étude 52. Cairo, 1972.

Graefe, Erhart. *Untersuchungen zur Verwaltung und Geschichte der Institution der Gottesgemahlin des Amun vom Beginn des Neuen Reiches bis zur Spätzeit.* 2 vols. Wiesbaden. 1981.

Green, Peter, ed. *Hellenistic History and Culture.* Hellenistic Culture and Society 9. Berkeley, 1993.

Grimal, Nicolas. *Quatre stèles napatéennes au Musée du Caire, JE 48863–48866: Textes et indices.* Mémoires de la Mission Archéologique Française au Caire 106. Cairo, 1981.

———. *La stèle triomphale de Pi(ankh)y au Musée du Caire, JE 48862 et 47086–47089*. Mémoires de la Mission Archéologique Française au Caire 105. Cairo, 1981.

Grimm, Alfred. *Die altägyptischen Festkalender in den Tempeln der griechisch-römischen Epoche*. Ägypten und Altes Testament 5. Wiesbaden, 1994.

Grimm, Günter, and Johannes Dieter. *Kunst der Ptolemäer- bis Römerzeit im ägyptischen Museum Kairo*. Mainz, 1975.

Hintze, Fritz. *Musawwarat es Sufra*, vol. 1: *Der Löwentempel*; vol. 2: *Tafelband*. Archäologische Forschungen im Sudan 1. Berlin, 1971.

———, ed. *Africa in Antiquity: The Arts of Ancient Nubia and the Sudan. Proceedings of the Symposium Held in Conjunction with the Exhibition, Brooklyn, Sept. 29–Oct. 1, 1978*. Meroitica: Schriften zur altsudanesischen Geschichte und Archäologie 5. Berlin, 1979.

Hölbl, Günther. *Geschichte des Ptolemäerreiches: Politik, Ideologie und religiöse Kultur von Alexander dem Grossen bis zur römischen Eroberung*. Darmstadt, 1994.

Husson, Geneviève, and Dominique Valbelle. *L'État et les institutions en Égypte des premiers pharaons aux empereurs romains*. Paris, 1992.

Jansen-Winkeln, Karl. *Ägyptische Biographien der 22. und 23. Dynastie*, Ägypten und Altes Testament 8/1. Wiesbaden, 1985.

———. "Der Beginn der Libyschen Herrschaft in Ägypten." *Biblische Notizen* 71 (1994): 78–97.

———. *Texte und Sprache in der 3. Zwischenzeit: Vorarbeiten zu einer spätmittelägyptischen Grammatik*. Ägypten und Altes Testament 26. Wiesbaden, 1994.

Jaros, Karl, Grete Swedik, and Marianne Leimlehner. *Ägypten und Vorderasien: Eine kleine Chronographie bis zum Auftreten Alexander des Grossen*. Linz-Vienna-Passau, 1976.

Jasnow, Richard. *A Late Period Hieratic Wisdom Text (P. Brooklyn 47.218.135)*. Studies in Ancient Oriental Civilization 52. Chicago, 1992.

Jenni, Hanna. *Das Dekorationsprogramm des Sarkophages Nektanebos' II*. Aegyptiaca Helvetica 12. Geneva, 1986.

Johnson, Janet H., ed. *Life in a Multi-Cultural Society: Egypt from Cambyses to Constantine and Beyond*. Studies in Ancient Oriental Civilization 51. Chicago, 1992.

Josephson, Jack A. *Egyptian Royal Sculpture of the Late Period, 400–246 B.C.* Sonderschriften des Deutschen Archäologischen Instituts Kairo 30. Mainz, 1997.

Kitchen, Kenneth A. *The Third Intermediate Period in Egypt (1100 to 650 B.C.)*. 2d ed. Warminster, 1973.

Kruchten, Jean-Marie. *Les Annales des prêtres de Karnak (XXI-XXIIImes dynasties) et autres textes contemporains relatifs à l'initiation des prêtres d'Amon*. Orientalia Lovaniensia Analecta 32. Leuven, 1989.

———. *Le grand texte oraculaire de Djéhoutymose, intendant du domaine d'Amon sous le pontificat de Pinedjem II*. Monographies Reine Élisabeth 5. Brussels, 1986.

Kuhlmann, Klaus Peter, and Wolfgang Schenkel. *Das Grab des Aba, Theben Nr. 36*. 2 vols. Archäologische Veröffentlichungen des Deutschen Archäologischen Instituts Kairo 15–16. Mainz, 1980.

Laskowska-Kusztal, Ewa. *Die Dekorfragmente der ptolemäisch-römischen Tempel von Elephantine*. Elephantine 15. Archäologische Veröffentlichungen des Deutschen Archäologischen Instituts Kairo 73. Mainz, 1996.

Leahy, Anthony. "Royal Iconography and Dynastic Change, 750–525 B.C.: The Blue and Cap Crowns." *Journal of Egyptian Archaeology* 78 (1992): 223–40.

———, ed. *Libya and Egypt c. 1300–750 B.C.* London, 1990.

Leclant, Jean. *Enquêtes sur les sacerdoces et les sanctuaires égyptiens à l'époque dite "éthiopienne" (XXVe dynastie)*. Bibliothèque d'Étude 17. Cairo, 1954.

———. *Montouemhat, Quatrième prophète d'Amon, Prince de la ville.* Bibliothèque d'Étude 35. Cairo, 1961.

———. *Recherches sur les monuments thébains de la XXVe dynastie dite éthiopienne.* Bibliothèque d'Étude 36. Cairo, 1965.

———, ed. *Ägypten III: Spätzeit und Hellenismus, 1070 v. Chr. bis 4. Jahrhundert n. Chr.* Munich, 1981.

Lefebvre, Gustave. *Le tombeau de Petosiris.* 3 vols. Cairo, 1923–24.

Manley, Bill. *The Penguin Historical Atlas of Ancient Egypt.* London, 1996.

Manuelian, Peter Der. *Living in the Past: Studies in Archaism of the Egyptian Twenty-Sixth Dynasty.* London, 1994.

Meeks, Dimitri. "Les donations aux temples dans l'Égypte du 1er millénaire avant J.-C." In E. Lipiński, ed., *State and Temple Economy in the Ancient Near East II: Proceedings of the International Conference Organized by the Katholieke Universiteit Leuven from the 10th to the 14th of April 1978,* vol. 2. Orientalia Lovaniensia Analecta 6. Leuven, 1978, pp. 605–87.

Mélèze-Modrzejewski, Joseph. *Les Juifs d'Égypte de Ramsès II à Hadrien.* Paris, 1991.

Merkelbach, Reinhold. *Isis regina—Zeus Sarapis: Die griechisch-ägyptische Religion nach den Quellen dargestellt.* Stuttgart, 1995.

de Meulenaere, Herman. "La famille du roi Amasis." *Journal of Egyptian Archaeology* 54 (1968): 183–87.

———. "La famille royale des Nectanebo." *Zeitschrift für ägyptische Sprache und Altertumskunde* 90 (1965) 90–93.

de Meulenaere, Herman, and Pierre Mackay. *Mendes II.* Warminster, 1976.

———. "Les Monuments du culte des rois Nectanebo." *Chronique d'Égypte* 35 [No. 69/70] (1960): 92–107.

———. *Le surnom égyptien à la Basse Époque.* Uitgaven van het Nederlands Historisch-Archaeologisch Instituut in het Nabije Oosten 19. Istanbul, 1966.

Minas, Martina, and Jürgen Zeidler, eds. *Aspekte spätägyptischer Kultur: Festschrift für Erich Winter zum 65. Geburtstag.* Mainz, 1994.

Montet, Pierre. *Lettres de Tanis, 1939–1940: La découverte des trésors royaux.* Monaco, 1998.

———. *La nécropole royale de Tanis,* vol. 1: *Les constructions et le tombeau d'Osorkon II à Tanis;* vol. 2: *Les constructions et le tombeau de Psousennès à Tanis;* vol. 3: *Les constructions et le tombeau de Chéchanq III à Tanis.* Paris, 1947, 1951, 1960.

Müller, Hans Wolfgang. "Der Torso einer Königsstatue im Museo Archeologico zu Florenz: Ein Beitrag zur Plastik der ägyptischen Spätzeit." In *Studi in memoria di Ippolito Rosellini nel primo centenario della morte,* 2 vols. Pisa, 1955, pp. 181–221.

———. "Ein Königsbildnis der 26. Dynastie mit der 'Blauen Krone,' im Museo Civico zu Bologna." *Zeitschrift für ägyptische Sprache und Altertumskunde* 80 (1955): 46–68.

Munro, Peter. *Die spätägyptischen Totenstelen.* Ägyptologische Forschungen 25. Glückstadt, 1973.

Myśliwiec, Karol. "A Lower Egyptian Sculptor's 'School' of the Late Dynastic–Early Ptolemaic Period." *Bulletin of the Middle Eastern Culture Center in Japan* 6 (1992): 191–220.

———. *Royal Portraiture of the dynasties XXI–XXX.* Mainz, 1988.

———. "Un naos de Darius roi d'Égypte." *Bulletin of the Middle Eastern Culture Center in Japan* 5 (1991): 221–46.

Naville, Edouard. *The Festival-Hall of Osorkon II in the Great Temple of Bubastis (1887–1889).* Tenth Memoir of the Egypt Exploration Fund. London, 1892.

Niwiński, Andrzej. *21st Dynasty Coffins from Thebes: Chronological and Typological Studies.* Mainz, 1988.

Onasch, Hans-Ulrich. *Die assyrischen Eroberungen Ägyptens*, Teil 1: *Kommentare und Anmerkungen*, Ägypten und Altes Testament 27, Teil 2: *Texte in Umschrift*. Wiesbaden, 1994.

Osing, Jürgen, et al. *Denkmäler der Oase Dachla aus dem Nachlass von Ahmed Fakhry*. Archäologische Veröffentlichungen des Deutschen Archäologischen Instituts Kairo 28. Mainz, 1982.

Parker, Richard A., Jean Leclant, and Jean-Claude Goyon. *The Edifice of Taharka by the Sacred Lake of Karnak*. Brown Egyptological Studies 8. Providence, 1979.

Posener, Georges. *La première domination perse en Égypte: Recueil d'inscriptions hiéroglyphiques*. Bibliothèque d'Étude 11. Cairo, 1936.

Quaegebeur, Jan. "Reines ptolémaïques et traditions égyptiennes." In *Das ptolemäische Ägypten: Akten des Internationalen Symposions 27.-29. Sept. 1976 in Berlin*, edited by Herwig Maehler and Volker Michael Strocka. Mainz, 1978, pp. 245–62.

Redford, Donald B. *Egypt, Canaan and Israel in Ancient Times* Princeton, 1992.

Russmann, Edna R. "An Egyptian Royal Statuette of the Eighth Century B.C." In William Kelly Simpson and Whitney M. Davis, eds., *Studies in Ancient Egypt, the Aegean and the Sudan: Essays in Honor of Dows Dunham on the Occasion of his 90th Birthday, June 1, 1980*. Boston, 1981, pp. 149–55.

——. *The Representation of the King in the XXV Dynasty*. Monographies Reine Élisabeth 3. Brussels, 1974.

el-Sadeek, Wafaa. *Twenty-sixth Dynasty Necropolis at Gizeh: An Analysis of the Tomb of Thery and Its Place in the Development of Saite Funerary Art and Architecture*. Beiträge zur Ägyptologie 5. Vienna, 1984.

Sauneron, Serge. *Esna*, vol. 1: *Quatre campagnes à Esna*; vols. 2–3: *Le temple d'Esna*; vol. 5: *Les fêtes religieuses d'Esna aux derniers siècles du paganisme*. Cairo, 1959, 1962, 1963, 1968.

el-Sayed, Ramadan. *La déesse Neith de Sais*, vol. 1: *Importance et rayonnement de son culte*. Bibliothèque d'Étude 86/1. Cairo, 1982.

——. *Documents relatifs à Sais et ses divinités*. Bibliothèque d'Étude 69. Cairo, 1975.

Schneider, Thomas. *Lexikon der Pharaonen*. Zurich, 1994.

Soudan: Royaumes sur le Nil. Catalog of the exhibition, Institut du Monde Arabe. Paris, 1997.

Steindorff, Georg. "Reliefs from the Temples of Sebennytos and Iseion in American Collections." *Journal of the Walters Art Gallery* 7–8 (1945): 39–59.

Thompson, Dorothy J. *Memphis under the Ptolemies*. Princeton, 1988.

Török, Lásló. *The Birth of an Ancient African Kingdom: Kush and Her Myth of the State in the First Millenium B.C.* Cahiers de recherches de l'Institut de Papyrologie et d'Égyptologie de Lille, suppl. no. 4. Lille, 1995.

——. *The Kingdom of Kush: Handbook of the Napatan-Meroitic Civilization*. Handbuch der Orientalistik, 1. Abteilung: Nahe und der Mittlere Osten, Bd. 31. Leiden, 1997).

——. *The Royal Crowns of Kush: A Study in Middle Nile Valley Regalia and Iconography in the 1st Millennium B.C. and A.D.* Cambridge Monographs in African Archaeology 18. Cambridge, 1987.

Traunecker, Claude, Françoise le Saout, and Olivier Masson. *La chapelle d'Achôris à Karnak*. Recherche sur les grandes civilisations, Synthèse 5. Paris, 1981.

Valbelle, Dominique. *Les Neuf Arcs: L'Égyptien et les étrangers de la préhistoire à la conquête d'Alexandre*. Paris, 1990.

Van Siclen Charles C. III. "Nectanebo II's Great Naos for Bastet." In *Essays in Egyptology in Honor of Hans Goedicke*, edited by Betsy M. Bryan and David Lorton. San Antonio, 1994, pp. 321–32.

Vassilika, Eleni. *Ptolemaic Philae*. Orientalia Lovaniensia Analecta 34. Leuven, 1989.

Vernus, Pascal. *Athribis: Textes et documents relatifs à la géographie, aux cultes, et à l'histoire d'une ville du Delta Égyptien à l'époque pharaonique.* Bibliothèque d'Étude 74. Cairo, 1978.

Vernus, Pascal, and Jean Yoyotte. *Dictionnaire des Pharaons.* Paris, 1996.

Vittmann, Günter. *Priester und Beamte im Theben der Spätzeit: genealog. u. prosopographische Untersuchungen zum thebanischen Priester- u. Beamtentum d. 25. u. 26. Dynastie.* Beiträge zur Ägyptologie 1. Vienna, 1978.

van Walsem, René. *The Coffin of Djedmonthuiufankh in the National Museum of Antiquities at Leiden,* vol. 1: *Technical and Iconographic/Iconological Aspects.* Leiden, 1997.

Welsby, Derek A. *The Kingdom of Kush: The Napatan and Meroitic Period.* London, 1996.

Wenig, Steffen. *Africa in Antiquity: The Arts of Ancient Nubia and the Sudan,* vol. 2: *The Catalogue.* New York, 1978.

Whitehorne, John. *Cleopatras.* London, 1994.

Winlock, Herbert E. *The Temple of Hibis in the El Khargeh Oasis,* vol. 1: *Excavations.* Publications of the Metropolitan Museum of Art, Egyptian Expedition 13. New York, 1941.

Winter, Erich. *Untersuchungen zu den ägyptischen Tempelreliefs der griechisch-römischen Zeit.* Österreichische Akademie der Wissenschaften, phil.-hist. Klasse, Denkschriften 98. Vienna, 1968.

Yoyotte, Jean. "Nectanébo II comme faucon divin?" *Kêmi* 15 (1959): 70–74.

——. "Les Principautés du Delta au temps de l'anarchie libyenne. Études d'histoire politique." *Mélanges Maspero,* vol. 1: Orient ancien, Cahier 4. Mémoires de l'Institut Français d'Archéologie Orientale du Caire 64. Cairo, 1961, pp. 121–81.

Yoyotte, Jean, Pascal Charvet, and Stéphane Gompertz. *Strabon: Le Voyage en Egypte.* Paris, 1997.

EGYPT	WESTERN ASIA
PREDYNASTIC (ARCHAIC) PERIOD Dynasties 1–2 (c. 3100–2686) Formation of the Egyptian state by uniting the northern and southern portions of the land, evidently in the reign of Narmer (Menes) **OLD KINGDOM** Dynasties 3–6 (c. 2686–2181) Construction of large pyramids in the Memphite necropolis. Composition of the Pyramid Texts. **FIRST INTERMEDIATE PERIOD** Dynasties 7–10 (c. 2181–2133) **MIDDLE KINGDOM** Dynasties 11–12 (c. 2133–1786) Kings with the names Inyotef, Mentuhotpe, Amenemhet, Senwosret. Flowering of Egyptian literature written in the classical language. Composition of the Coffin Texts. **SECOND INTERMEDIATE PERIOD** Dynasties 13–17 (c. 1786–1567) Hyksos in the north of Egypt: Dynasties 15–16. Last ruler of Dynasty 17: Kamose. **NEW KINGDOM** Dynasties 18–20 (c. 1567–1085) Kings with the names Amenophis and Tuthmosis (Dynasty 18) as well as Ramesses and Sethos (Dynasties 19–20). Akhenaten's "monotheistic" heresy. Return to orthodoxy under Tutankhamun (Dynasty 18). Expansion at Thebes: temple of Amun-Re at Karnak, tombs and mortuary temples on the west bank. Growth and decline of Egypt's imperial power. Composition of the Book of the Dead. Late Egyptian language.	

EGYPT	WESTERN ASIA
THIRD INTERMEDIATE PERIOD	

THIRD INTERMEDIATE PERIOD
Dynasty 21 (1085–945)
Kings at Tanis:
Smendes
Amenemnisu/Neferkare
Psusennes I
Amenemope
Osorkon the elder
Siamun
Psusennes II
High Priests of Amun at Thebes, including Pinudjem I, Masaharta, Menkheperre, Smendes II, Pinudjem II, Psusennes III.
Dynasty 22 (c. 945–745)
Libyan kings at Bubastis:

Shoshenq I	c. 945–924
Osorkon I	c. 924–889
Shoshenq II	c. 890
Takelot I	c. 889–874
Osorkon II	c. 874–850
Harsiese	c. 870–860
Takelot II	c. 850–825
Shoshenq III	c. 825–773
Pami	c. 773–767
Shoshenq V	c. 767–730
Osorkon IV	c. 730–715

Dynasty 23 (c. 818–715)

Pedubaste I	c. 818–793
Iuput I	c. 804–783
Shoshenq IV	c. 783–777
Osorkon III	c. 777–749
Takelot III	c. 754–734
Rudamun	c. 734–731
Iuput II	c. 731–720
Shoshenq VI	c. 720–715
(identification uncertain)	

Dynasty 24 (c. 730–715)
Kings at Sais:

| Tefnakhte I | c. 727–720 |
| Bocchoris | c. 720–715 |

Dynasty 25 (c. 747–656)
Kushite domination of Egypt
Partially contemporary with Dynasties 23 and 24:

Piye	c. 747–716
Shabaka	c. 716–702
Shebitku	c. 702–690
Taharqa	690–664
Tantamani	664–656

WESTERN ASIA

Saul, the first king of the Israelite state, fights against the Philistines and other neighboring peoples.
David of the tribe of Judah, king of Israel, unites the kingdoms of Israel and Judah and makes Jerusalem his capital. David's son Solomon, king of Israel and Judah, erects the Temple in Jerusalem. High point in the development of the Jewish state.

After the death of Solomon (c. 930 B.C.E.), the state breaks up into the southern kingdom of Judah, with its capital at Jerusalem, and the northern kingdom of Israel, with its capital at Shechem and later Samaria.
Shoshenq I conquers and plunders Jerusalem. Egypt assists Israel in its struggle against Judah.

Jeroboam II, king of Israel beginning 784, is the last important ruler of this state. Israel loses Galilee to the Assyrians in 734. Israel becomes an Assyrian province in 722.

Egypt and Judah defeated in battle against Sennacherib in southern Palestine.
Gyges, king of Lydia, lends military assistance to Egypt in its struggle for unification.

MESOPOTAMIA/PERSIA	GREECE
Assyrian conquest of Babylon (c. 1100 B.C.E.).	Migration of the Dorians (c. 1100 B.C.E.), who settle on the Aegean Sea, conquer the Achaeans, destroy the centers of Mycenaean culture, and assume rule over nearly all the Peloponnesus, forcing the Ionians out of mainland Greece to the west coast of Asia Minor.
Appearance of the Medes in northwestern Iran (Media) c. 900 B.C.E.; their dependence on Assyria. Assurnasirpal II, king of Assyria, defeats the Arameans and subjects the Phoenician harbor cities, c. 883. Egypt unsuccessfully supports Syria against Assyria.	The city states (*polis*) develop what was to be the typically Greek life style. Greek colonization of Italy. Sparta becomes the predominant power in Greece after subjecting Messenia (730).
Adadnirari III, king of Assyria until 782, assumes rule over Babylon and fights against Syria, c. 806. Tiglathpilesar III, king of Assyria, conquers Damascus (745), deports rebellious peoples, subjects Syria and Phoenicia (732), and conquers Babylon (729), which now becomes a part of the Assyrian state. Assyria conquers Isreal and leads its population (about 30,000 people) into captivity. Sargon II, king of Assyria until 705, conquers the Hittite state in northern Syria (717). End of the Neo-Hittite culture. Sennacherib, king of Assyria until 681, erects magnificent buildings and city walls at Nineveh. In the course of the next two centuries, the Assyrians subject all of western Asia. Rebellion of Babylonia against Assyria (703). Sennacherib conquers and destroys Babylon (689). Esarhaddon, king of Assyria until 669, conquers Egypt (671). Apogee of Assyrian power. Decline of political power and of cultural and intellectual development in Assyria in the reign of Assurbanipal (until 630).	Greek colonies in Italy, Sicily, and on the Black Sea.

[221]

EGYPT	WESTERN ASIA
LATE PERIOD Dynasty 26 (c. 664–525) at Sais: Psammetichus I 664–610 (after 656, king of all Egypt) Necho II 610–595 Psammetichus II 595–589 Apries 589–570 Amasis 570–526 Psammetichus III 526–525 Dynasty 27 (525–404) First Persian occupation capitals at Susa and Persepolis: Cambyses 525–522 Darius I 522–486 Xerxes 486–465 Artaxerxes I 465–424 Darius II 424–405 Artaxerxes II 405–359 Dynasty 28 (404–399) at Sais: Amyrtaios 404–399 Dynasty 29 (398–378) capital at Mendes: Nepherites I 398–393 Mutis I (?) 393–391 Psammuthis 391–390 Hakoris 390–378 Nepherites II 378 Dynasty 30 (378–341) capital at Sebennytos: Nectanebo I 378–360 Teos 361–359 Nectanebo II 359–341 Dynasty 31 (343–332) Second Persian occupation: Artaxerxes III 343–338 Arses 338–336 Darius III 336–332	Necho II attempts to conquer Syria and supports the collapsing Assyrian realm. He suffers a defeat in battle against the Babylonians and the Medes and loses Syria. Apries unsuccessfully supports Syria's rebellion against Babylon. Nebuchadnezzar II conquers Judah, destroys Jerusalem, and leads its population into the "Babylonian Captivity." A rebellion of the Greek colonies in Asia Minor against the Persians, with the assistance of Athens, is the cause of the Persian War. The Persians conquer Miletus and suppress the rebellion of the Ionic Greek states.

MESOPOTAMIA/PERSIA	GREECE
Babylonia becomes an Assyrian province (648). Appearance of an independent kingdom of Media, east of Assyria. Nabopolassar, king of Babylonia, frees his state from Assyrian rule and allies himself with the Medes. The Medes and Babylonians destroy Assur (614) and Nineveh (612). End of Assyrian power. Rise of the Neobabylonian state (c. 605).	Tyrants rule in many Greek states. Codification of Athenian law by Solon (c. 594). Peisistratus, tyrant of Athens, wins power with the help of the poorest citizens (560–527). End of Greek colonization in the western Mediterranean.
The Persians, a mountain people, vassals of the Medes, found a kingdom in the region of Susa (576). Cyrus, the first king of the Old Persian state, frees his land from the overlordship of the Medes (c. 550) and conquers Babylon (539). End of the Neobabylonian state. End of the "Babylonian Captivity"; the Jews return to Palestine. Conquests of Darius I. The Persian state stretches from the Indus River to Macedonia and to Egypt and Libya. Division of the empire into 20 satrapies. The Persians conquer and destroy Babylon (479). After many struggles against the Persians, Egypt regains its independence (404).	Themistocles commands the Athenians in the war against the Persians. At Athens, Cleisthenes reforms the social order in a democratic spirit (509). Development of Athenian culture in the time of Pericles (500–429). Greek victories over Persia at Marathon (490) and Salamis (480). Freedom of the Greek states in Asia Minor (479). Peace assuring Greek rule in Europe and Asia Minor.
	Corinthian War pitting Corinth, Athens, and Thebes against Sparta (395–387). The Persians dictate peace conditions: the Greek states of Asia Minor and Cyprus fall under Persian rule. Time of Demosthenes, Greek orator and statesman.
	Philip II, king of Macedon (359–336). Demosthenes' speeches (the "Philippics") against Philip at Athens.
	After his victory over the allies of Athens at Chaeronea (338), Philip assumes command of the Greek army in the struggle against Persia. Greece under Macedonian rule.

EGYPT	GREECE
MACEDONIANS AND PTOLEMIES	
Macedonian kings (332–305):	After the death of Philip II (336), Alexan-
Alexander the Great 332–323	der the Great becomes king of Macedon.
Philip Arrhidaeus 323–317	Alexander campaigns against the Per-
(Ptolemy Lagos rules as satrap)	sians and is victorious over Darius III at
Alexander IV, son of Roxane	Issus (333). After conquering Asia Minor
317–305	and Syria, Alexander gains control over
Ptolemaic Dynasty (305–30)	Egypt without a struggle and founds
Ptolemy I Soter 305–285	Alexandria.
Ptolemy II Philadelphus 283–246	
Ptolemy III Euergetes I 246–221	After the death of Alexander (323), his
Ptolemy IV Philopator 221–205	realm is divided into states ruled by his
Ptolemy V Epiphanes 205–180	commanders.
Ptolemy VI Philometor 180–145	Egypt under the rule of the Macedonian
Ptolemy VII Neos Philopator 145	Ptolemies.
Ptolemy VIII Euergetes II 145–116	
Ptolemy IX Soter II 116–107	
Ptolemy X Alexander 107-88	
Ptolemy IX (again) 88–81	
Ptolemy XI Alexander 81–80	
Ptolemy XII Neos Dionysus 80–51	
(Auletes)	
Cleopatra VII Philopator 51–30	
ROMAN RULE	
(30 B.C.E.–323 C.E.)	
BYZANTINE PERIOD	
(323–641 C.E.)	

Index

Ablutions, 204
Abu Simbel, 71, 104
Abydos, 42
Achaemenes, 155, 159
Achaemenid dynasty, 131–32, 146; subject
    peoples of, 149–51. *See also Persia; and
    specific rulers*
Adoption Stela, 112–15
Aga Ayat, Mustafa, 36–37
Agesilaus (king of Sparta), 169
Ahmose, 37, 69
Ahuramazda, 154
Akanosh, 79
Akhenaten/Amenophis IV, 40, 64, 97, 133
Alara, 71
Alexander IV, 178–79
Alexander Severus, 188
Alexander the Great, xiii-xiv, 163, 173,
    175–76, 198; conquest by, 178–79; tombs
    of, 185–87, 193
Alexandria, 180, 185–86, 189, 193,
    209–10
Amarna revolution, 14, 15
Amasis (general), 137
Amasis (king), 62, 129, 131, 132, 158;
    Herodotus on, 123–27
Amaunet, 6, 138, 139
Amduat, 39
Amenemhet I, 21, 69
Amenemope, 30
Amenhotpe (high priest), 18, 19
Amenhotpe son of Hapu, 191–92, 197
Amenirdis I, 57, 67, 90, 94
Amenirdis II, 111, 112, 114, 116
Amenophis I, 5, 39, 69
Amenophis II, 15, 35, 45, 70

Amenophis III, 7, 8, 15, 61, 64, 191; statues
    of, 189; stone scarab of, 95, 96
Amenophis IV/Akhenaten, 40, 64, 97,
    133
Amenothes. *See* Amenhotpe son of Hapu
Amun, 6, 42, 52; in Nubia, 71, 72, 98, 104.
    See also God's Wife of Amun
Amun-Re, 11, 15, 27, 39, 165; cyclical rebirth
    of, 2, 6, 95, 96; and Piye, 78–79, 84; in
    Report of Wenamun, 22, 24; and
    Shabaka, 86–87; temple at Karnak of, 15,
    17–18, 45, 88, 119; —, Adoption Stela at,
    112–15; —, under Taharqa, 94, 95–96;
    temple at Tanis of, 27; at temple of Hibis,
    142–43. *See also* Theban clergy
Amyrtaios, 159
Animals: burial of, 61–62, 98–99;
    conquerors' treatment of, 61, 135, 177;
    fantastic, 94–95; figurines of, 98–102. *See
    also specific animals*
Ankhnesneferibre, 131
Antalcidas, Peace of, 164
Antinous, 188
Antiochus III, 208
Anubis, 2, 11, 51
Aphrodite, 192, 200, 202. *See also* Isis
Apis bulls, 49–50, 59–63, 130, 186; during
    Persian occupation, 135, 137
Apries, 123–24, 128
Aramaic texts, 156–57, 159
Archaeology, xvi; at Alexandria, 193; at
    Deir el-Bahri, 37–39, 92–93, 191–92; at
    Minshat Abu Omar, 194–95; at Naqlun,
    194; in Nubia, 68, 102–3, 104, 194; and
    Saite Period, 127–30; and search for
    Alexander's tomb, 185–87, 193; of the

Archaeology (*continued*)
    Serapeum, 58–59, 61; and Tanite kings, 27–29, 30–33, 38–39. *See also* Athribis
Architecture. *See* Temples
Ark of the Covenant, 45
Arsames, 159
Arses Bagoas, 177
Art: under Alexander the Great, 173, 175–76; alteration of, 28, 96–97, 133; archaized, 97, 111–12, 128–29, 133, 203–4; under Bubastid kings, 38, 44, 45, 64–67; dating and authenticating, 97, 128–29, 132–34, 201; Egyptohellenic style in, 176, 178, 183–84; erotic, 202; during Kushite period, 85–88, 92, 94–97, 118–20; —, animal figurines, 98–102; —, in Nubia, 97–98; under Nectanebo I, 170–71; under Nectanebo II, 171–74, 176; New Kingdom influence on, 39, 44, 45, 64, 92–93, 111; painted, 4, 6, 39, 92–93, 200; proportions in, 18, 117; during Saite Period, 111–12, 117–19, 128–29, 132–34. *See also* Terracotta figurines
Artaxerxes I, 156, 158–59
Artaxerxes II, 159, 164, 169
Artaxerxes III Ochus, 153, 177
Artists and artisans: in Athribis, 200–202; under Persians, 140, 153–54
Asasif, the, 38
Asclepius. *See* Imhotep
Assurbanipal, 107–9, 117
Assyria, 57, 105–9, 111, 116–17
Aswan, High Dam at, 68, 71, 182, 194
Aten, 40
Athribis, 80, 195–200; baths at, 202–7; Dionysiac cults in, 204–8; political symbolism in, 207–11; workshops in, 200–202
Atum, 2, 6, 39, 120; kings' identification with, 11–14, 151–52, 154–55; and sacred animals, 59, 99–100, 102
Atumet, 6
Avaris, 27, 31, 32–33

Bab al-Gasus cachette, 38
Baboons, 165–66
Basa, 112
Bastet, 42, 46
Baths, 202–4; cultic aspect of, 204–7
Battle of Qadesh, 16
Beards, 14, 120
Behbeit el-Hagar, 168, 172–74, 182
Bekenmut, coffin of, 5
Berenike I, 192
Bes, 207
Bible, the, 28–29, 41, 44–45, 93, 106
Bietak, Manfred, 32, 131

Birds of Re, 161–62
Bocchoris, 57, 67, 85, 106–7
Book of the Afterlife, 39
Book of the Dead, 39
Borkowski, Zbigniew, 193
Bothmer, Bernard V., 132
Bresciani, Edda, 192
Bronze figurines, 98–102
Brugsch, Emil, 37
Bubastid dynasty. *See* Dynasty 22
Bubastid Portal of Osorkon II, 46–47
Bubastite Portal (Karnak), 43, 51–52, 64. *See also* Chronicle of Prince Osorkon
Buchis bulls, 59, 171–72
Bulls, 17, 59, 171–72. *See also* Apis bulls
Burial practices, 1; Kushite, 84–85, 104–5; for sacred animals, 61–62, 98–99
Buyuwawa, 62
Byzantine era, 190

Cachettes, 35–40, 119
Caligula, 188
Cambyses, 61, 127, 132, 134, 135–36
Canals, 120, 136
Canopus Decree, 181–82
Carians, 157–58
Cassander, 179
Chababash, 177
Chabrias (general), 164, 169
Christianity, 189–91
Chronicle of Prince Osorkon, 51–56
Civil war. *See* Rebellions
Cleomenes of Naukratis, 178
Cleopatra I, 208, 209, 210–11
Cleopatra II, 208
Cleopatra VII, 186, 188
Clergy, 15, 17–22, 40, 47–48; and Ptolemies, 180–81, 199. *See also* Theban clergy
Coins, 199, 201, 202–3, 210–11
Colossi of Memnon, 188–89
Copts, 190–91
Corruption, 17
Crowns. *See* Headdresses, royal
Cybele, 206
Cyrus, 159, 163

Daressy, Georges, 38
Darius I, 136–37, 144–46. *See also* Hibis, temple of; Susa, statue of Darius from
Darius III Codomanus, 178
Daszewski, Andrzej W., 193
David (king of Israel), 41
Debod, temple of, 194, 196
Deir el-Bahri, 21, 35–39, 92–93, 191–92
Deities: dualism of, 1, 2, 4, 6; Graeco-Roman adoption of, 182–84, 188, 189–90, 192–93; Persian, 154; syncretization of, 39–40, 59,

141–42, 192–93; theriomorphic representations of, 98–102, 165–66. *See also specific deities*
Demotic Chronicle, 162–63, 164
Demotic language and script, 117, 181, 190, 192
Dendara, temple of, 189
Dendur, temple of, 194, 195
Diadochi, xiv. *See also* Ptolemaic Dynasty
Diodorus, 60, 90, 163
Dionysus, cult of, 204–8
Diplomatic marriages, 33–34
Divine Adoratrices. *See* God's Wife of Amun
Djanet. *See* Tanis
Djed-Hor, 197–98, 204
Djoser, pyramid of, 58, 186, 187, 191
Donadoni, Sergio, 104
Dream Stela of Tantamani, 107–8
Dualism, 1–6. *See also* "Lord of the Two Lands"; Unification iconography
Dynasty 1, 69
Dynasty 3, 58
Dynasty 12, 21, 28, 69, 70, 97
Dynasty 17, 69
Dynasty 18, 14–15, 33, 39, 44, 69; art during, 64, 92–93. *See also specific rulers*
Dynasty 19, 16, 32, 37. *See also specific rulers*
Dynasty 20, 16, 18, 32. *See also specific rulers*
Dynasty 21, 22, 26, 27–29, 44, 47; cachettes from, 35–40; and Israel, 40–41; and Theban clergy, 33–35; tombs from, 29–31, 32
Dynasty 22, 28, 29, 31, 41–44; and Chronicle of Prince Osorkon, 51–56; domestic policy during, 47–51; warfare during, 44–46. *See also specific rulers*
Dynasty 23, 49, 56–57. *See also specific rulers*
Dynasty 24, 57. *See also* Bocchoris; Tefnakhte
Dynasty 25. See Kushite kings; and specific rulers
Dynasty 26, xvi; archaeology of, 127–30; art during, 111–12, 117–19, 128–29, 132–34; and Assyrians, 106–7, 108–9; fall of, 131–32; Herodotus on, 121, 122–27; Thebes during, 130–31. *See also specific rulers*
Dynasty 27. *See* Persia; *and specific rulers*
Dynasty 28, 159
Dynasty 29, 93, 162–65
Dynasty 30, 59, 163, 166–69. *See also specific rulers*

Eels, 99, 100
Egyptian Antiquities Service, 35, 37

Egyptian unification. *See* Unification iconography
Elephantine: Jewish settlement at, 156–57, 159; scandal at, 17
Elibaal (king of Byblos), 46
Esarhaddon, 107, 108
Evagoras, 164

Faience, 31–32, 201
Faras, 194
Fertility cults, 60, 96, 205
Figurines, bronze, 98–102. *See also* Terracotta figurines
Freed, Rita, 129–30

Gebel Barkal, 8, 70, 72, 92, 102–4. *See also* Victory Stela of Piye
Gem(pa)aten. *See* Kawa
Gender dualism, 6
Geography (Strabo), 58
Giza, 1
Godlewski, Wlodzimierz, 192, 194
Gods. *See* Deities
God's Wife of Amun, 6, 33–34, 57, 58; and Kushite kings, 72, 94, 110; during Saite Period, 112–16, 130–31
Gold mines, 68
Graeco-Roman period. *See* Ptolemaic Dynasty; Roman era
Greece, and Egypt allied, 159, 163–64, 169
Greek language, 190, 191
Gyges (king of Lydia), 116

Habachi, Labib, 31–32
Hadad, 41
Hadrian, 188
Hakoris, 93, 163, 164, 165
Hakoris Chapel, 164–65
Harem conspiracy, 17
Harendotes, 50, 144
Harpokrates, 193, 205, 210
Harsiese (god), 138
Harsiese (king), 51
Hathor, 60, 174, 181, 192, 200
Hatiba, 25
Hatshepsut, 98; temple of, 38, 39, 191–92
Headdresses, royal, 118, 140; Bubastid, 46, 64, 66–67; Kushite, 87–88, 91–92, 120; Ramesside, 91
Heliopolis, 11, 15, 90, 151–52, 160
Henuttawy, 34
Herakleopolis, 41, 48, 163
Herihor, 18–21, 22, 24, 34, 35
Herishef, 48
Hermonthis, 11
Hermopolis, 166–68

Herodotus, xv, 61, 90, 158, 159; on Assyrian campaign, 106; on Saite kings, 121, 122–27
Hezekiah (king of Judah), 106
el-Hiba. *See* Teudjoi
Hibis, temple of, 137–40; portrayal of Seth at, 140–42; sanctuary reliefs at, 142–43
Hieroglyphics, 6, 146, 148–50, 181
Homer, 157, 202
Horakhty, 39
"Horn of the Earth," 103. *See also* Gebel Barkal
Horus, 39, 56, 67, 108, 193; and Athribis, 197, 205, 206, 210; and mongoose, 99, 100; and Nectanebo II, 176, 177; and Seth, 1, 6, 141, 144; and transfer of power, 161
Hyksos kings, 27, 31, 32, 69

Iliad (Homer), 202
Imhotep, 191–92
Imperialism, 14–16; against Nubia, 14, 69–70, 121; against Palestine, 14, 44–46, 121; Persian, 131–32, 163–64, 169, 177; during Saite Period, 117, 120–21. *See also* Kushite invasion; Warfare
Inaros, 158–59
Inscriptions, as sources, xiv
Irta, 95
Ished-tree ceremony, 8, 10–11, 64–67
Isis, 179, 182–83, 188, 189–90, 192; at Athribis, 200, 202, 206, 208–10, 211
Islam, 190
Isocrates, 164
Israel-Palestine, 14, 41, 44–46, 121
Iuput, 50, 51, 79, 81, 84

Jakobielski, Stefan, 194
Jeroboam (king of Israel), 44, 46
Jews, in Egypt, 156–57, 159, 199
Justinian, 188, 190

Kamose, 69
Karnak, 176; Babustite Portal at, 43, 51–52, 64; temple of Khons at, 12, 18, 19–20; temple of Mut at, 115–16; temple of Osiris Heqadjet at, 10, 64–67. *See also* Amun-Re, temple at Karnak of
Karomama, royal women named, 57–58
Kashta, 57, 67, 71–72, 90
Kawa, temples in, 97–98
Kematef, 95
Kendall, Timothy, 102
Kerma culture, 69, 70
el-Kharga Oasis. *See* Hibis, temple of
Kheded, 65
Khepri, 39
Kheruef, tomb of, 7, 9

Khnemibre of Heliopolis, 152, 154
Khnum, temple at Elephantine of, 17
Khons, 11, 34; temple at Karnak of, 12, 18, 19–20
Khuit, 197
Kings: dating reigns of, 62–63; ritual confirmation of, 159–62
King's Son of Kush, 69–70
Kolataj, Wojciech, 193
Kryzyżaniak, Lech, 194
Kush, origin of name, 70
Kushite invasion, 73–76; of Memphis, 78–79; representation of, 83–84; and tribute of the defeated, 76–78, 80–83
Kushite kings, 71–72; art under, 85–88, 92, 94–97, 118–20; —, animal figurines, 98–102; —, in Nubia, 97–98; headdresses of, 87–88, 91–92, 120; representations of, 84, 85–88; temples under, 88, 89–90, 93–98; and Theban clergy, 110–11; throne names of, 90. *See also specific kings*

Ladice, 127
Lagide dynasty. *See* Ptolemaic dynasty
Łajtar, 192
Laskowska-Kusztal, Ewa, 192
Late Period, xvii; sources regarding, xiv–xvi. *See also Dynasties* 26–31
Legrain, Georges, 112, 119
Leontopolis, 49
Libya, and Saite dynasty, 116, 117
Libyans, 21, 26, 35, 41, 49, 50; and Kushite conquest, 82. *See also* Dynasty 22; *and specific rulers*
Lipińska, Jadwiga, 92
Literature, xiii, 6; and imperialism, 15. *See also specific writings*
"Lord of the Two Lands": Bubastid kings as, 42; Darius I as, 136, 138–40, 146, 152–53; Kushite kings as, 85, 88, 108; and Macedonian conquest, 178–79; and Ptolemies, 183; Saites as, 109, 111, 115. *See also* Unification iconography
Lower Egypt, 2; Atum as symbol of, 11–14; historical sources in, xv–xvi; military vulnerability of, xvi. *See also* "Lord of the Two Lands"; Unification iconography

Maatkare (daughter of Psusennes II), 47
Maatkare-Mutemhet (daughter of Pinudjem), 34
Macedonian conquest. *See* Alexander the Great; Ptolemaic Dynasty
Madamud, 94
Mahes, 49
Manetho, 22, 42, 56, 106–7, 182
Mariette, Auguste, 27, 38–39

Marriages, diplomatic, 33–34
Maspero, Gaston, 35–36, 37
Ma tribe, 21, 35, 41, 49, 82
Maximus (general), 189
Medinet Habu, temple of, 3, 16, 51, 95, 96, 116
Memnon, 188–89
Memphis, 49–50; Alexander's tomb at, 186–87; during Kushite Period, 78–79, 89–91, 93; and Ptolemies, 199; during Saite Period, 128–30; Serapeum of, 58–63, 90, 93, 130
Memphis, Tennessee, 129–30
Memphite Theology, 89–90
Menkheperre, 35, 38
Meref-nebef, mastaba of, 187
Merneptah, 30, 104
Meroites, 182
Meshwesh (Ma) tribe, 21, 35, 41, 49, 82
Michalowski, Kazimierz, 68, 193, 194, 195
Middle Kingdom, xiii. *See also* Dynasty 12
Mikasa, Takahito, 155
Military, 156, 198; clerical role in, 34–35; under Saite kings, 116–17, 121. *See also* Imperialism; Warfare
Minshat Abu Omar, 194–95
Mnevis bulls, 17, 59
Mongooses, 99–102
Monotheism, 14, 40
Montemhet, 111, 118–19
Montet, Pierre, 28–29
Montu, 11, 12, 39, 59, 94
Müller, Hans Wolfgang, 133
Mummification, of animals, 61, 98–99
Mummy caches. *See* Cachettes
Mut, 11, 84; and Bubastite Portal, 43, 52; temple at Karnak of, 115–16; at temple of Hibis, 138, 139
Mutnodjmet, Queen, 30
Mythological Papyri, 40

Nabopolassar, 117
Namart. *See* Nimlot
Naoi: from Dynasty 30, 170–71, 172; at Tuna el-Gebel, 144–46
Napata, 70–71, 102, 104
Naqlun, 194
Naukratis, 121, 126
Navy, 121
Nebuchadnezzar II, 121
Necho I, 108, 109
Necho II, 120–21, 136
Nectanebo I, 96, 162–63, 166–69, 187; art and architecture under, 170–71
Nectanebo II, 59, 163, 169, 187, 198; art and architecture under, 171–74, 176, 177
Nefertari, 71

Nehmetawai, 166
Neith, 49, 62, 127–28, 136, 192
Nepherites I, 163, 164
Nepherites II, 164
Nephthys, 48
Nesamun, 18
Nestent, 75
Nesubanebdjed. *See* Smendes
New Kingdom, xiii, 14–17; artistic influence of, 39, 44, 45, 64, 92–93, 111; decline of, 17–22; and Report of Wenamun, 22–26. *See also* Dynasties 18–20; *and specific rulers*
Nile delta. *See* Lower Egypt
Nile River, 33, 93
Nimlot (father of Shoshenq I), 42
Nimlot (king), 75, 76–77, 83, 84
Nimlot (son of Shoshenq I), 48
Nitocris I, 112–16, 131
Nitocris II, 131
Niwiński, Andrzej, 38
Nodjmet, 19, 34
Nubia, 14, 18, 57, 116, 121; archaeology in, 68, 102–3, 104, 194; artistic influence of, 118–19; Egyptian interests in, 68–71; Kushite Period art in, 97–98
Nut, 30, 31, 32

Ogdoad, 76, 81n, 95
Old Kingdom, xiii. *See also* Pyramids
Olympias, 179
Onuris-Shu, 173
Opening of the Mouth ritual, 61
Oracles, 40, 42, 165
Osiris, 2, 30, 35, 39, 46, 56; and Apis bull, 49, 59, 61; cult center of, 42; heart of, 197; Hellenization of, 59, 61, 182, 184, 192, 205–6; during Kushite Period, 90, 94, 95
Osiris Heqadjet, temple of, 10, 64–67
Osorkon, Prince, 50; chronicle of, 51–56
Osorkon I, 41, 45–46, 47, 49, 52, 58
Osorkon II, 8, 49, 51, 52, 58; Bubastid portal of, 46–47; tomb of, 48
Osorkon III, 56–57, 58, 72; representations of, 10, 64, 65
Osorkon IV, 80, 84

Pabasa, 112
Painting, 4, 6, 39, 92–93, 200
Palermo Stone, 7, 69
Palestine, 14, 41, 44–46, 121
Panehsy, 18
Pasenhor (priest), 62
Pasha, Daud, 37
Patarbemis, 123–24
Peace of Antalcidas, 164
Pedestals, decoration of, 92
Pediese, Prince, 79, 80–81, 82

Pedubaste, 56
Pef-tjau-(em)-aui-(en)-Bastet, 84
Persia: and Egypt compared, 154–55;
    Egyptian artists in, 153–54; first conquest
    by, 131–32; and foreigners in Egypt,
    156–58; rebellions against, 136, 155,
    158–59; ritual transfer of power under,
    159–62; second occupation by, 169, 177;
    and Sparta, 163–64. *See also specific rulers*
Petemenope, 112
Petosiris, tomb of, 183–84
Petrie, William Matthew Flinders, 27,
    128
Phanes of Halicarnassus, 132
Pharaoh (Prus), 21–22
Pherendates, 177
Philae, 179, 180, 182–83, 189–90
Philip Arrhidaeus, 175, 178–79, 198
Phoenicia, Wenamun's mission to, 22–26
Piankh, 34
Pinudjem I, 34
Pinudjem II, 34, 35, 38, 40
Piriamsese, 31
Piye, 57, 72, 94, 104, 106, 197; burial of,
    84–85. *See also* Victory Stela of Piye
Polycrates of Samos, 132
Pottery, 201. *See also* Terra-cotta figurines
Praxiteles, 200
Priests. *See* Clergy; Theban clergy
Prus, Boleslaw, 21–22
Psammetichus I, 109, 110–12, 118, 158;
    Herodotus on, 122–23; military reforms
    of, 116–17; and Nitocris, 112–16
Psammetichus II, 114n, 119–21, 131
Psammetichus III, 131–32
Psammuthis, 164
Psusennes I, tomb of, 29–30, 31, 32
Psusennes II, 42, 47
Psusennes III, 34
Ptah, 59, 89–90, 91, 120; temple at Memphis
    of, 49, 50, 60, 129, 180
Ptolemaic dynasty, 62, 88, 179–84, 198–202;
    baths during, 202–7; political theology of,
    207–11. *See also specific rulers*
Ptolemaic *exedra*, 186–87
Ptolemy I Soter, 178, 179, 192, 198, 199
Ptolemy II Philadelphos, 180, 199, 201
Ptolemy III Euergetes I, 134, 181–82
Ptolemy IV Philopator, 208
Ptolemy V Epiphanes, 180, 181, 210
Ptolemy VI Philometor, 176, 192, 201, 202;
    representations of, 208, 209, 210
Ptolemy VIII Euergetes II, 192, 209, 210
"Pure Mountain." *See* Gebel Barkal
Pyramids, xiii, 58, 186, 187, 191; Kushite,
    84–85
Pyramid Texts, 6, 11, 59

Qadesh, Battle of, 16
Qantir, 31–32

Ramesses I, 16
Ramesses II, 16, 21, 37, 62, 104; crown of, 91;
    representations of, 13, 28, 29, 176; temple
    at Napata of, 71
Ramesses III, 16–17; temple at Medinet
    Habu of, 3, 16, 51, 95, 96, 116
Ramesses IV, 12, 57, 64–67, 105
Ramesses IX, 18, 71
Ramesses XI, 18, 19–21, 22, 26, 34
Ramessesnakht, 18
Ramesside Period, 16–17, 30, 33, 91
Rams, 71, 98, 177
Raphia, battle of, 208
Rassam, Hormuzd, 107
el-Rassul, Ahmed Abd, 36
el-Rassul, Mohammed Abd, 36–37
Re, 17, 99, 161–62. *See also* Amun-Re
Rebellions, 18; against Bubastid kings,
    52–56; against Kushite kings, 82–83, 89;
    against Persia, 136, 155, 158–59
Rehoboam (king of Judea), 45
Repeating of Births, 21
Report of Wenamun, 22–26
Roman era, xiii-xiv, 188–91, 204
Rosetta Stone, 181
Ruszczyc, Barbara, 195

Sacred animals. *See* Animals; *and specific
    animals*
St. Phoibammon, monastery of, 192
Sais, 49, 50, 57, 127–28, 140
Saite Period. *See* Dynasty 26
San el-Hagar. *See* Tanis
Saqqara, 1, 186–87. *See also* Serapeum of
    Memphis
Sarapis, 58, 59, 61, 182, 183, 192
Saul (king of Israel), 41
Scarabs, 95, 96
Sculpture. *See* Art
Sebennytos. *See* Behbeit el-Hagar
Second Intermediate Period, 27, 32, 69–70
Sed-festival, 7–8, 10–11, 46–47
Sema-tawy sign, 7, 8–9, 92, 136, 138
Senacherib (king of Assyria), 106
Senwosret I, 69, 70
Senwosret III, 69
Serapeum of Memphis, 58–63, 90, 93, 130
Seth, 1, 6, 22, 24, 25n, 144; and temple of
    Hibis, 140–42
Sethnakhte, 17
Sethos I, 21, 37, 91, 104, 193
Sethos II, 18, 116
Shabaka, 85–89, 96; piety of, 89–91
Shebitku, 67, 88, 93

Shed-su-Amun, coffin of, 4
Shepenwepet I, 57, 64, 67, 72
Shepenwepet II, 94, 110–11, 112, 113, 114, 116
Shoshenq (high priest), tomb of, 49, 50, 51
Shoshenq I, 41–43, 49, 52, 58, 62; Palestinian campaign of, 44–46; sons of, 48, 50, 51
Shoshenq II, 47
Shoshenq III, 56
Shoshenq IV, 62
Shoshenq V, 56, 63
Siamun, 38, 40, 41
Silenus, 204–5
Sinuhe, Story of, xiii
Smendes, 22, 23, 26, 34
Snofru, 69
Solomon (king of Israel), 41, 44, 45
Southern Harem (Luxor), 88
Sparta, 163–64
Sphinxes, 58–59, 98, 134, 170
Step Pyramid of Djoser, 58, 186, 187, 191
Story of Sinuhe, xiii
Strabo, xv, 58, 61
Susa, statue of Darius from, 146–49, 153–55; inscriptions naming subject peoples on, 149–51; political theology of, 151–53

Taharqa, 8, 91, 92, 110; animal figurines from reign of, 98–102; and Assyria, 105–7; Gebel Barkal under, 102–4; pyramid of, 104; temples under, 93–98; ushabtis of, 104–5
Takelot I, 46, 52
Takelot II, 50, 51, 52, 58
Takelot III, 10, 64, 66
Tanis, 27–31, 32, 33, 48, 49; decline of, 40–41. *See also* Dynasty 21
Tantamani, 107–8, 111, 116
Ta (vizier), 16–17
Tefnakhte, 57, 67, 73–74, 82; descendants of, 75, 85, 106
Tell Atrib. *See* Athribis
Tell el-Daba, 31, 32
Temples: animal fables on, 94–95; under Cambyses, 135–36; during Kushite Period, 88, 89–90, 93–98; under Nectanebos, 166, 168, 170–73; under Ptolemies, 179–80; Roman, 188, 189–90; symmetry of, 2. *See also* Art; Tombs; *and specific temples*
Tentne (singer), 25
Teos, 168
Terra-cotta figurines, 200, 202–7; and Ptolemaic political theology, 207–11
Teudjoi, 35, 41, 42, 44, 50
Theban clergy: cachette of, 38–39; military function of, 34–35; power of, 17–22, 42, 110–11; royal children as, 50–51; and royal marriages, 33–34. *See also* God's Wife of Amun
Thebes, xiii; Piye's conquest of, 75; during Saite Period, 130–31
Theodosius I, 189
Third Intermediate Period, xvii, 31. *See also* Dynasties 21–25
Thoth, 138, 144, 146, 165; temples of, 166, 168
Tiberius, 188
Titus, 188
Tjekerbaal, 23, 25
Tombs, xiii; of Alexander, 185–87, 193; of Apis bulls, 61–62; of Kheruef, 7, 9; of Petosiris, 183–84; during Saite Period, 111–12; of Shoshenq, 49, 50, 51; at Tanis, 29–31, 32, 48; violations of, 16, 17, 35. *See also* Cachettes; Pyramids
Tottori, Hisa, 155
Trade, with Nubia, 69
Trajan, 189
Tuna el-Gebel, 144–46, 183–84
Tutankhamun, tomb of, xiii, 7, 29
Tuthmosis I, 70, 103
Tuthmosis III, 37, 39, 45, 70, 104; conquests of, 14–15; temple at Deir el-Bahri of, 38, 92–93; temple at Karnak of, 176; temple at Medinet Habu of, 88
"Two Lands." *See* "Lord of the Two Lands"; Unification iconography

Udjahorresnet, 135–36
Udjarenes, 111
Udjat-eye, 144, 145
Undjebaundjed (general), 30
Unification iconography, 1–2, 3, 6–7; and Atum, 11–14; on crowns, 12–13, 46, 87–88; *ished*-tree ceremony, 8, 10–11, 64–67; and Kushite invasion, 73; *sed*-festival, 7–8, 46–47; *sema-tawy* sign, 7, 8–9, 92, 136, 138; at temple of Hibis, 138–40; at temple of Osiris Heqadjet, 67. *See also* "Lord of the Two Lands"
"Uniting of the Two Lands," year of, 7–9, 73
Upper Egypt, 1–2; gods symbolizing, 11, 12. *See also* "Lord of the Two Lands"; Unification iconography
Usermaatre setepenumun, 57
Ushabtis, of Taharqa, 104–5

Valley of the Kings, xiii, 1, 16, 17, 35
Valley of the Queens, 1, 71
Victory Stela of Piye (Gebel Barkal), 73–76; illustration of, 83–84; and Memphis, 78–79; and tribute of the defeated, 76–78, 80–83

Wadi Allaqi, 68
Wadjit, 99, 100, 101
Wahibre. *See* Psammetichus I
Warfare, xvi, 14–16, 26, 117. *See also*
 Imperialism; Kushite invasion;
 Rebellions
Wenamun, Report of, 22–26
Werekter, 25n
Wildung, Dietrich, 194
Winnicki, Krysztof, 192

Wipszycka-Bravo, Ewa, 194
Workshops, in Athribis, 200–202
Writing systems, 6, 117, 146, 148–50, 181;
 Carian, 158; evolution of, 190; Meroite,
 182

Xenophon, 163
Xerxes I, 155

Zeus-Ammon, 192, 211